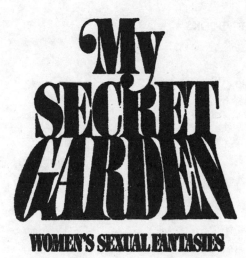

My SECRET GARDEN

WOMEN'S SEXUAL FANTASIES

Books by Nancy Friday

My Secret Garden: Women's Sexual Fantasies
Forbidden Flowers: More Women's Sexual Fantasies

Published by POCKET BOOKS

FOR BILLY

*who believed in this book
when it was just a fantasy*

N. F.

NANCY FRIDAY

My SECRET GARDEN

WOMEN'S SEXUAL FANTASIES

POCKET BOOKS

New York   London   Toronto   Sydney   Tokyo   Singapore

POCKET BOOKS, a division of Simon & Schuster Inc.
1230 Avenue of the Americas, New York, NY 10020

ISBN: 0-671-74252-3

POCKET and colophon are registered trademarks of
Simon & Schuster Inc.

Cover design by Designed To Print

Printed in the U.S.A.

CONTENTS

vii

ix

x

FOREWORD
by "J," author of the Sensuous Woman

☐ I've never met Nancy Friday, but I feel that I know her, for I still have pictures of her wedding tucked away in a drawer. She had what I consider a perfect wedding—romantic, glamorous, inexpensive and private—and the reason I know about it is that *Cosmopolitan* Magazine covered the event in its April 1966 issue.

The article was titled "Marry the Man Today . . . in Rome," and when the manuscript of *My Secret Garden* was sent to me for comment, I dug out *Cosmopolitan* and took another look at the author. My memory was accurate. Nancy Friday looks like a former Miss America—pretty, wholesome, well-scrubbed, glowing. *This* girl has written a book on women's sexual fantasies?

There couldn't be a more perfect author, for it's time that we removed the veils of misunderstanding from this subject and made it respectable. Too many people assume that anyone who has sexual fantasies is mentally sick or oversexed—or both! Ms. Friday's healthy attitude and common-sense comments will do much to alleviate guilts, fears and ignorance, and the fact that she is somewhat of a girl-next-door type will be comforting to readers who feel that sexual fantasies aren't well-bred.

Admittedly, the reader will at times have to fight off shock, prurient interest and distaste while reading *My Secret Garden*. This is no coffee-table book. Nor should it be left around where children might pick it up. *My Secret Garden* could bring plain brown paper wrappers back into vogue, for not only is it a serious, informative study of a facet of human sexuality that has been largely ignored, it

xi

is also painfully personal, uncompromisingly candid and unabashedly erotic. There has never been anything quite like it. You are going to have to force yourself at times to remember that this is a clinical work.

I began to be interested in sexual fantasies several years ago when I realized how much you could learn about the person you love by examining his or her fantasies. For it is pretty certain that sexual fantasies do reflect one's secret vision of ideal sexual activity. That doesn't mean I think you should take your lover's dreams literally (most fantasies feature highly exaggerated behavior), but you should become aware that buried in his or her favorite sexual fantasy is a core of desire to experience a special psychological attitude or activity and the accompanying physical sensations. You won't really know your lover until you have unearthed those hidden desires. Nor will you have achieved complete trust and intimacy until you have been able to share your fantasies with each other and have them accepted. Perhaps this book will break the barrier of silence.

Very little space was devoted to sexual fantasies in *The Sensuous Woman*. Most of the women I interviewed were uninhibited in their discussions of the subject and I incorporated some of their comments into several chapters. I even considered doing a separate section detailing the fantasies that were repeated to me most often, but I dropped the idea when the companion chapter on men's fantasies proved so difficult. That was one of the shortest chapters in my book, for, much to my astonishment, asking a man about his sexual fantasies triggered a response similar to that of hitting an exposed nerve. In both individual and group interviews the men reacted as if I had suggested rape, and clammed up immediately. Even swingers and habitual orgiasts seemed to be struck by a bolt of instant amnesia. After *The Sensuous Woman* was published, I got a number of letters from women saying they thought the chapter on men's fantasies was interesting, but not one comment was ever received from men. My heart goes out to the poor soul who attempts to compile the first book on men's fantasies. It would be easier to train turtles to out-run greyhounds.

In all fairness, I should mention that my own sex has its area of sensitivity. I had an extremely difficult time getting many women to discuss masturbation. They would volunteer every detail of their lovemaking, acknowledge extramarital affairs, etc., without embarrassment, but be unable to even say the word masturbation, much less admit to engaging in this very normal activity. Only when they were describing a sexual fantasy were these women able to relax enough to speak of masturbation.

I mention all this to explain my opinion that men and women will react very differently to *My Secret Garden.* I suspect that women generally will be fascinated by the revelations in this book, but not surprised. Nor will these readers have trouble in acknowledging that they too fantasize. Those women, however, who consider sexual intercourse unpleasant and/or unsatisfying will be revolted by the explicit and enthusiastically carnal sexual daydreams of the women in this book and will reject and deny their own fantasies both to the world and to themselves.

And how will the male react? The first man I gave *My Secret Garden* to was so turned on by the book that he went on a lovemaking marathon. But, unfortunately for the women in America, I suspect that this reaction was not average. The next few male readers were much like the men Nancy Friday tells us about. Since many of the women in this book regard their sexual fantasies as more intimate than the sex act itself, the men felt that their masculinity was threatened (how could any dream be more satsifying than me?). These readers were especially furious at the fantasies where women imagined that their husbands were movie or sports stars during their lovemaking. (A common male fantasy, by the way, is to imagine while he is making love to his wife or girlfriend that she is Raquel Welch, Ava Gardner or whoever else excites him. The double standard seems to extend even to dreams.)

Some men, already unnerved by the onslaught of women's lib, will be angered that they are treated as sex objects in most women's fantasies and be shocked and frightened by some of the contributors' lusty, dominating, twisted dreams. The possibility that Susan, his demure little wife, could imagine even one of the outrageous acts in *My Secret Garden* will be more than this type of man can handle emotionally, and my advice to Susan is that she let him know that she approves of the book but keep her fantasies to herself until he matures a little more. Women are going to have to do most of the work of helping men acknowledge that it isn't freaky to fantasize.

I know I haven't told you any of my fantasies. I'm not about to. So much of my sex life was revealed in *The Sensuous Woman*, all I have *left* are my fantasies! Variations of them are in *My Secret Garden* though (the first thing I did when I got the manuscript was look through it to see if I was represented), and I bet your secret garden is here, too. Nancy Friday has collected enough fantasies so that there is something for everyone.

Whether you like it or not, *My Secret Garden* is a milestone in sex education, for it explores one of the last uncharted areas of female sexuality and forces us to acknowledge the probability that fantasies are as necessary to our sexual well-being as dreams are to healthy sleep. More scientifically oriented books will follow as sex researchers start to give fantasies the attention they deserve, but I doubt if the experts' book will be as human and readable as *My Secret Garden*.

December 10, 1972   "J," author of *The Sensuous Woman*

CHAPTER ONE

"TELL ME WHAT YOU ARE THINKING ABOUT," HE SAID.

☐ In my mind, as in our fucking, I am at the crucial point:
. . . We are at this Baltimore Colt–Minnesota Viking
football game, and it is very cold. Four or five of us are
huddled under a big glen plaid blanket. Suddenly we jump
up to watch Johnny Unitas running toward the goal. As he
races down the field, we all turn as a body, wrapped in our
blanket, screaming with excitement. Somehow, one of the
men—I don't know who, and in my excitement I can't
look—has gotten himself more closely behind me. I keep
cheering, my voice an echo of his, hot on my neck. I can
feel his erection through his pants as he signals me with a
touch to turn my hips more directly toward him. Unitas is
blocked, but all the action, thank God, is still going toward that goal and all of us keep turned to watch. Everyone is going mad. He's got his cock out now and somehow
it's between my legs; he's torn a hole in my tights under
my short skirt and I yell louder as the touchdown gets
nearer now. We are all jumping up and down and I have
to lift my leg higher, to the next step on the bleachers, to
steady myself; now the man behind me can slip it in more
easily. We are all leaping about, thumping one another on
the back, and he puts his arm around my shoulders to
keep us in rhythm. He's inside me now, shot straight up

1

through me like a ramrod; my God, it's like he's in my throat! "All the way, Johnny! Go, go, run, run!" we scream together, louder than anyone, making them all cheer louder, the two of us leading the excitement like cheer leaders, while inside me I can feel whoever he is growing harder and harder, pushing deeper and higher into me with each jump until the cheering for Unitas becomes the rhythm of our fucking and all around us everyone is on our side, cheering us and the touchdown . . . it's hard to separate the two now. It's Unitas' last down, everything depends on him; we're racing madly, almost at our own touchdown. My excitement gets wilder, almost out of control as I scream for Unitas to make it as we do, so that we all go over the line together. And as the man behind me roars, clutching me in a spasm of pleasure, Unitas goes over and I . . .

"Tell me what you are thinking about," the man I was actually fucking said, his words as charged as the action in my mind. As I'd never stopped to think before doing anything to him in bed (we were that sure of our spontaneity and response), I didn't stop to edit my thoughts. I told him what I'd been thinking.

He got out of bed, put on his pants and went home.

Lying there among the crumpled sheets, so abruptly rejected and confused as to just why, I watched him dress. It was only imaginary, I had tried to explain; I didn't really want that other man at the football game. He was faceless! A nobody! I'd never even have had those thoughts, much less spoken them out loud, if I hadn't been so excited, if he, my real lover, hadn't aroused me to the point where I'd abandoned my whole body, all of me, even my mind. Didn't he see? He and his wonderful, passionate fucking had brought on these things and they, in turn, were making me more passionate. Why, I tried to smile, he should be proud, happy for both of us. . . .

One of the things I had always admired in my lover was the fact that he was one of the few men who understood

2

that there could be humor and playfulness in bed. But he did not think my football fantasy was either humorous or playful. As I said, he just left.

His anger and the shame he made me feel (which writing this book has helped me to realize I still resent) was the beginning of the end for us. Until that moment his cry had always been "More!" He had convinced me that there was no sexual limit to which I could go that wouldn't excite him more; his encouragement was like the occasional flick a child gives a spinning top, making it run faster and faster, speeding me ever forward toward things I had always wanted to do, but had been too shy even to think about with anyone else. Shyness was not my style, but sexually I was still my mother's daughter. He had freed me, I felt, from this inappropriate maidenly constraint with which I could not intellectually identify, but from which I could not bodily escape. Proud of me for my efforts, he made me proud of myself, too. I loved us both.

Looking back over my shoulder now at my anything-goes lover, I can see that I was only too happily enacting *his* indirectly stated Pygmalion–D. H. Lawrence fantasies. But mine? He didn't want to hear about them. I was not to coauthor this fascinating script on How To Be Nancy, even if it was my life. I was not to act, but to be acted upon.

Where are you now, old lover of mine? If you were put off by my fantasy of "the other man," what would you have thought of the one about my Great Uncle Henry's Dalmatian dog? Or the one member of my family that you liked, Great Uncle Henry himself, as he looked in the portrait over my mother's piano, back when men wore moustaches that tickled, and women long skirts. Could you see what Great Uncle Henry was doing to me under the table? Only it wasn't me; I was disguised as a boy.

Or was I? It didn't matter. It doesn't, with fantasies. They exist only for their elasticity, their ability to instantly incorporate any new character, image or idea—or, as in dreams, to which they bear so close a relationship—to contain conflicting ideas simultaneously. They expand,

3

heighten, distort or exaggerate reality, taking one further, faster in the direction in which the unashamed unconscious already knows it wants to go. They present the astonished self with the incredible, the opportunity to entertain the impossible.

There were other lovers, and other fantasies. But I never introduced the two again. Until I met my husband. The thing about a good man is that he brings out the best in you, desires all of you, and in seeking out your essence, not only accepts all he finds, but settles for nothing less. Bill brought my fantasies back into the open again from those depths where I had prudently decided they must live —vigorous and vivid as ever, yes, but never to be spoken aloud again. I'll never forget his reaction when timidly, vulnerable, and partially ashamed, I decided to risk telling him what I *had* been thinking.

"What an imagination!" he said. "I could never have dreamed that up. Were you really thinking *that?*"

His look of amused admiration came as a reprieve; I realized how much he loved me, and in loving me, loved anything that gave me more abundant life. My fantasies to him were a sudden unveiling of a new garden of pleasure, as yet unknown to him, into which I would invite him.

Marriage released me from many things, and led me into others. If my fantasies seemed so revealing and imaginative to Bill, why not include them in the novel I was writing? It was about a woman, of course, and there must be other readers besides my husband, men and other women too, who would be intrigued by a new approach to what goes on in a woman's mind. I did indeed devote one entire chapter in the book to a long idyllic reverie of the heroine's sexual fantasies. I thought it was the best thing in the book, the stuff of which the novels I had most admired were made. But my editor, a man, was put off. He had never read anything like it, he said (the very point of writing a novel, I thought). Her fantasies made the heroine sound like some kind of sexual freak, he said. "If she's so crazy about this guy she's with," he said, "if he's

4

such a great fuck, then why's she thinking about all these other crazy things . . . why isn't she thinking about him?"

I could have asked him a question of my own: Why do men have sexual fantasies, too? Why do men seek prostitutes to perform certain acts when they have perfectly layable ladies at home? Why do husbands buy their wives black lace G-strings and nipple-exposing bras, except in pursuit of fantasies of their own? In Italy, men scream "Madonna mia" when they come, and it is not uncommon, we learn in *Eros Denied*, for an imaginative Englishman to pay a lady for the privilege of eating the strawberry cream puff (like Nanny used to make) she has kindly stuffed up her cunt. Why is it perfectly respectable (and continually commercial) for cartoons to dwell on the sidewalk figure of Joe Average eyeing the passing luscious blonde, while in the balloon drawn over his head he puts her through the most exotic paces? My God! Far from being thought reprehensible, this last male fantasy is thought amusing, family fun, something a father can share with his son.

Men exchange sexual fantasies in the barroom, where they are called dirty jokes; the occasional man who doesn't find them amusing is thought to be odd man out. Blue movies convulse bachelor dinners and salesmen's conventions. And when Henry Miller, D. H. Lawrence and Norman Mailer—to say nothing of Genet—put their fantasies on paper, they are recognized for what they can be: art. The sexual fantasies of men like these are called novels. Why then, I could have asked my editor, can't the sexual fantasies of women be called the same?

But I said nothing. My editor's insinuation, like my former lover's rejection, hit me where I was most sensitive: in that area where women, knowing least about each other's true sexual selves, are most vulnerable. What is it to be a woman? Was I being unfeminine? It is one thing not to have doubted the answer sufficiently to ever have asked the question of yourself at all. But it is another to know that question has suddenly been placed in someone else's mind, to be judged there in some indefinable, unknown, unimaginable competition or comparison. What

5

indeed was it to be a woman? Unwilling to argue about it with this man's-man editor, who supposedly had his finger on the sexual pulse of the world (hadn't he, for instance, published James Jones and Mailer, and probably shared with them unpublishable sexual insights), I picked up myself, my novel, and my fantasies and went home where we were appreciated. But I shelved the book. The world wasn't ready yet for female sexual fantasy.

I was right. It wasn't a commercial idea then, even though I'm talking about four years ago and not four hundred. People said they wanted to hear from women. What were they thinking? But men didn't really want to know about some new, possibly threatening, potential in women. It would immediately pose a sexual realignment, some rethinking of the male (superior) position. And we women weren't yet ready either to share this potential, our common but unspoken knowledge, with one another.

What women needed and were waiting for was some kind of yardstick against which to measure ourselves, a sexual rule of thumb equivalent to that with which men have always provided one another. But women were the silent sex. In our desire to please our men, we had placed the sexual constraints and secrecy upon one another which men had thought necessary for their own happiness and freedom. We had imprisoned each other, betrayed our own sex and ourselves. Men had always banded together to give each other fraternal support and encouragement, opening up for themselves the greatest possible avenues for sexual adventure, variety and possibility. Not women.

For men, talking about sex, writing and speculating about it, exchanging confidences and asking each other for advice and encouragement about it, had always been socially accepted, and, in fact, a certain amount of boasting about it in the locker room is usually thought to be very much the mark of a man's man, a fine devil of a fellow. But the same culture that gave men this freedom sternly barred it to women, leaving us sexually mistrustful of each other, forcing us into patterns of deception, shame, and above all, silence.

6

I, myself, would probably never have decided to write this book on women's erotic fantasies if other women's voices hadn't broken that silence, giving me not just that sexual yardstick I was talking about, but also the knowledge that other women might want to hear my ideas as eagerly as I wanted to hear theirs. Suddenly, people were no longer simply *saying* they wanted to hear from women, now women were actually talking, not waiting to be asked, but sharing their experiences, their desires, thousands of women supporting each other by adding their voices, their names, their presence to the liberating forces that promised women a new shake, something "more."

Oddly enough, I think the naked power cry of Women's Lib itself was not helpful to a lot of women, certainly not to me in the work that became this book. It put too many women off. The sheer stridency of it, instead of drawing us closer together, drove us into opposing camps; those who were defying men, denying them, drew themselves up in militant ranks against those who were suddenly more afraid than ever that in sounding aggressive they would be risking rejection by their men. If sex is reduced to a test of power, what woman wants to be left all alone, all powerful, playing with herself?

But if not Women's Lib, then liberation itself was in the air. With the increasing liberation of women's bodies, our minds were being set free, too. The idea that women had sexual fantasies, the enigma of just what they might be, the prospect that the age-old question of men to women, "What are you thinking about?" might at last be answered, now suddenly fascinated editors. No longer was it a matter of the sales-minded editor deciding what a commercial gimmick it would be to publish a series of sexy novels by sexy ladies, novels that would give an odd new sales tickle to the age-old fucking scenes that had always been written by men. Now it was suddenly out of the editors' hands: Women *were* writing about sex, but it was from their point of view (women seen only as male sex fantasies no more), and it was a whole new bedroom. The realization was suddenly obvious, that with the liberation

7

of women, men would be liberated too from all the stereotypes that made them think of women as burdens, prudes, and necessary evils, even at best something less than a man. Imagine! Talking to a woman might be more fun than a night out with the boys!

With all this in the air, it's no surprise that at first my idea fascinated everyone. "I'm thinking of doing a book about female sexual fantasies," I'd say for openers to a group of highly intelligent and articulate friends. That's all it took. All conversation would stop. Men and women both would turn to me with half-smiles of excitement. They were willing to countenance the thought, but only in generalities, I discovered.

"Oh, you mean the old rape dream?"

"You don't mean something like King Kong, do you?"

But when I would speak about fantasies with the kind of detail which in any narrative carries the feel of life and makes the verbal experience emotionally real, the ease around the restaurant table would abruptly stop. Men would become truculent and nervous (ah! my old lover— how universal you are) and their women, far from contributing fantasies of their own—an idea that might have intrigued them in the beginning—would close up like clams. If anyone spoke, it was the men:

"Why don't you collect men's fantasies?"

"Women don't need fantasies, they have us."

"Women don't have sexual fantasies."

"I can understand some old, dried-up prune that no man would want having fantasies. Some frustrated neurotic. But the ordinary, sexually satisifed woman doesn't need them."

"Who needs fantasies? What's the matter with good old-fashioned sex?"

Nothing's the matter with good old-fashioned sex. Nothing's the matter with asparagus, either. But why not have the hollandaise, too? I used to try to explain that it wasn't a question of need, that a woman is no less a woman if she doesn't fantasize. (Or that if she does, it is not necessarily a question of something lacking in the

8

man.) But if a woman does fantasize, or wants to, then she should accept it without shame or thinking herself freaky—and so should the man. Fantasy should be thought of as an extension of one's sexuality. I think it was this idea, the notion of some unknown sexual potential in their women, the threat of the unseen, all-powerful rival, that bothered men most.

"Fantasies during sex? My wife? Why, Harriet doesn't fantasize . . ." And then he would turn to Harriet with a mixture of threat and dawning doubt, "Do you, Harriet?" Again and again I was surprised to find so many intelligent and otherwise open-minded men put off by the idea of their women having sexual thoughts, no matter how fleeting, that weren't about them.

And of course their anxiety communicated itself to their Harriets. I soon learned not to research these ideas in mixed company. Naively at first, I had believed that the presence of a husband or an accustomed lover would be reassuring and comforting. Looking back now, I can see that it had been especially naive of me to think he might be interested, too, in perhaps finding out something new in his partner's sexual life, and that if she were attacked by shyness or diffidence, he would encourage her to go on. Of course, that is not how it works.

But even talking to women alone, away from the visible anxiety the subject aroused in their men, it was difficult getting through to them, getting through the fear, not of admitting their fantasies to me, but of admitting them to themselves. It is this not-so-conscious fear of rejection that leads women to strive to change the essence of their minds by driving their fantasies down deep into their forgotten layers of mind.

I wasn't attempting to play doctor in the house to my women contributors; analyzing their fantasies was never my intention. I simply wanted to substantiate my feeling that women do fantasize and should be accepted as having the same unrealized desires and needs as men, many of which can only find release in fantasy. My belief was, and is, that given a sufficient body of such information, the

9

woman who fantasizes will have a background against which to place herself. She will no longer have that vertiginous fright that she alone has these random, often unbidden thoughts and ideas.

Eventually, then, I developed a technique to enable all but the shyest women to verbalize their fantasies. For instance, if, as in many cases, the first reaction was, "Who, me? Never!" I'd show them one or two fantasies I'd already collected from more candid women. This would allay anxiety: "I thought my ideas were wild, but I'm not half as far out as that girl." Or it would arouse a spirit of competition which is never entirely dormant among our sex: "If she thinks that fantasy she gave me to read is so sexy, wait till she reads mine."

In this way, without really working at it too hard, I had put together quite a sizeable, though amateur, collection. After all, everything to date was from women I knew, or from friends of friends who would sometimes phone or write to say they had heard of what I was doing and would like to help by being interviewed themselves. Somewhere along the way, though, I realized that if my collection of fantasies was going to be more than just a cross section of my own narrow circle of friends, I would have to reach out further. And so I placed an ad in newspapers and magazines which reached several varied audiences. The ad merely said:

FEMALE SEXUAL FANTASIES
wanted by serious female researcher.
Anonymity guaranteed. Box XYZ.

As much as I'd been encouraged by my husband and also by the spirit of the times in which we live, I think it was the letters that came that marked the turning point in my own attitude toward this work. I am no marcher, nor Red-Crosser, but some of the cries for help and sighs of relief in those letters moved me. Again and again they would start, "Thank God, I can tell these thoughts to someone; up till now I've never confided mine to a living

10

soul. I have always been ashamed of them, feeling that other people would think them unnatural and consider me a nymphomaniac or a pervert."

I think it fair to say that I began this book out of curiosity—about myself and the odd explosive excitement/anxiety syndrome the subject set up in others; the male smugness of my rejecting lover and that know-it-all editor kept me going; but it became a serious and meaningful effort when I realized what it could mean, not only to all the sometimes lonely, sometimes joyful, usually anonymous women who were writing to me, but to the thousands and thousands who, though they were too embarrassed, isolated, or ashamed to write, might perhaps have the solitary courage to read.

Today we have a flowering of women who write explicitly and honestly about sex and about what goes on in a woman's mind and body during the act. Marvelous writers like Edna O'Brien and Doris Lessing. But even with women as outspoken as these, they feel the need for a last seventh veil to hide acknowledgement of their sexuality; what they write calls itself fiction. It is a veil I feel it would be interesting and even useful to remove as a step in the liberation of us all, women and men alike. For no man can be really free in bed with a women who is not.

Putting this book together has been an education. Learning what other women are like, both in their fantasies and in their lives—it is sometimes difficult to separate the two—has made me gasp in disbelief; laugh out loud occasionally; blush; sigh a lot; feel a sense of outrage, envy, and a great deal of sympathy. I find my own fantasies are funnier than some, less poetic than others, more startling than a good number—but they are my own. Naturally, my best fantasies, my favorites of the moment—numbers 1, 2, and 3 on my private hit parade—are not included here. One thing I've learned about fantasies: they're fun to share, but once shared, half their magic, their ineluctable power, is gone. They are sea pebbles upon which the waters have dried. Is that a mystery? So are we all. □

CHAPTER TWO

"WHY FANTASIZE WHEN YOU HAVE ME?"

FRUSTRATION

☐ Most people think women's sexual fantasies fill a need, a vacancy; that they are taking the place of The Real Thing, and as such arise not in moments of sexual plenty, but when something is missing. Since frustration, therefore, is the beginning of popular understanding of why women fantasize, let's begin with two fantasies from frustrated women.

Madge

What a relief it is to admit to fantasies and to tell them to someone as understanding as you obviously are. I have a regular fantasy brought on by lack of interest by my husband. He fucks me every five or six weeks, and it is always the same: We are in bed with the lights out and he starts to play with his prick. This goes on often for half an hour or even longer. (He used to get me to do it, but he doesn't bother now.) I feel him start to really rub hard and breathe heavily, then he pulls up my nightie (still under the sheet), says, "Open your legs," and after about two seconds he comes inside me, rolls off, and goes to sleep. All this time, and especially afterward when I know he's asleep—I play with myself then—I really enjoy my fantasy.

12

I find myself at the door of a big house; the door opens and a very big black man with a buxom black woman behind him are inside. He grabs me and pulls me inside, with the woman pushing, helping him. They drag me into a room in which a large Alsatian—very obviously male in the full sense!—is tied up with a boy of about fourteen. The boy is naked. I am ordered to strip naked. "Let's see what you've got," the black man leers at me. I protest and he produces a whip while his wife forcibly undresses me and ties my hands behind my back. She takes his trousers off and exposes his prick, which is abnormally big and stiff as she rolls his foreskin back and forth. I am forced to kneel in front of him, and when he tells me to, I am forced to use the words "cock" and "prick" to describe it. I am made to beg to be fucked and he makes me say the word "fucked" several times to emphasize it.

Then the dog is unleashed, and I am forced on my back while the dog is coaxed so that my head is by his cock and he licks my cunt. I have to feel its cock and rub it gently. Finally I am made to turn around and suck the dog's cock as the black man watches me to make sure I really suck it. Then I'm made to lie on my back on a long stool and the woman gets the dog between my legs, held wide open, and guides his prick and I feel it go right inside me. I am watched by the boy and the wife is naked now. I have to beg for a fucking as the man rubs his prick against my mouth until it becomes big and wet. I am made to lick it and suddenly he holds my head and forces his massive prick in my mouth and holds my nose so that I am forced to suck and swallow his come. It seems to squirt endlessly down my throat. As a final act, I am forced to suck his wife's tits and finally to lick her cunt until she is completely satisfied, while the boy jerks himself off over my cunt and belly. The fantasy fades and I am wet as my finger urgently strokes my cunt to orgasm.

Do you suppose this is all due to lesbian tendencies and my secret desire to be watched by a young boy? [Letter]

☐ As is so often the case when human beings are faced

with a mass of unexplained or bewildering experience they have been taught not to discuss, not only does Madge not have the answers, she doesn't even know the right questions. The inadequacy of her final paragraph, wondering about the meaning of her fantasy, is almost heartbreaking. □

Dot

Although we have been sleeping together regularly for two years, and I have had three short affairs during that time, my husband and I have been married only eight weeks. I thought I was well prepared for all the postmarital disillusionments that young brides are prone to, but one took me by surprise. Prior to our wedding, our sex life had been varied, quite spontaneous and imaginative. Although I had masturbated since puberty, it was only a year ago that I discovered my clitoris and experienced my first orgasm. Since that time, my mate had been only too anxious and willing to make use of that knowledge, and in his consideration, never failed to masturbate me to orgasm either immediately before or during intercourse.

Since we have been married, however, our mutual sex life has come to a standstill in relation to the life we had beforehand. Granted, we are now on stricter schedules and he is often too tired, but even on Sunday afternoons (what used to be our spend-one-day-in-bed-fucking day) the most I can expect is an uneventful nap. Now this hasn't been going on long enough for me to become angry or even frustrated, so I will deal with this myself. All this rambling has been my disorganized way of building up to the subject of fantasies.

When my husband does decide to get down to business, it generally becomes a slam-bam-thank-you-ma'am affair. Here's where my imagination comes in. I found that no matter how long I concentrated on achieving an orgasm, he was simply not giving me the time. So gradually I discovered that it was quicker to snap together a mental vision, a situation that would give me a quick dose of eroti-

14

cism that would carry me through. Second, I discovered after trying several fantasies, that the process was much quicker and more effective if I relied on one fantasy each time. And the more use the fantasy gets, either during intercourse or masturbation, the more vivid and realistic it becomes.

This particular fantasy is brief, and I generally repeat it several times in my mind, omitting the finale until I feel the wave of my orgasm. It consists of a room of men, well-dressed, wealthy, and at least middle-aged. One man acts as my husband or guardian—he is anonymous and I never really assigned him any specific relationship to me. He is in command of my actions and seems to be the leader of the men. I appear in this room of men dressed in a lovely summery dress, light and full-skirted. The man tells the men that I am easily embarrassed but am basically an exhibitionist. He tells me to undo the bodice of the dress, leaving my bare breasts exposed. He then has me lie face down across the coffee table with my breasts hanging freely at one end and my rear at the other. He tells the men that I am aroused by anything icy and wet and suggests that they cup their half-full champagne glasses around my breasts. (When my husband and I were having better days and nights, we often applied ice to one another.) The fantasy goes on as he slips his hand under my dress and underwear and massages my rear. He does not pay any attention at all to my clitoris or vagina, only my rear. He speaks to the other men and tells them what a marvelous white broad ass I have, and would they like to see it? He feels my rear some more and then slowly lifts my dress to expose my butt, still in panties. He rubs it some more, praises it to the men. By this point, my orgasm is beginning to build and when I am ready, I imagine him very slowly peeling my panties down my thighs. If I have not experienced my climax by now, I either repeat the fantasy from the point of the champagne glasses, or else I add to the ending a light spanking. During the spanking, he explains to the men that he enjoys seeing my white cheeks turn pink.

15

This fantasy originated while I masturbated in the bathtub. Now it gets used almost daily, if not in bed with my husband, in the tub with a well-aimed stream of water. I'm curious to know how long this one fantasy will suffice before it becomes boring. I'm beginning to think that just the concept of this fantasy is what turns me on—sort of a reflex action. But as long as it works, it's keeping our marriage—including our sex life—joyful. [Letter]

INSUFFICIENCY

☐ Before we go on to more provocative reasons for fantasy, positive reasons with which I personally identify but about which I still feel—even after putting together this book—an odd mix of excitement and anxiety, let me give you four more variations on this theme of frustration; it is one of the great and universal themes of sexual loneliness, one whose reality we can all understand. The first interview below is with forty-five-year-old Louella, a totally sexually deprived woman; the second with Irene, twenty-five, who might as well be. Next comes a letter from Annette, who was young enough—nineteen—and frantic enough to have probably done something about her frustration by now. I think the violence and alienation of some of the themes these women explore is a measure of how much the human being will rage against sexual famine. The well-fed diner will idly choose between this dessert and that; the starving person will dream of "eating a horse." ☐

Louella

Perhaps the basis for my fantasy about my stepson is the humiliation I feel because my husband only married me to be a housekeeper and in order to look after his son. My husband is sexually impotent, but the boy is blatantly sexual. Sometimes I feel I cannot tear my eyes away from

16

the bulge in the boy's trousers. I know what's there, it seems to run the full length of his belly.

In my fantasy I call for him to get up out of bed, I know he isn't sleeping. I listen outside the bedroom door and know he is lying there playing with himself. I am about to call him again but another boy, a school friend, comes to call and I let them go off by themselves because I know what they are up to.

They go into the woodshed, and after a little time I creep down and peek through the planks. They are standing facing each other, their cocks out, stroking each other. I feel so bloody cross, but yet I still feel myself getting wet. I go back to the house and shriek for him to come in. I still feel like hitting him over the head. He comes in half ashamed and sneering; I myself sit down with my legs trembling. I see he has a big bulge there, he seems to be sticking it out more, then, I don't know, I open his buttons and pull his shirt up. I didn't think it was so big. I stroke him, it is hot and throbbing and he comes as quick as that, covering my hand. Later I take him to my bedroom, he sits on the edge of the bed, I play with him, pulling his skin right back. I am shaking with sex, I pull my dress off and he sucks my tits, then I back up to him and guide it in, with my thighs closed. But he comes too soon, and I send him away. I watch him go down the lane and get out my dildo, it is thicker and goes all in. [Letter and interview]

Irene

My husband is studying for his master's degree, but I have only about one year's worth of college credits which I have earned by attending college part time. I am twenty-five and my husband is one year younger. We do not have any children and I believe I would prefer not to have any.

My husband talks a lot about sex, but he is not very active sexually. As you can probably guess, I am sexually unsatisfied, and have never had an orgasm. Only lately

17

have I thought of someone other than my husband during sex. I imagine what it would be like to have sex with a man who could continue long enough for me to be satisfied. I know several men who I think could do this. Unfortunately, sex with my husband lasts for such a short time I don't get much of a chance to even fantasize for very long.

He often asks me about my thoughts during sex, but I wouldn't dare tell him about the other men. I'm sure it would just make things worse if he knew I was pretending that he was another man. Anyway, when I do make up innocent little sexual thoughts to tell him, he just gets more excited and comes even more quickly.

I often search for "fantasy partners" when I'm in public. If I see a man who interests me, I imagine that my large breasts are bare. Seeing them, he is unable to resist me and he takes me then and there, and finally and fully satisfies me. I even look at attractive couples, wondering whether or not the man can satisfy the woman, and what it must be like for her to have an orgasm. That usually just leaves me feeling jealous though.

I have also tried thinking of other women, not frequently but sometimes. I imagine having sex with a girl like myself. We know each other's desires better than any man could, and we are far better able to satisfy them. The fantasies include cunnilingus because I have heard that is a good way to help a woman have an orgasm. My husband will not do it to me though.

I've tried masturbation, but even with fantasy I've not been able to reach a climax. During masturbation, I've tried imagining that it is a young, good-looking man doing it to me. I close my eyes and imagine his head pressed against my breasts and that my fingers are his lips. Or I imagine that an entire fraternity house has kidnapped me for an orgy. I am the only girl there. I imagine them one by one taking their turn with me, in the dining room, in various beds, on the floor, everywhere and with everyone watching. They come at me one right after the other and this way I imagine I can finally have an orgasm . . . but I never really do reach one.

My latest and most unusual fantasy is that I am both a woman and a man and that I am having sexual relations with myself. I imagine that I am able to give myself all the sexual satisfaction I have ever desired. It is a complicated fantasy to work out, but I think eventually it will work. [Letter]

Annette

I have never confided my sexual fantasies to a living soul, but I feel I must tell someone about them, and so I welcome the opportunity to unburden myself. I have always been ashamed of them, because I feel that other people would think them unnatural, and consider me a nymphomaniac, or something similar.

I am nineteen years old, and have been married for a year now; my husband is twenty-three. We have a satisfying sex life when he is at home, and indulge in every kind of sexual activity, including long sessions of oral lovemaking. The trouble starts when my husband is away from home, which is sometimes as much as two weeks at a time, as he travels abroad on business quite a lot and cannot always take me with him.

By the end of the second week, or sometimes sooner, I am getting desperate for intercourse, and I have to resort to masturbation, as for various reasons I do not wish to get involved with other men. At first, I used to fantasize that my husband was with me, and he was fondling my breasts and my vulva, licking and sucking my clitoris, and—as I thrust a banana or the smaller end of a cucumber into my vagina—I closed my eyes and pretended it was my husband's penis that was penetrating me.

This was sufficient to give me a satisfying orgasm at first, but after a while I found it more difficult to reach one. So, I started to imagine that two men were making love to me—my husband and a man I strongly fancy at the tennis club. I imagined that one was kissing my breasts and sucking my nipples while the other was loving me with his mouth between my legs. Then, as I pushed the banana into my vagina, I imagined that the other man was fucking me while my husband put his penis in my mouth.

Now it has gone a step further, and to get my orgasm, I lie down on my back across our double bed, with my legs apart and a two-inch-thick cucumber thrust into my vagina, and close my eyes while I imagine that four men are making love to me all at once. As I thrust the cucumber in and out with a screwing motion, I imagine that one man kneels between my legs, kissing my slit, which is hairless, by the way; another kneels beside the bed above my head kissing my mouth; and two others kneel on the bed each side of me, sitting on their heels, and leaning forward to suck my nipples, while I stretch out my hand and take hold of their penises to masturbate them.

From there the fantasy progresses. I tip my head back over the side of the bed, and the man there inserts his penis in my mouth. The man between my legs gets onto the bed and inserts his penis in my vagina, and with my mouth, my hands, and my vagina, I make all four of them come at once. After a while, when I start to want another orgasm, I imagine that I am taking them on one at a time for a session of *soixante-neuf*. One by one, I suck them to erection, and proceed to drain them dry; swallowing each offering of semen from four men, leaving them limp and impotent (for the time being), thrills me immensely, and I enjoy a whole series of wonderful orgasms in this way.

I know that if ever I had the chance to make my fantasy come true with four virile men, without the possibility of my husband getting to know about it, I would grab the chance. I feel that once I had experienced the sensation, which I am sure would be out of this world, I would no longer be tormented with the need to fantasize about it.

I shall be interested to hear of other women's fantasies, and to know if I am alone in having such wicked thoughts. And if you know of four *strong*, sexy men who want to take part in an orgy with an attractive, passionate woman (37" 24" 37"), send them along to me! [Letter]

Maria

I have been married three years. I think my husband would mostly react with surprise if he found out that I think about other men sometimes when we are having intercourse. I have led him to believe that I do not often think about sexual things. If anything, he might have his feelings hurt by such a revelation because he often expresses doubts about his sexual attractiveness to women.

I sometimes try to imagine my husband being so sexually excited about me that he would tear my clothes off and "rape" me. His actions when we have intercourse are so much the opposite of that, though, that it is almost impossible for me to imagine. Often, lately, I have resisted having sexual intercourse with my husband when he wants it (which is only about once a month anyway) so that he will have to force me to have it with him, in the hope that he might sort of rape me. So far, though, he has not done so. [Letter]

SEX ENHANCEMENT

☐ If you like, you can read almost any female sexual fantasy as a cry of frustration. We are all prepared to think of women, any woman, as potentially frustrated simply because it is our historic sexual role. Traditionally, we are the frustrated sex—less experienced, less mobile, and less accepted sexually. We have spent less time at it, and been less informed by art, literature, and commerce (to say nothing of our parents and husbands) as to just what our sexual role is—except usually that of desireless virgin or prisoner. Even the most daring sexual adventuress I've talked to admits that her role in her fantasies may still lag behind her real sexual activity: somewhere, even in her wildest, most sexual fantasy, she still plays the inhibited

21

role her mother taught her. In her life she may feel perfectly free to initiate sex, to play the active seducer's role, to take on a man for a guiltless, one-night stand just for the fun of it, but her fantasy will often still be of the "it is not my fault, he made me do it" type: She was doped, or raped, or subjected to cruel and overwhelming domination. Ideas like these, so deeply rooted in the mind no matter what the relatively free body does, will take another generation to outgrow.

But it would be too simple to say that anyone whose sexual imagery conflicts with her sexual reality isn't getting what she wants, that all sexual fantasy is dominated by real frustration. Some of the happiest, most sexually satisfied women I've talked to fantasize, and are all the more sexually satisfying partners because of it. What I am saying is simple: that we women are traditionally prone to and expert at fantasy; that even when we are being fully fucked our minds can imagine the sexual exploration and variables that our bodies are accustomed to do without; *that sex itself—and not only lack of it—can inspire fantasy;* and that for some women there is almost a chain reaction between sexual fact and fantasy, that the one feeds and stimulates the other. □

Patricia

□ Patricia is a tall, blond American beauty who lives in Rome. For the past year she has been separated from her husband and living with Antonio, an Italian. Patricia and her wealthy English husband have an agreement that when they're tired of their individual adventuring they will leave Rome, that nothing either of them has done there will have counted, and that they will return to New York or London together. Because, as Patricia says, "We really love one another. We simply want to explore now, without guilt." □

When he is going down on me I close my eyes and imagine myself at some incredibly proper place, some very elegant restaurant, for instance. On the surface, it's like a hundred different "smart" dull evenings we've spent at as many smart, dull restaurants: the men are in dinner jackets, the women divinely coiffed, the headwaiter aching with savoir faire. (I think this fantasy is my own rerun of the old Paulette Goddard story.) We are all sitting around this table with its glittering crystal and silver on a very deeply hemmed, heavy linen tablecloth—the tablecloth is important because it hides the man underneath who is between my legs. I chat away amiably with the people on either side. How has this man got under the table? Interesting you should ask. Because in my fantasy I've taken care of that detail. Either he has quietly slipped under the table on the pretense of picking up a dropped napkin, or he's excused himself—supposedly gone to the gents—but in fact raced to the cellar below only to emerge through a trapdoor at my feet, there gently to part my willing legs. It's funny how little time during a fantasy it takes to sort out the mechanical details . . . but time, during a fantasy, is not like normal time. Sometimes this man is black, more often he is unknown. Perhaps he is a new face in our dull little group, a face I have responded to all evening, as I respond to his touch on my thighs. I want him, this fantasy man, as much as I want the man who is actually between my legs.

There is always the most amazing amount of detail in the fantasy at this point: me, casually arranging the tablecloth over my lap so that no one can see he has raised my skirt, or see his head tight up against me, or his tongue . . . yes, there is a lot of the lips, actually seeing them, and the tongue. Or there is the intricate arranging of feet, like a ballet, under the table, with me praying that no one will bump into him with their feet! Funny thing is, all this detail makes it even more exciting. But mostly there is the fear—sweet agony—that someone may ask me to dance! Or, worst of all, that the man under the table will stop . . . that someone will call for the bill and say, "Okay, everybody up, let's go." What I am really afraid of, I suppose, is that the real man, the man who is making love to me, will stop, will tire. I do take a long time to reach a climax . . . mostly because I enjoy getting there so much. And there have been men in the past, lovers, who get impatient, who will suddenly stop before I have reached an orgasm, when I already know that I am going to . . . and you know what a letdown that is.

All of this suspense in my fantasy, of course, heightens the *real* excitement, and what ultimately makes the pleasure excruciating is the thrilling fear of what in the hell I am going to do in the fantasy restaurant when the man between my legs makes me come. So I put one hand on his head—don't stop!—and with the other hand I accept a cigarette or toy with my salad, always this perfect social smile on my face, but always the clutch: What am I going to do when I come? (I'm pretty noisy.) The closer I get to actually coming, the realer the suspense in the fantasy becomes, until, thank God, there is a sudden power failure in the restaurant. All the lights go out. Then pow! In the darkness and shouting of the fantasy restaurant, I have my very real, very loud orgasm. [Taped interview]

☐ I realize how much anxiety is aroused by the mention of fantasy during sex . . . but was there anything threatening in that fantasy? It's an exciting little scenario, and it's also fun; as a follow-up, Patricia states that it made her real lover feel and enjoy her own excitement . . . without ever having to know what caused it. (And as he was Italian it would be better that he never did know.) Most people—men and women—understandably don't like to hear that their lover's minds are on anything but them during sex. Anxiety in bed is one of the most contagious emotions going; the smart woman will know just how much her lover wants to hear. The only way Patricia's lover will ever know about her fantasy is through the added emotion that fantasy communicates to him through her body. Because you don't always feel that it would be an unalloyed joy for your partner to hear about your fantasies doesn't mean you yourself should not have them. How much she tells

24

and how much she keeps to herself is a true measure of a woman's subtlety.

Patricia and the other women who contributed to this book are admittedly in a minority; the average woman is not consciously aware of her fantasies, and if she is, would not dream of telling anyone. Most women never get beyond this; their fantasies are not merely unspoken but unacknowledged even to themselves, never deliberately put at the service of their sexual lives. In the end, both these women, and their men, lose what fantasy might have added.

I know there will be some men who will say that Patricia's fantasy is no example of how sex can be enriched by sexual fantasy, for the simple reason that when a man goes down on a woman, it is not real or complete sex at all; that of course a woman *has* to fantasize in that position: She isn't getting the full benefit of him. If she were—if he were giving her a good old-fashioned man-into-woman fuck—she'd have no need to fantasize at all.

For myself, when Patricia says her fantasies make her (and her lover) enjoy sex more, I feel I have nothing to add. However, if that is not enough, here is Suzanne's letter which argues the case for fantasy in all positions. □

Suzanne

When I was sixteen, I read a sex instruction book in which there was a case history that had a great effect on me. This girl described how she was alone in the cloakroom at a dance, bending forward, when a man came in behind her, lifted her dress, put his penis into her (obviously before the days of tights) and had intercourse with her without her looking around or even knowing who the man was.

This excited me. I had not had intercourse at this stage, but I would think about what I had read while masturbating and, of course, after awhile I started to put myself in the girl's place, imagining that it was happening to me.

This basic fantasy went on for a long time. I started having intercourse when I was seventeen, but I am sure you will agree that to carry through a fantasy while having intercourse it is necessary that neither partner should talk too much or the theme is lost. As this was not the way it usually went in those early days, I did not fantasize very much during intercourse, but I always did when masturbating.

I met my husband when I was nineteen and married him at twenty. Once we had settled into a pattern of prolonged intercourse, I found I could have fantasies, which of course increased my pleasure, also my husband's. I was able to tell my husband of these fantasies, and he was very understanding and encouraging.

The fantasies expanded from the original, but there were always similarities. The idea of the anonymous approach from behind continues to excite me, but the fantasies took on more scope, although the man would always do whatever he wanted without any form of lead up or courting. I am rarely nude, usually wearing a dress, but never panties or tights so that I show myself very easily and am always available. The scene is usually at least partly public, at a party, in a park, at the office so that other people see what happens. They never get in the way or object in any way.

A typical example: We are at a party, all nice attractive people standing around talking. I am talking to two men. I am wearing a dress just long enough to cover my crotch, with nothing else. They each put an arm around me and play with my breasts. One puts his hand between my legs. The other people carry on as before while I am led over to a settee where I am laid down, my dress pushed up, my legs spread and I am entered by one, then the other, and then by all the other men in the room, last of all my husband. At this point where the fantasy is returning to fact, my husband and I will work up to a wonderful climax.

I would like to say that we do not use the expression "making love" as we feel that love is the feeling we have for each other all the time, and the enjoyment of sex is something else, so that while we love each other while we are having sex, which includes me thinking of other men, of being fucked by other men, we prefer to use other words. I feel sure you agree. I have never felt there was anything unusual in fantasies. I cannot imagine masturbating without them, and my husband's attitude during intercourse was a big help.

No doubt you have given some thought to the connection between fantasy and fact, where one might try to make the fantasy come true. In many cases where perhaps unobtainable people are involved, this would not be possible. In my case, whereas the people are just ordinary, the circumstances are larger than life, so it would still be very difficult to do what I fantasize, impossible really to fuck with maybe ten men in full view of passersby. Even going around without panties can be risky, although I realize that a great many men, including my husband, are turned on by the idea of women doing this, so that when I do have intercourse with another man it is usually under fairly conventional circumstances, which I later enlarge on in fantasy. I have at times been able to have sex in some degree like my fantasies, but invariably it has been contrived to some extent, so that it is not quite the real thing.

We have tried group sex for this purpose, and in this way I have had sex with up to five men in one evening. I do not want to make too much of the panties thing, but going back to the original incident I read about, which was not only before tights but before minis too, it simply said that her dress was lifted, without any reference to whether she wore anything below, as if they were the wide-legged type that would not get in the way. But whatever, there was no obstacle, and this is very important in my fantasies. I have read of girls saying they go out every day without panties, but frankly I haven't the nerve for this, although my husband supports the idea, so I tend to pick occasions when I feel there will be no danger, as when I am in the company of people I know will approve. Simply, I love sex, but I don't want to be raped.

27

I would just repeat that I get much pleasure from my fantasies, and wish you well. [Letter]

FOREPLAY

□ In my desire to lessen the anxiety about fantasy during sex, I don't mean to imply that if you don't have sexual fantasies there is something wrong with you, or even that you yourself may not prefer it that way. What I am trying to do is establish a more acceptable climate for fantasy, so that women who do fantasize will not feel so alone, so estranged, and will realize that there is nothing wrong with it —that in fact, for them as well as for women still unaware of their fantasies, a more conscious use of them can add an exciting new dimension to sex.

But we all respond differently to different stimuli, and some people, I realize, do not fantasize, just as there may be some rare people who do not dream. I happen to believe, however, that most *do*—and that while reading this book, many will, in fact, discover theirs beneath the thin skin of childhood training or prudery—call it what you will.

I've already said why I think women's fantasies are often far richer and more adventurous than men's. They are a true women's underground. But just as some people do and some do not fantasize, some fantasies are meant to be shared and others not. By opening up the underground, I am not suggesting we have to tell or act out all our fantasies to be sexually happier; just accept them without anxiety for what they are.

For example, no one objects to the idea that certain props like a martini, music, low lights—elements outside the man—can get a woman "in the mood"; then why should he feel threatened by what is going on in her mind? Some people get warmed up looking at erotic pictures or reading a bit of porn; does it matter that the people in the pictures are other people or that the words that excite her were written by another man? Then why should it matter what, or of whom a woman is thinking? A woman doesn't need an erection to have sex; she can be entered at any time, and a man can have an orgasm while his wife's thinking about the grocery list. Is that preferable? Wouldn't they both enjoy it more if, say, at the outset, during the preliminaries, she deliberately changed mental reels, put on something a little more highly charged than what to give the kids for supper tomorrow? And would it really matter whether her imagery were a rerun of one of their own earlier more erotic sessions together (such as in Bertha's fantasy which follows), or if she got her sexual charge by imagining that she was being fucked by some tennis stars she doesn't even know (as does Bellinda)? What matters is the quality of the real sex, and if a private screening of her own favorite erotica gets her in the mood quicker than a martini, and ultimately gives him a better fuck, then why not? It's not telling him your fantasy that's important, it's telling yourself it's okay to have it. For some women, fantasy is the strongest sexual foreplay of all; what they should both remember is that it's the real man she really wants—or presumably she wouldn't be there. ☐

Bertha

While having intercourse with my husband, I will sometimes go over our past lovemaking sessions in my head, ones that were particularly exciting, where we both did and said things we don't normally do. I'd like it to be that way all the time, of course—with the bed practically torn apart and us ending up on the floor, wet and sticky and happy—but of course it doesn't always happen that way. So I re-create it, rolling him over in my mind when, say, all he's really doing is lying there on top of me and thrusting away.

We've had some incredible times in bed—and out, especially in the shower playing catch-me-if-you-can with

29

our bodies covered in Sardo oil. Those are the times I remember. I do it especially if I'm not particularly excited and it helps me to reach the aroused state I want. Then when I get there he does, too. My husband knows of this and fully approves; I sometimes think he even relies on it, say, when he's tired. It's as though he were saying, "Come on, baby, remember how it was, get us up there."

We've been married two and a half years and enjoy a good sex life. But I've invariably found that re-creating these scenes with my husband (in my mind) leads to a more erotic session, which in turn gives me new material for the next time. For me, my fantasies are money in the bank, if you know what I mean. [Taped interview]

Bellinda

☐ While I was putting this book together, I met and talked with Dr. Robert Chartham, psychologist and author of *The Sensuous Couple*. He showed me a letter he'd received from a woman we'll call Bellinda, in which she complained that her sex life was dreary, that her mind wandered to the day's trivia during sex, and that she felt guilty that the only sexually exciting thoughts she seemed to have were of tennis star John Harrison's thighs:

"Last year," she wrote, "I went to the Albert Hall to watch John Harrison in person play indoor tennis. I was sitting on purpose near the umpire's chair so I could be near his legs. I just could not take my eyes off him, and when he was toweling down, he stared back for a lovely long moment, our eyes were really locked. He may have been wondering what this stupid woman (me) was looking at, but I prefer to think that my message got through, which was, 'My God, I'd like you to thrust yourself inside me.' If it's possible for a woman to say that with her eyes, then I said it."

Dr. Chartham's advice to her and her subsequent reply follow. ☐

Dear Bellinda:
By believing yourself to be, as you put it, a "sexual dud," you are making yourself one.

You have quite the wrong attitude toward lovemaking, and your husband seems no better.

You have got yourself all worked up about sexual responses and the quality of them, when you ought to be fully relaxed, and letting things just happen to your body. Instead of thinking about next day's lunch while you are being made love to, why don't you think of John Harrison's thighs, or better still imagine that those are John Harrison's hands and mouth caressing you, and John Harrison's cock that is up you. Try it and see what happens. Let me know.

We call it fantasizing, and nearly all of us, men and women, have our sexual fantasies—at least from time to time. It's quite a legitimate way of awakening our sexual senses. The only thing is, don't let on to your husband that you are imagining that he's John Harrison; he might be hurt.

Best wishes,
Robert Chartham

Dear Dr. Chartham,
Thank you so much for your letter. I am perfectly certain you were aware of the effect that phrase "John Harrison's cock that is up you" would have on me. Of course I have thought of this and longed for it, but being able to tell some one and see the words written down was somehow extra exciting. In my thoughts I have used the word penis, but your phrase sent a sort of electric shock through me. All that day (last Friday) I felt very odd, warm and sort of open and receptive. I bought a black scanty garment because I know that color turns my husband on. I just couldn't wait until we were in bed, as we have two children around. I was in bed first, so my husband hadn't seen the little black thing I was wearing.

I must say it had a dramatic effect! He came into me right away and in a few seconds had come off. Needless to say, I couldn't quite match his speed, but came soon afterward and it was more intense than usual. We made love

31

twice that night and again in the morning, and were both in a daze of well-being the next day. It is thanks to you, and I feel that it's now much more likely that I shall not have to fight for my orgasms in the future. To make things even more sexual for me, there was John Harrison himself on television doing a "Bisto" commercial! Not a very erotic product, but I wasn't watching the gravy! I just hope I behaved naturally, as my husband was watching and it came as a bit of a shock.

The orgasm in the morning was the best, as I threw all guilt to the winds and imagined John Harrison begging me to let him make love to me. In this fantasy he is completely unable to control himself and is holding his penis in an effort to suppress his erection. He fails, and comes while he is standing there, the semen spurting through his fingers onto me.

I agree with you that this must be kept from my husband, as it would hurt him and might wreck future developments.

I have never told anyone these things in my life before and I thank you for releasing thoughts which made me feel so guilty. My husband says he never thinks of me as a wife but as a mistress, so I suppose that is his fantasy. I shall have to be careful to keep your letter hidden; I don't want to lose it, as it is stimulating to see "John Harrison's cock up you" written down.

I realize I can't feel this way every day of the year, but I have made a start and shall now enjoy my fantasies instead of trying to push them away.

APPROVAL

☐ I said earlier that I didn't want to act too strongly as advocate in this book, that I wanted to let the material speak for itself. Aside from believing in sexual fantasy as an interesting side of women's sexuality—being a fantasist myself—I had little to say on the subject before I began collecting this material. I've learned a lot from the women who contributed to this book; in fact, all I have to say comes directly from what they've told me, and have imaginatively illustrated for me in their fantasies. But if I haven't interfered with the fantasies themselves, I have selected certain ones to appear in the book, and grouped and classified them in a definite order of progression.

Any number of people could have done this according to whatever arbitrary system of classification they might have chosen. That I have chosen this order therefore means to me that I am acting as advocate after all. This book is designed to win you over, unequivocally, first to the idea of female sexual fantasy as an introduction to love play, and eventually to the validity of sexual fantasy at any time.

I began by thinking that it was *obvious* that it doesn't matter what a woman is thinking of during sex; if it excites her, it's good, and thus adds to the joy of both. But I know how the material in this book has been received even by friends I'd call sophisticated and "liberated." Their reactions tell me how difficult it will be for other people to accept, even to believe, some of the sexual images women say they have, especially during sex. Even harder to believe will be the statements of these women that these fantasies occurred during happy, satisfying sex with men they loved.

That is why I broached the topic of fantasy during sex with the easily understood idea of fantasy as sexual foreplay; I assume we are all in favor of that, of anything that leads to sex. As the next step, I would also assume that we are all in favor of anything that gives us stronger feelings of reassurance or approval during sex. (I need not explain to my women readers the misapprehension in the idea widespread among men, who have done most of the writing on sex, that because women don't have the outward giveaway of inner sexual anxieties—the limp cock—that women suffer less and need less reassurance.) Therefore, in the fantasies you are about to read, the fact that women like Sally, Vicki, and Sondra get the desired approval from such universal judgment figures as Mother, the doctor,

33

and even Jesus Christ, should strike a sympathetic chord. If you can understand and accept the idea of female fantasy as a form of sexual foreplay and excitement, the idea that fantasy, by allaying anxiety, can allow the excitement to grow cannot be too strange a progression of thought. □

Sally

□ My friend Sally owns her own small boutique. She's in her early twenties, has long, multilayered black hair, and the kind of figure that looks perfect under one of her own flowing chiffon designs. She recently finished a yearlong affair with a man twice her age. who, as a parting gesture, set her up in the boutique business. She considers this latest affair "the greatest education of my life." She is still terrifically fond of Alan, her benefactor. and talks of him with enthusiasm. Having known him briefly, and knowing Sally's zest for anything new, I would imagine that the "education" Sally refers to would include some fascinating new chapters in sexual exploration. She admits that he will be a hard act for any new man in her life to follow; "I really am so bored with younger men now," she says. □

I've thought about this fantasy quite a bit, ever since I started having it, dreaming it. I've analyzed it ten different ways, but I'm still not quite sure what it means. I don't think I had it before I knew Alan, but maybe I did. He brought me out in many different ways, so maybe the fantasy had been there all along, but I just never acknowledged it until him. It's really a very simple fantasy on the surface; I have a variety of twists I add to it depending on my mood Basically, it's that while I am making love I have this image of me lying there, naked, just as I really am, with the man, or men, and while we are fucking I'm talking on the telephone to my mother. Isn't that weird? What I have to do, of course, is control my voice, talk to her normally as if nothing unusual is going on. Every now and then she'll ask, "What was that I heard?" Every time she becomes suspicious, I get wildly excited, but even dur-

34

ing those long periods while she and I just chat—far more amiably than we do in reality—I lie there in a great warm bath of arousal. It's very comfortable talking to her like this, also wildly exciting.

She used to come on very heavily with Alan—after all, they're about the same age. She's an incredible flirt. Also, she never really approved of me and Alan; either that or she was jealous. But she's always very sweet and understanding to me on the fantasy telephone.

The funny thing is, when I do come, when I reach an orgasm and I can't control my voice any longer, she doesn't scold or hang up as you would expect, she just keeps on chatting in this kind of nice warm voice that she never uses with me in reality. [Taped interview]

Vicki

☐ Vicki is thirty-two and single, just out of her second divorce. Her exotic good looks appeal to a variety of men, but Vicki's own preference has always been limited to the rat bastards. She's already set her sights on her next conquest (I mean victimizer) and is the first one to laugh at the hard knocks that lie ahead for her. "That's how I am," is how she puts it, adjusting the fall of a tight little T-shirt over her boyish figure, before sailing forth to meet her Waterloo.

When she's not being knocked, Vicki's generally to be found in the archives of some far-flung museum; she is a well-established art historian, appears regularly on TV, and writes for art publications in half a dozen countries. You would think she'd seen enough suffering on the cross without adding her own. ☐

Interesting you should ask, my dear, because I'm sure I've got you to thank—or blame—for these strange new thoughts that have entered my sex life ever since we talked about this book of yours last year. That's how long they've been going on. No, wrong, I'm sure they were there all along, but it was our talking about fantasies that brought

35

them to the surface. Nowadays I can't seem to go to bed with a man without having this image that he is my doctor. I can't really say whether this focused fantasy has really heightened sex for me or not. All I know is that there he is, cap and mask, bearing just the slightest resemblance to my real doctor. Or is it just the cap and mask? You know the old line about doctors: They all look alike when you've got your feet in the stirrups. Not that I've had one of those examinations for years. Okay, I know it's dumb when you're over twenty-five not to, but I've always hated those check-ups. Remember how you screamed at me in college for not seeing a doctor when I hadn't had a period for six months? And me still a virgin. Well, that turned out all right, didn't it?

You know, the only thing that bothers me about this doctor fantasy is that I don't understand the association. I've never had a romance with a doctor. God knows, I've never been excited during one of those examinations. I never even went through the ritual childhood games of Doctor and Nurse with the neighborhood boys. But get me in bed with a man these days and there we all are—me and the guy in bed, and me and the doctor in my head. The more excited I get, my legs up, the doctor between them—my lover I mean . . . well, you know what I mean —anyway, the more intent the examination, the more intense the excitement. The closer the doctor gets to his prognosis, the closer I get to orgasm. And then, without fail, right before orgasm, the doctor's masked face zooms in close to mine and those loving eyes tell me even before he speaks that I'm in great shape, everything's just where it should be.

Now that I think of it, tell it out loud, I realize I should edit what I said earlier, the part about blaming you for bringing all this up. Whatever it means, all I know is my sex life has never been better. [Taped conversation]

Francesca

☐ Francesca is a pretty Jewish mother of three. Her sweet disposition goes a long way in running a house constantly teeming with her teen-age children's friends and her non-stop husband's business associates, who seem to fly in hourly from all over the world. Under her quiet but firm hand, all generations and nationalities meet and merge around the family dining table. Her mother lives with them three months of the year. "I have very ambivalent feelings about my mother," she says. "I suppose I love her and accept her more now than I ever did, but it's very rare that I can even kiss her on the cheek. I used to sort of shrink from being touched by anyone, but now I'm much more liberated . . . with everyone except my mother. I've often wondered if there was anything homosexual about this fantasy; when I was nineteen I had an unfulfilled lesbian experience in Paris. But I don't know, as often as I fantasize about women, I fantasize about men, and my real sexual life is very much only with men."

(This interview with Francesca shows how women often talk about their fantasies. Even though Francesca was an interested volunteer, she begins by trying to tell it all in one semiabstract sentence. Only as she reworks the almost unconscious images again and again in her mind as she tells it to me, will she remember the elaborate details.) ☐

I'm afraid my fantasies are just the usual ones. This is my favorite: I am brought at the age of thirteen or fourteen, as a pubescent girl, by my mother to be sold to an Oriental potentate.

Actually, it's a faceless mother, not really *my* mother, because I rather have this thing against my mother. But she's somebody of authority and she's brought me here to sell me. She's told me in advance exactly what I am to do. In fact, she's trained me herself since childhood to perform sexually, she's raised me as a purely and perfect sex-

37

ual object, demonstrating on me herself to show me just how everything should be done. She's performed cunnilingus on me, done everything to me, and showed me with her own body. Actually, it gets a little confusing here as to whether it's a mother or who it is . . . but it is a woman.

We enter the palace. And there is the potentate sitting on his throne like a great Buddha, a rajah. I have been instructed by my mother exactly what I must do; there is no hesitation on my part, I *must* perform well, it is the culmination of my training, or I will not be bought. And it is a great honor to be bought. My mother begins by describing my abilities to the Rajah. In fact, she begins by demonstrating on him herself just what it is she has taught me to do. She fucks him, sitting on top of him on his throne, she goes down on him, she plays with him all the while talking to him of me.

Then she performs on me, she goes down on me, she fucks me, but not with any apparatus—there's never any of that—she does it with her finger. I lie there, responding just as I should as her finger or her tongue enter me, my beautiful body reacting perfectly.

It gets confused here . . . let me think . . . The Rajah himself is passive throughout all of this. But he's pleased with my performance, very pleased, that's the most important thing, of course.

He says, "Yes, she will do, she's marvelous, she will have a high position in the court . . ."

It never has anything to do with "She'll be the most bejeweled or the richest"; it's not that kind of harem. The idea is that I've performed beautifully and that I'm the most sexual figure he's ever seen and he wants me there by his side. (I suppose this all has to do with pleasing the man, but it does get me worried afterward sometimes just why he is so passive, why I'm always doing to him. Let me try to remember more.)

He, the Rajah, never leaves his throne. He sits up there and my mother and I perform below him on a kind of stage, a platform. We are naked at this point, but when I was brought in I was beautifully robed. I was taken to him

and he parted my robes and murmured appreciation. But
it's my mother who undresses me, pointing out all the
beautiful parts of my body as she uncovers them, "Look at
this body, the beauty of the breasts . . ." (That's another
thing; I used to be very hung-up about being flat-chested
—I'm over that now—but certainly in fantasies I'm beautifully endowed.) "Look at how I've nurtured her," she
continues, her hands moving over my hips, parting my ass
for him to see, "look how beautifully she's shaped, just to
please you."

Then she has me lie down and she parts my legs, exposing my cunt so that he can see how perfect it is. This is
when she performs on me. All this time he's masturbating.
And so are the courtiers, oh yes, it's a big M-G-M court,
with Nubians standing around holding torches (they're
very tall and they aren't masturbating, but the others are,
and the women courtiers too).

Then I go and sit on the Rajah's lap, he just parts his
gown, and I fuck him . . . after I've gone down on him. I
sit there naked on his cock on his throne and through it all
he does nothing, nothing to me, nothing for me. I do all
the work . . . which is what I've been trained to do, so in
the fantasy it doesn't matter, but now that I think of it, it's
strange that there's really nothing in it for me sexually.
What matters is that I'm the best, I'm accepted. The sex
part with the Rajah isn't what counts—whether he's big or
skillful or anything; I have other fantasies where size and
skill and three men at once are what turns me on—but
this one, and it's my favorite, it's all about being accepted.
What I mean is, if I'm being fucked in real life, and I have
this fantasy . . . it's the greatest pusher in the world.
[Taped interview]

Sondra

☐ Sondra has a funny habit of always feeling that new
women she meets are more "jealous natured" than most
other people think they are. Perhaps this is mild projection

on Sondra's own part—she keeps a very fond, but very careful eye on her husband Tom. Actually, I like her; she is very pretty, bright, has a funny acid wit and a good reputation as a literary agent. Both she and Tom were married before, and their large house is filled with half a dozen kids from each of their previous marriages. As for Tom, he himself shares Sondra's interest in jealousy; they play a game in which he comes on with other ladies, and she— well, as Tom put it abruptly one night, "I suppose you're wondering why my eye is red?" I said No, I hadn't noticed. "Sondra did it," he snorted. "We had one hell of a fight last night." After that it occurred to me that I rarely see them when one of them isn't bandaged or bruised. ☐

Music is playing on the record player. As I sit listening to the plucking of the harpsichord, I wonder if Dali must have dreamed up this fantasy to torment me. You see, one of my fantasies concerns him . . . not that I want a wispy end of his mustache to tickle my cunt (a word I prefer to *clitoris,* which sounds so clinical, or *clit,* which is so flip) but I want that big black octopus to take me in every way all at once, with every tentacle going full force at the same time—since I tire so easily.

The big black octopus, I must explain, was in a gallery off Fifth Avenue. It was a Dali *vernissage* and included a huge painting of Jesus preaching his Sermon on the Mount. Well, exactly opposite this hedonism were several beautiful and erotic drawings, and the one I really fancied was this octopus having a girl. As I stared at it, I lived it . . . each black rhythmic finger in and out of her body and my body, winding all the way up (because I'm a very deep person) and ending in a thin point—not like a knife, but all the same gentle and definite. A corkscrew arrangement follows the end of the point with a kind of rubbing, twisting power and force; it makes me reel and scream with delight. One after the other, each tentacle makes me come again and again, many comings per black thing, and there is Jesus still talking to these poor infidels from his lofty place, but really He is watching me while I gaze into the eyes of my taker, this huge body-head like the end of a giant orchid penis as it fucks me and engulfs the whole of me with those spent fingers but with many more still poised, still ready to come as I come again and again . . . aaaahhhhh! "Bless you, my child . . ." [Conversation]

EXPLORATION

☐ The next three fantasies are from women who are sexually happy in their beds. At least they say they are, and I'm prepared to accept what a woman tells me about her sex life. The alternative is to say that because each of these women fantasizes beyond what is actually happening, it follows that the real sex is inadequate and she dissatisfied. But that would be playing more than amateur psychiatrist, it would be playing God. No thank you.

For many women, fantasy is a way of exploring, safely, all the ideas and actions which might frighten them in reality. In fantasy they can expand their reality, play out certain sexual variables and images in much the same way that children enter into fantasy as a form of play, of trying out desires, releasing energies for which they have no outlet in reality. Thinking about it, even getting excited over the image, doesn't mean you want it as your reality . . . or else we all, night dreamers that we are, would be suppressed robbers, bisexuals, murderers, or even inanimate objects. ☐

Karen

I have this fantasy quite often while Ben is fucking me. In fact, I'd say I have it during our best sessions, when my body is most relaxed and inventive. Ben gets so excited when I'm into this fantasy it's as though he were having it too. Yet I know if it were to really happen it would scare the hell out of him—and out of me. I don't think we have any room in our lives for any kind of group scene; it simply wouldn't fit in; we wouldn't know how to handle it. But in fantasy, it's fantastic.

The three of us are in the living room, me, Ben, and my friend Helen. Our living room, here at home. Only the windows are larger, big bay windows with large panes and no drapes, no curtains, the way those windows are in the endless little houses all lit up along the endless roads that stretch across the countryside, the people's lives exposed, like . . . We have just come in from shopping, the three of us, and as I go into the kitchen to put away the groceries and start dinner, I see Ben help Helen out of her coat. I stand at the sink, watching them behind me reflected in this huge polished window. Ben is standing behind her with his hands on her shoulders, on her coat, but she takes his hands quickly and slips them down, cupping them around her breasts, holding them there. They don't realize that I can see, as their backs are to me. I make little noises with the groceries to reassure them that I am busy putting things away. I run the water in the sink, giving them time to go on. Ben hesitates, letting her press his hands against her breasts. Then she presses back against him, rubbing against his groin. I can feel the rush of excitement that charges Ben, that gets him instantly erect as I can get him, as I so often have by rubbing my bottom against him.

I go back into the living room, but first I clear my throat and start talking so they will know I am coming. I walk through the room, telling them I'm going up to have a quick bath, telling Ben to fix Helen a drink and keep her company. But I don't go upstairs. I stand just outside the door and wait, watching them. Ben sits on the sofa, shy as always, and it is Helen who moves in, kneels in front of him, unzips his fly and takes his penis in her hand, puts it into her mouth. Ben's hands start to push her away. He looks quickly in the direction I've gone. But the pleasure is too much. He sees Helen, sees her lips round his penis, her mouth full of him, her lips bulging around it as though she's going to swallow it. He reaches for her breasts again and fondles them; they seem to grow in his hands, to swell in size. Until they are as large as mine. Her blond head moves faster and faster, up and down on his penis, pushing her lips back so that Ben can see her teeth, small and white, moving as though she is eating some delicious piece of meat. The tip of it slips farther and farther down into her throat; Ben is practically paralyzed with ecstasy. He falls back against the sofa, his hands reaching for his trouser front, unfastening it altogether so that she can really get at him. He is no longer the Ben I know at all. Helen undoes her blouse, never letting his penis rest, sucking away on it. She takes her breasts in her own hands, and kneads them so that drops of milk gush from them onto Ben's pubic hairs, soaking them. I move quietly into the room, knowing they won't stop now, and wanting to watch them more closely. They have forgotten now that I am even in the house. Ben is about to come in her mouth, but he wants the milk even more and he lifts her, drags her onto the sofa, so that he can suck her breasts while his hands undress her, fondle her until she moans for him to put it into her, there on our sofa, their clothes half on, half off, in front of the huge picture window. I shake off my clothes and naked I go over to them. I get on the sofa behind Ben. I want so badly to join them, to give Ben even more pleasure in return for all the pleasure he is giving Helen—who is really part me and part Helen—and suddenly I have this warm wet thing to put into him, a penis, my penis. I press it into him slowly, but all the way in. Ben gasps with excitement, and I feel the same wild sensation as though it really was a part of me going into him, as if it really were my penis. Firmly, quickly, I move it in and out in rhythm with his fucking Helen, whose pleasure I can also feel. Having it both ways, having everything, it is overwhelming. I can't stand it, it is too much, and I press deeper and deeper into my husband until it seems my penis goes through Ben and into Helen, into me myself, and I die with pleasure. [Conversation]

43

Abbie

I've been thinking more and more about my fantasies lately. I've even tried talking to my husband about them, that is, the ones I think wouldn't make him angry. I wouldn't dare tell him that I often think of my old boy friend, of how it used to be with him, nor of my thoughts of some unknown man who has forced himself upon me, which in my imagination I seem to enjoy.

For some *odd* reason, while having sexual relations with my husband I prefer him to be fully clothed, and while we are in bed, I'd rather not see his "parts." I'd rather we have sex when I didn't have to see his penis. Although he enjoys studying my "areas," I cannot bring myself to do the same. It turns me on more when things are left to the imagination. But my husband tends to parade his "parts" in front of me, even though I've asked him not to, and mentioned that our sex life might improve if he didn't.

You may therefore find it strange that in my latest fantasy I tell my husband that I *think* I would enjoy watching him having sex with another woman. Not really someone we know—preferably some strange female. That way we'd know no relationship could come of it. But if it were to come true I don't know if I'd have the nerve to allow it. Yet I keep thinking it would be fun.

I also have fantasies of me with other women. But these women have no face. I mean they are no one in particular. These occur usually during masturbation, which is maybe two, three times a month. I don't *really* have lesbian fantasies, because for me to do the act on a female, to me it seems repulsive, but the idea of a female doing it to me seems pleasurable. (Selfish, perhaps?)

I know I began this letter by saying I do discuss some fantasies with my husband, but I'm afraid that even that is a fantasy! I can't think of any fantasy we've discussed, but then we have a communication problem! [Letter]

Hilda

I am thirty-seven years of age. My marriage is a happy one and the sexual part of our life together extremely satisfying. I like to think of my husband's penis as being small but very powerful. I often get on top of him, squatting in a knees-up position. He strokes my buttocks and caresses my anus while he thrusts from underneath. When I feel his fingers exploring my bottom, my fantasy is that a very long but delicately thin penis is penetrating my anus. I can feel this thin shaft penetrating me from behind and the feel of the palms of his hands pressing against my buttocks reminds me of another male attacking me from behind. This causes me to relieve the muscular tension which I have built up in my pelvis as though to admit this second party to my body. As my husband and I come to our climax, I imagine that this thin shaft inside my rear is pulsating and thrusting to fill me with a double ration of semen, thus ensuring that the act of intercourse, if not successful by my husband, has been achieved by the fantasy "thing" behind me. I have no feelings of who might be the owner of this aggressor from behind me. He or It is a nothing in my mind, but is a very real sensation of additional intrusion within my body. Sometimes the tension in my rear is so great that I lose all control, and the moment after my husband has come, my bladder relaxes completely and I pee, flooding back to him the semen that he has just shot into me. We have only once tried to have anal intercourse, but because of the thick dimension of his mighty dwarf I just could not take him. The fact of my involuntary release of just a little urine gives my man a tremendous thrill.

I have seen cows being served by a bull on a farm that belongs to some friends. One particular bull is very broad across the back, like the flat top of a table. My husband and I frequently have sex in the lounge or the kitchen after the children are in bed or away for the weekend. Then I imagine that I am lying on the back of the bull, while the

45

bull is mounting a cow. I experience a distinct feeling of the kitchen table or the lounge settee on which I lie heaving up and down. My hands automatically go down on either side of the table to grasp the legs, to prevent myself from falling off the back of the frantic bull as he works away at the cow. I can feel my body thrusting up and down in time with the thrusts of the bull into the cow. Sometimes my husband has extreme difficulty staying inside me. Invariably I experience a climax before my husband in these situations, and his continuing action to bring off his own climax results in me having a second orgasm, which I imagine in my mind to be the bull flooding the cow with his sperm. On these occasions I imagine my husband's penis to be even greater in girth than it really is. In fact, I imagine it as thick as the bull. To make this even more realistic, I sometimes insert a finger into my vagina at the moment of his climax to swell his real dimension to what I imagine would represent the bull's erection. My husband enjoys this routine, feeling that my finger's there to help stimulate him. However, it is my desire to feel filled by an enormous penis that is really the key to the whole situation. [Letter]

Heather

I'm twenty-two and very shy, and group gropes aren't my scene at all. But my imagination isn't the least bit shy. When my husband and I are making love, or when I masturbate, I visualize my husband screwing another woman while I am screwing another man. We're all in the same room, or in two double beds, and I can see what they're doing in a big mirror. It excites me very much. I can't remember when this started or what started it, but I very rarely reach orgasm without thinking about it. [Letter]

Kitty

Sometimes during sex, or just during the day, I think of what it would be like to trade husbands, that is, for me and my husband to have sex with a couple with whom we are good friends . . . me with the guy and my husband with the other wife. This can be one of several couples that we know, or any new couple we meet and hit it off with.

I often tell my husband of these "group sex" fantasies, that is, of imagining trading off with our friends and imagining what they look like naked, and he reciprocates. We often talk of what it would be like to swap with Virginia and Dick or Fran and Ernie for instance, but never do so, and are quite sure we never will. It's just the imagining it, thinking of what it might be like, and their bodies, what we all might do that is so exciting. But if I happen to be around a friend when she is dressing or nude, which of course doesn't happen often, I make mental notes and then describe to him in great detail her feminine charms. He does the same for me if he happens to see someone I know in the men's room. We both thoroughly enjoy having this nude mutual fantasizing about our friends; we find it very stimulating and exciting, even if it will never happen . . . especially so, I guess. You can go so much further in fantasy than you can in reality. [Letter]

SEXUAL INITIATIVE

☐ Society encourages women to find sexual partners; a woman without one is disturbing, she is only half a woman (spinsters and nuns are downright creepy to some people). Society demands she have sex (a marriage must be consummated to be legal), yet she is barred from initiating sex. She is granted sexual desires, urged to fulfill them, but discouraged from taking the active role . . . except in fantasy, where, in her own way, in her own time, she can take what she's been told is hers rightfully as a woman.

What is meant by "She's a real woman"? Men say it with such loaded admiration that every woman within hearing distance freezes in envy and anticipation of finding out, at last, what it is that the "real" woman has. (Women don't say "She's a real woman" of one another; how would we recognize one? We've been trying to find out what it is to be a woman since we were born.)

Information is so scarce and contradictory on the vital essentials of womanhood, you would think someone (Mother?) was intentionally trying to mislead us from the beginning. Not only contradictions within, but contradictions without; the clues we do get seem to go directly against what we feel, what we want to do.

Our first toy is a baby, a doll baby; our first "play" role is that of Mother, and while we dimly know this all has something to do with our sex, we are given no clues about that. Some step seems to have been left out, and the anger and anxiety our mothers show beneath their fixed smiles when we ask questions about it show it was left out deliberately, and we'd better Keep Off that particular grass. We play house with our play babies, but it's a daddyless house. Little boys don't play house; it's not an accepted role. Nor is there any accepted play role in which the little mothers can explore their first sexual drives, which often come so unexpectedly. Little girls with lots of suddenly newfound energy, who want to run and holler, swing in trees and climb walls, are called tomboys. Clearly, spontaneity and action are not the quickest route to womanhood. But if it is not an acceptable outlet for these mysterious, perhaps troubling new energies, what is? We are not told. We only know there is a mystery here. We can go wrong somewhere. All about us is silence. We learn to be still. Passive.

Eventually a girl grows out of doll babies and begins to get her first signs of having miraculously arrived at womanhood. (Without understanding how she got there, because to her knowledge she has done nothing, learned

48

nothing, experienced nothing at all. Can *this* be it? Doing nothing, avoiding the mystery, being passive and ignorant —is that being a woman?) Whatever the answer is, boys are apparently aware which girls have solved the problem. They begin to ask those girls out on dates. Dates lead directly and naturally to those desires and urges she's been stifling. And wonder of wonders, the way to get asked out most (to be the most womanly?) is to do what you really want to do, and stifle nothing at all! Freedom, excitement and "real" womanhood suddenly and magically seem united and integrated, beckoning at last.

Wrong. Once again it is pointed out—by Mother and the other girls, if you're slow in catching on—that action, the seemingly easiest way to womanhood, is not the nicest way. Is maybe not the way at all. In fact, once again, it seems womanhood has something to do with *not* doing what you want to do, with frustration and passivity. Suddenly childhood's vague distinction between "nice" little girls and girls who were not "nice" becomes a decided hard-line distinction between women: there are two kinds. The ones boys like to go out with, and the kind they marry. But which of the two is the "real" woman? The choice is more bewildering now that she's had a taste of the forbidden fruit: Whether to reach out and respond, or to hold back, to hold out for marriage.

No one is taking any chances: Marriage is now painted —by Mother?—as the glorious answer to every maiden's prayer, the end of the rainbow, the beginning of "happily ever after . . ." And just to be sure the marriage sticks and the maiden doesn't wander, the "real" woman is further defined as not only married, but also a mother. Or to put it another way—Mother's way—one isn't a real woman until one *is* a mother.

But just as with baby doll toys that arrived out of a sexless void, a vital step between herself as she is now and this new "real" womanhood has been passed over in silence. With each new man in her life she could have learned something new, maybe contradictory things (one man's real woman is another man's dull or cutting tool), but always something that might have brought her closer to the enigma of herself and of what womanhood could indeed be for her. The prospect of this exploration of the variousness of men and women and life itself is fascinating, frightening, and forbidding—if not forbidden (by Mother and the other girls).

I'm convinced this is why so many women marry early: For every woman who holds out for the unknown, for sexual exploration, there are hundreds who anxiously grab marriage, motherhood, and the symbolic surface manifestation that she has at last arrived: She is a *real* woman. The wedding ring certifies it and motherhood guarantees it. Who is there in the world to doubt these majestic reassurances? Only herself, the self in her fantasies who picks up where her real self left off in trying out and trying on women's various sexual roles.

One role she's been denied from the beginning is that of sexual initiator, innovator. A woman may ask a man to dinner, but she may not ask him to dance. She may ask him to pass her the salt if she wants more of it, even reach across the table to get it, but she may not put her hand on his knee under it. She will coax him to try her new dishes and urge him to have more because Mother told her his stomach was a quicker (nicer) way to his heart than the telephone. Traditionally, women wait to be asked, or acted upon. To reach out for the man you want is to be aggressive, and to reach out for the way you want him in bed isn't just aggressive, it's unfeminine. The fact that he might enjoy what follows her first move isn't what's at issue; the point is that it isn't done, hasn't been done, and won't be done until men and women are convinced that changing the traditional sexual roles doesn't constitute a threat.

Meanwhile, if he's too shy to telephone, or perhaps less imaginative or worn out in bed than she (might be, given the chance), then two people who'd like to never do get started and the sheets barely get rumpled. He never knows what he's missed; she does, but only in her fantasies. And if in those fantasies, as in so many in this book, she comes

50

on like a tiger, in a startlingly aggressive role—she tying him down on the bed, etc.—don't hastily put the little lady down as a secret dominating sexual sadist: Sometimes you have to shout just to be heard.

Even as sexually self-accepting a woman as Carol (below) has to fantasize a sex-instruction class where an imagined instructor *tells* her to take the initiative before she can, in reality, do something as loving and natural as climb on top of her husband. Faye's fantasy, which follows Carol's, of initiating her lover into a three-way sex scene, is something she has always longed to do and feels he would enjoy too, but only if she took him by the hand. Why not? Think how much more active the dance floor and the bedroom might be if women (and men) felt easier about taking the first step, making the first move, assuming a second position . . . or a third, or a fourth. □

Carol

My husband and I are expatriate New Zealanders. We live in Papua. My husband is fifty-five years old and I am nearly thirty-eight. We have been married 18 years. We have two children, and have had and continue to enjoy a highly satisfactory sex life together.

My fantasy, which often occupies me, is that we are a demonstration couple for a class of young couples being instructed in the art of intercourse. I can hear the instructor telling the class of our progress toward climax. Every so often the instructor wants us to change position so that his pupils can get a better view between my legs. At this point I usually climb on top of my husband, sometimes adopting a squatting attitude over him to enable our audience to see our connected organs together. Sometimes I hear the instructor tell me to take the active part, whereupon I actually tell my husband that I want our movements to come only from me until he ejaculates. He will usually cooperate, unless I have misjudged his progress and he is about to come off anyway, in which case I will mentally apologize to the instructor. But on most of the occasions when my mind runs this way, I can hear the instructor accurately telling the audience my feelings while we are having each other, and he keeps talking the whole time in a soft voice so as not to distract the pair of us. Every time he instructs his class to watch more closely I become even more excited, feeling their eyes on us. The instructor's voice, as he calmly tells me to do all the things I want to do, is not like any voice I know, no particular friend or acquaintance. But he is a friend in that his role in my fantasy is that of benefactor, someone who is looking after me and knows my every desire. He and I have a wonderful rapport. [Letter]

Faye

I'm not sure what got me started on this fantasy. I really like Richard; in a way we're more than just lovers, we're great friends. Marriage will never be our scene; we could go ages without seeing one another, but whenever we are together it's as lovers, and we can pick up wherever we left off. I do love him, but maybe it's because I love him without the possessiveness that so often goes with love that I have this fantasy. I don't think Richard's ever had a conscious queer notion in his head, I mean I don't think he'd ever acknowledge being attracted sexually to another guy. But I think there's a bit of the bisexual in all of us, and in some way I think I bring it out in Richard. Maybe it's because I want to. You see, I really get turned on by this idea of me and Richard making it with another guy. I'd just love to see him expressing some of that good solid love he has for sex, for women—sharing it with men too.

And I'd love to be the one that makes it happen. That's it, I guess: I'd really love to initiate him into a happy little group scene, and as long as I'm there, involved, I think he'd do it and enjoy it. What's interesting is I know I'd never be turned on with this idea if Richard and I were serious about each other, because I am too damn jealous and possessive. But I'd love to turn him on, him and another man and me. It would be so friendly and exciting.

I am kneeling in front of a fireplace, poking the embers back to life. Only it's not a real fire, it's papier-mâché, and the room is like that chalet we once rented in Switzerland; in fact the room is a set, a stage. Because of the stage lights I can't see the audience, but I know they're out there. Also, the fake fire throws out a semicircular pink glow that surrounds me, making it hard to see who the other man is.

He has just come into the room with Richard and they stand in the shadows behind me, talking. As Richard goes into the other room to mix us all a drink, the other man starts to follow him, then changes his mind and comes and stands behind me. He puts his big sheepskin coat around me, as I'm shivering. Then he kneels beside me and takes the poker, but keeps my hand under his, pressing it hard around the grooved handle. I watch my fingers whiten under the pressure of his. Richard's voice comes warm and happy from the other room, and the sound of the ice clinking in the glasses. I can smell the other man's warm brandy breath and feel the hardness of his thigh against me, and the unrelenting pressure of his hand. I let the coat slip from my shoulders, feeling the pain in my nipples as they harden visibly under my sweater The audience murmurs appreciatively. Now I reach for a log to put on the fire and in the movement let my nipples graze his shoulder. My gesture lets him know I won't resist; his pressure on my hand lessens. The audience claps very quietly, approving. Squatting as he is, I can see the sudden bulge in his trousers as I acquiesce. His cock moves like a quick heartbeat, just above that mysterious place between a man's legs where all the seams of his trousers meet. Behind us is the familiar sound of Richard's voice, like a hum. He is humming as he puts on the music. Shirley Bassey's voice, heavy breathing music-to-get-laid-by, Richard calls it. With his finger, just the finger tip the man lifts my sweater and bends his head to press his warm lips around my breast, holding me in his mouth, just his tongue flick-

53

ing the nipple until I gasp. And the audience gasps, too. My body begins to move with the music, my body and this man's mouth in a dance, all wet and warm now. With my finger I begin to trace the seam between his legs and his mouth responds, his tongue circling downward as my hand spreads round his crotch, the fingers arched and separated over the pressure beneath. In one motion I unzip his fly, setting him free like some giant bird. Now his tongue is in my hair, reaching for it just below the top of my low-slung pants. His hands tug to ease them down so that he can get at me. I can feel his breath just above my clitoris and can feel him inhale the scent of me; I am wet with my own juices. His hands work quickly at the fastening on my pants and I am free, too, his mouth open wide now, his tongue full out for where I want it. I lean back, resting on my hands, raising myself up to him, and he holds my buttocks, pressing my upturned cunt to his mouth like some big, wet persimmon. The lips of my cunt seem to move like real lips in anticipation, begging him for his tongue until I feel it, warm and full on that little spot, sucking it in a kiss. I strain, arching my back to give him that whole part of my body, the music all around me, Shirley wailing away for more, my head thrown back, so far away from that other part of me, so lonely, until I open my eyes and see Richard watching us, fascinated, his own erection big and eager to share. "Come," my own lips form the word, and he is on us, on top of me, his grateful mouth on mine, his cock dangling in front of the other man's face. But only for a second, as the man raises his mouth from my cunt to Richard's cock, while thrusting his own cock into me with such force that my scream of pleasure is drowned in the thunderous ovation from the audience. [Taped interview]

INSATIABILITY

☐ Why do women fantasize about sex when they've got it, when they're right in the midst of it, Why do unashamed and sexually satisfied women like Carol and Faye imagine more sex when they already have their hands (etc.) full? Maybe because physically women, most women, are never full, never sated sexually beyond their imagination.

It need have nothing to do with reality, with whether the real man can (or even would if he could) totally satisfy her; as I said earlier, to reduce fantasy to the "nothing but" kind of thinking, which says it is "only" frustration, is too simple. Fantasy, by definition, is about something that isn't happening, and some of the most vivid fantasies I've collected are from women who are clear about not wanting their fantasies to be reality.

No, rather than a frustrated cry for more real sex, I think that a lot of female fantasy is a psychic need for a more complete exploration of everything that was kept from them as girls, of everything that conceivably could be thought sexual.

"The Road of Excess leads to the Palace of Wisdom," wrote William Blake, and the unconscious mind knows this is true. Fantasy means more involvement, more spontaneity. more take as well as give, more focus on herself, and maybe more noise, more black men. women, dogs, audiences, parents, experiences, attitudes, roles. For women, sex is still the infinite and inexhaustible variable, the one way she can unravel the mystery of what it is to be and feel a woman. I think women have enormous sexual appetites—far greater than is publicly acknowledged.

Of course, these appetites could be fed in reality; often they are not. But they do exist and can be made known to the woman herself in fantasy. ☐

Clarissa

When my husband first begins to make love to me, just feeling me and kissing me, there is one imaginary scene that comes to my mind, and that is that I am an African fertility image or statuette with long pointed breasts grotesquely exaggerated in size, and that instead of my husband I am being loved by the male counterpart, a fertility figure with an enormous penis far out of proportion to his body.

This image seems to turn itself on without my trying or doing anything about it, almost as soon as I am sure we will have intercourse, and continues until I have had an orgasm. It has nothing to do with my being dissatisfied with my husband's penis, which is a very good-sized one that fully satisfies me. I just somehow seem to imagine that this enormous, long, thick penis (with a giant knob on the end) is entering me. When we are just starting, I imagine this huge organ is rubbing my enormous breasts, and especially is more or less dueling with them, trying to slide up between them and poking at first one and then the other, and that I am holding it off from me by sticking my huge breasts in the way. This is when my husband is stroking or sucking my nipples. Again, it is not jealousy on my part or any feeling of inadequacy, since I am quite sure he thinks I am adequate in this respect.

For example, I'll try to describe our very relaxed and loving habits with one another and our happy appreciation and acceptance of one another's bodies: We sleep nude, and he almost always is in bed before my hair is put up. I do this in the nude, standing in front of the large dresser mirror in our bedroom. He watches because he likes to see my breasts lift as I raise my arms to put in curlers, and then lower them. While we ordinarily are very old fashioned in our language, he almost invariably tells me, "You sure have yummy tits, kid," at such times. When I am done, I walk to the bed, bend over so he can nibble each

nipple in turn for a moment, then turn the covers down so
he is exposed, and bend over and give his penis a quick
kiss. We do this every night, although we have sex only
every second or third night on the average. If he already
has an erection or a partial one, I linger longer on his
penis since I know this is "the" night. If it is not, but I feel
I would like a little loving and don't think he is tired or
worried or something, I will work on his penis a bit more
to see if he responds. But many nights it is only a wifely
kiss and nothing more happens. (Of course we kiss mouth
to mouth before going to sleep, too.)

So you can see by the above that my fantasy of these
over-enlarged sex organs doesn't come from any feeling of
frustration or lack of appreciation. Looking further back,
I can't remember any fantasy as a child other than that of
erect penises. Although I don't do it much now, I can't remember when I wasn't masturbating some as a child . . . I
am sure it was as young as eleven years old, because my
mother caught a girl friend and me doing it together with
candles when we were twelve, and I had been doing it a
long time then. The candles were my friend's idea, since
she had found some of those wicked comic books in her
brother's room, showing Dagwood and Blondie and Harold
Teen and Lillums and others having sex, both genital
and oral, with the man in each case always endowed
with an enormous and constantly erect penis. I kept that
image in my mind the whole time I masturbated . . . the
sort of scary and exciting pictures of those huge comic
book penises. Actually, they weren't scary in the forbidden
sense; sex was not a forbidden topic in our house. My
mother had given me very full and complete sex instruction from a very early age, including the fact that sex is
fun, which most parents never mention. Mother didn't
scold us and didn't even tell my friend's mother what we
had been up to. She just made us stop and told us to be
careful not to hurt ourselves using candles or anything like
that. Although I did not experience my first intercourse
until I was fourteen, I always was definitely interested in
boys' penises from that day on, as well as before. I do not

know if this has anything to do with my African sex-god fantasy or not. It may have, I suppose.

I might mention that I've never told my husband of this fantasy, and I'm afraid I never will, because he would think I thought he was too small, and I really don't at all. [Letter]

Annabel

My fantasy is nearly always the same: I am being raped by not one man, but three or four. But the strange thing is that as each man takes his turn, I have to take a bigger penis. Some of the sizes of them in my fantasies are nine and twelve inches. And as I have to open my legs wide to take them, the erotic pleasure I have always brings on the most wonderful orgasm. The pleasure I get is so intense that my husband also gets added pleasure, thinking that it is he alone who is giving it to me. [Letter]

Iris

I am twenty-three years old, have been married two years, and have two children.

The earliest fantasies I can remember were when I was nine or ten years old; I would imagine that the boys in my class were looking at me and touching me and discussing my anatomy. Nowadays my fantasies are similar. I often fantasize that the man I am with is closely examining my sexual organs, not as a doctor, but as a lover. Sometimes I imagine he's discussing me with a friend while they both examine me and bring me to orgasm manually while they watch. I often practice this fantasy in front of a mirror while masturbating.

It was only recently that my husband and I admitted to one another that we had fantasies. We have never described them, just simply acknowledged their existence. I do sometimes think of other men while my husband and I are making love. I most often imagine men we know whom I find particularly attractive. I usually imagine that these men have begged me to have an affair with them and I've finally given in.

I don't think my husband would be jealous if I told him of this fantasy. Perhaps if I fulfilled it, he would be. He does know that I enjoy thinking about men; and that I always wish I knew what's behind the zipper of every man I look at. [Letter]

Nora

My husband is not an imaginative man and our lovemaking is not at all varied. I used to attempt to get him to try different things, but he never wanted to. The reason that I was more advanced was not that I'd had more experience before marriage than he had, but I had had *some*, and I guess what took place was what the man wanted, in all cases. Anyway, he was clearly offended, for example, when I tried once to push his head down toward my cunt, and he stubbornly pushed it up again to give me a conventional kiss on the mouth. He doesn't even seem happy with me on top, although he lets me once in a while.

In every other area except bed I consider him an ideal husband—or at least a good one, so I'm determined to reconcile myself to a somewhat deprived sex life. The way I do it is I achieve variety with my fantasies, and I achieve an orgasm almost every time by using them. I think variety is the key to the whole thing, and the reason so many marriages go stale is that they just do the same thing over and over. Well, so do we, but in my head it's different every time.

I do it all quite deliberately. I can tell, when I'm getting ready for bed, whether my husband is in the mood or not, and if he is I get myself all sexed up mentally, even before I get near the bed, while I'm brushing my hair and undressing and so forth. Sometimes I linger longer in the bathroom just so I can get to the right point in my fantasy.

Then, when we're having the same old version of sex, I'm having my old Arabian Nights. I mean it; it's like the one thousand and one nights, with me as Scheherazade telling myself a different sex story each time. For the first dozen or so times, it was just me and a man; I'd describe all the different things we did. Then I went on to think of different settings, like doing it on the kitchen floor (maybe with a delivery boy) or in my neighbor's garage when I went to borrow a tool (Freudian slip). Then I got involved for a long time with doing sixty-nine with people watching. Then I started thinking of myself with two men, and just lately I've been in a whole group, both men and women (but the women were involved with the other men, not touching me). I've never imagined myself with a woman, but other than that I'll try anything—mentally. I'm able to pace the flow of my thoughts to what's really going on, and this way it works for me almost every time. [Letter]

DAYDREAMS

☐ You could say that a woman's life was made for fantasy. All those idle hours, the boring repetitive jobs that her hands do automatically, the endless opportunities to reflect, construct and reconstruct. In a sense we were born to dream, to stay at home . . . it is how most men dream of us. Even today's superwomen who leave the house to go to work have at least as much opportunity for the odd idle fantasy as the guy at the next desk (and more natural talent and practice at it)—the tedious subway rides, the dull business conferences, hungover days when you just can't concentrate on anything except the erotic possibilities of the boss's moustache, the provocative way the new account executive dresses on the right, last night's abandoned fuck with Harry, the prospect of tonight's with George.

Does the adage "The idle mind is the devil's playground" indeed apply only to one sex? Why do advertisers consistently use a picture of a pretty girl with a faraway look in her eye to sell almost anything? Because it's universally accepted that women, dreamers all, dream the good pure thoughts that hold us all together—especially material things connected with the home. (And homemaking.) Whereas men, those lusty scoundrels, will dream only of things that might make their naughty dreams come true. What are men in advertisements wistful for? Automobiles, whiskey, rugged pipe tobacco . . . anything that might lead them more successfully to sex.

I suggest that next time you see that pretty female face with the Mona Lisa smile you consider, just consider, that she may not be thinking of a knight on a horse, just the horse.

This lifelong habit of rumination is what makes women so good at fantasy; daydreams are often as close as they ever get to what they really want. A man finding desire upon him can pick up the phone, go see someone, ask a girl out, or order one. But it is not so easy for a woman to reach out as readily and shamelessly for what she wants— to take his clothes off, take him to bed, take him from above, below, and if he won't take her from behind, take a whore to bed who will. . . .

Instead, women dream about it. □

Corinne

This fantasy really happened. What I mean is that it was told to me by the guy involved; it happened to him and another girl. But I've always loved the story so, and I like him so much, even though we've never made it together, that I fantasize that I am the girl, that he and I do make it in this very jolly way. Sometimes I'll be on the subway and find I have this foolish smile on my face as I think about this fantasy. I wish it would happen. Even if it never does it's helped me pass a lot of otherwise boring hours.

61

I've agreed to help a bachelor friend paint his new apartment, and since it's a hot day we've both shed our clothes to do the job. He's up on a high ladder slapping paint on the ceiling with a broad brush, while I'm standing below painting the walls with a roller. It's a water paint, pale grey; and at one point as we are laughing at some joke—we've been smoking a joint, and the record player is on loud—I glance up at him as he grins down at me, and from below his balls look so funny (and nice) even though he and I have never been to bed together and I don't really know him well enough to know how he'll take it—even so I reach up with my roller dripping grey paint and slather his bouncing balls, and on up to his collarbone. He lets out a yell, and risking his life he's down the ladder like a flash and lets go—slap! slap!—with his brush, on my tits, left then right, and I go spinning around and he whops me on the can, left then right, with his big, fat brush. So I run my roller up one of his sides from the ankle to the armpit, so he dabs me in the navel, and I double over laughing and he's on top of me, and we go down in a puddle of grey paint, writhing and wrestling and struggling and both of us suddenly aroused, hot as hell and panting and I'm saying "Put it in" and he's trying to get me in position so he can, and I get my legs up around his neck in a frenzy so he can find my cunt and it's all impossible with all the goddam paint, and suddenly I see his eyes widen with panic and I feel it the same second: the paint is burning us up, but it's only the first second we mind it, then it becomes the greatest sensation in the world and we both start sliding together and the slimy stuff on all our surfaces glues us together and we get it in, and we slide around fucking and fucking and FUCKING and *FF-FUUUCCCKKKIIINNNGGG* . . . [aaaaarrrrrgggggghhhhh] [Taped interview]

Molly

☐ Molly specified that this fantasy is not something she

thinks about during sex, but that it's more of a daydream, a little episode she likes to think about while driving to pick up the kids, or while she's doing housework. As Molly puts it, "It keeps my sexual machinery charged." She has never been a teacher, nor does she want to be, but she does admit to finding the young men her kids bring home attractive. She was married at 18.

"Maybe," she admits, "a little too early for an imaginative girl. Sometimes I think there is so much I've missed." □

The scene is a one-room schoolhouse, somewhere out West. The teacher is about my age, thirty-five, or even older. But she is a virgin, a frustrated old maid. She has kept one of the pupils after school, a strong, six-foot-tall boy who isn't too bright. She goes through a stern lecture with him about how he's not been paying attention during class, etc. She asks him two or three tough questions, and when he can't answer says she's going to have to punish him. She tells him to take down his pants; he's embarrassed but she insists. She sits down on a chair and makes him lie down over her lap, face down, with his pants pulled down around his knees, and she starts spanking him. He gets an erection and she spanks harder, but at the same time more caressingly. Then she starts fingering his penis with her other hand and she keeps spanking. He gets a bigger and harder erection. She asks him if he's ever fucked a girl and he says no and she moves around on the chair to get her skirt up; she has no pants on. She also moves him about until she can maneuver his penis into her cunt, and at this point she goes back to the lecturing tone she'd had earlier, and tells him all about how he's going to have to improve his work, etc., while she's still spanking him, but the spanking is more of a pushing him into her. She's also moving her pelvis back and forth rhythmically, very actively, so she's controlling the whole thing for her own mounting pleasure but also giving him a fantastic time.

He starts shouting, "Oh, teacher!" over and over as his climax begins, and she keeps trying to lecture him but the words fuck and cunt keep popping up in the middle of her lecture. They both work up to a noisy climax, by which time they've slid off the chair onto the floor. Afterward, she primly buttons her clothes and very mock-disapproving tells him he's going to have to stay after school again the next day unless he can bring his school work up to scratch, and he agrees that he certainly has been lazy, etc., and he just doesn't seem to be able to do the work. [Letter]

Alicia

☐ Alicia has never really left school. She is thirty-four, an associate professor at a Midwestern university, and is to go to Africa to complete one of her many papers on anthropology. When you meet her, it's hard to believe she is so professional and self-sufficient, as she looks as vulnerable and appealing as Mississippi honeysuckle. But behind those violet eyes, there is a mind like a precision tool. She has a penchant for difficult men, types who beat her up either physically or mentally. I've never known her to be attracted to a "nice guy," and I get the feeling that there's something in her that would turn even a nice guy into a bastard. I do know one of her former lovers, and he's as much as said she invites or incites a put-down reaction from her men, that there is something in her that brings out the worst in a guy: "Maybe it's just that you always know with Alicia that she isn't sexually satisfied. No matter how often you tell yourself it's her and not you yourself that's sexually unsatisfied or unsatisfying—that there must be something wrong with her because you know, always, that you've not really moved that dame—still, a guy can't help feeling inadequate with her in bed. She just isn't all there." ☐

I don't fantasize during sex. My fantasies fall more into occasional daydreams. I like to imagine that I am a unique creature of the future. Ethereally beautiful, of course, but this isn't central to the idea. What is important is that I am the triumph of some incredibly advanced geneticist's work aimed at breeding a strain of people equipped for the ultimate in exquisite sensual pleasures—with nerve endings and sensory circuitry so highly pitched that they can experience ecstasies unimaginable for normal, limited human beings.

For me, for those like me (and are there others like me? The excitement of this is that I don't know; I'm living my intense life in the midst of people who appear to be enjoying the same crude little pleasures as their ancestors and no more) . . . for me, the touch of a tip of a feather on my knee can produce—if my mood is erotic—a sensation so intense that it would be like twenty orgasms at once for another woman. I experience this all right, but it is invisible, secret, known only to me. It's not simply a hypersensitivity over all my surfaces—no, I can be impervious, I can make my way through a jostling crowd with only the usual discomfort at the unwelcome human contact. I'm inexhaustibly tuned up exclusively for sensuality, for carnality, for all the feeling and desires of the sexual animal. My sexuality, while animal, is capable of such subtlety that a glance, received a certain way from a man I fancy even mildly, can bring on wave after wave of the sort of piercing sensation that would cause gasps and moans and even screams from another woman. All I may show is a small smile in his direction, but what I am enjoying inside—just in a split second—is like the sum total of anyone else's lifetime of erotic experience.

The climax of this fantasy, of course, will be when I meet up with a man whose senses are as fantastically heightened and refined as mine, but I haven't gotten to that point yet. There's too much going on here, and I'm only getting started. He'll come along a few chapters from now, and then I'll really get going. [Taped interview]

Lily

Joe and I have been living together for three years now,

65

but we've been making it for eight years. I think we've got a pretty imaginative sex life together, and I enjoy discussing my fantasies with him. Unless I were to tell him that I'd been thinking of another man during a particularly passionate session, I don't think he would ever be jealous of my fantasies.

But I can truthfully say that I've never had fantasies of another man while Joe was making love to me. I think most of my fantasies are of the daydream type. I have had several recurring ones:

1. I never had an affair with my ex-boss, but he was extremely attractive and had a moustache. At times I'd find myself staring at him and wondering what it would be like it he were to fondle and kiss my breasts with his moustache rubbing across my nipples. I imagined it would be a very erotic sensation to have him suck my nipples and feel his moustache next to my skin.

2. I find myself staring at well-dressed black men on the subway. I begin by looking at their hair, then their faces, then I let my eye slowly, casually move down their bodies. I try to judge from the bulge just how large their penises are and with a little imagination I see them undressed and feel them inside me. I judge them as lovers individually. Occasionally I will do this with white men, but generally they are black. Joe is black, but I don't think this is why I do this.

3. Sometimes on my way to work I think about the way Joe made love to me the night before and I get quite aroused. I can feel my clitoris get hard and it starts throbbing. It is always a sudden jolt back to reality when I suddenly see the crowd of people squeezing out of the station.

I enjoyed answering your request. Yours is a great idea.
[Letter]

Eliza

Even when going about my household chores I sometimes think of how it feels to have a man run his hands all over my body. I often remind myself of the pleasure of having a firm penis sliding in and out of my mouth and try mentally to recreate any delicious experience. [Letter]

Esther

I daydream a lot, which probably accounts for the fact that I enjoy sex so often. I do my housework in the tops of baby-doll pajamas, stay in a half-hot mood most of the time, what with touching myself, or rubbing against different objects. The nozzle of the vacuum cleaner hose, for instance, played lightly over the pubic area is terrific and will bring on an orgasm if desired. Sometimes I wear a dildo inserted while doing housework. I imagine it to be my boxer dog's prick. [Letter]

Shirley

I am a nurse and have been married ten years. During boring lectures at the hospital, I often fantasize going down on the lecturer. I try to imagine just how long he could go on talking all that mumbo-jumbo while I was kneeling there in front of him with his penis in my mouth.

I also often find myself fantasizing about those patients who fill my particular fantasy type—usually strong, overwhelming, cavemen types with great staying power. It's funny: there they are, lying helpless in their little white beds or on the table, but when I'm looking at them and imagining, it's *me* who feels helpless and small, as they protect me and give me pleasure.

This has nothing to do with not loving my husband. I do. [Letter]

Lillian

Sometimes when I'm, say, peeling potatoes, I imagine

that Bill will come up behind me, bend me over and enter me, right there at the kitchen sink. [Conversation]

Viola

When I'm making love, I don't think of anything else but satisfying my lover. Would he be jealous if he knew I were thinking of someone else? Probably. Which is why I concentrate wholly on making love.

I save my fantasizing for when I'm alone. I wait till evening, take a couple of drinks, and curl up in bed with a sexy book. Then when the drinks take hold I can imagine my hands are those of my lover.

Other fantasies are just daydreams, which I have constantly. My favorite daydream is of me cooking or washing dishes, my lover comes in, puts his arms around me, and as we kiss and press against one another and our passion builds, I just reach behind me and turn off the stove, the dishes are forgotten, everything left wonderfully unfinished in this very interrupted state, as we go off to the bedroom to make love. [Interview]

MASTURBATION

☐ Not all idle minds drift to sexual fantasy, as not all sexual fantasy (and idle hands) leads to masturbation. In fact, it's the old chicken-and-the-egg routine. Fantasy and masturbation: which comes first? But one thing seems certain: that masturbation without fantasy is unlikely, unhappy, unreal. Masurbation doesn't just require fantasy, it demands it. Without fantasy, masturbation would be too lonely. I don't even want to think about it.

In my researches I didn't find one woman who said she had never masturbated. You could say that this has something to do with the nature of my subject, that the kind of people who talked to me were bound to be more sexually

candid. Perhaps my surprise at finding that all the women
I talked to masturbated is more a comment on me than my
contributors. Possibly. But you see, it wasn't that I didn't
expect women to masturbate—to have tried it or stumbled
upon it at some point in their lives—I simply didn't think
my own experience was all that universal. It goes back
again to how little women know about one another, how
inclined we are to feel isolated, different, not like the other
girls, because we don't know about other girls.

We all know about men; they masturbate. Little boys
and masturbation are a normal, even charming part of the
women's magazine stories as to how little boys are. I suppose that's it; we've all read so much about it, about little
boys discovering it, and being discovered. It's charming.

But women? We're as hidden as our clitorises. By the
time we've found them, hidden away up there, we're guilty
at having located them. If it were meant to be found and
enjoyed, wouldn't it be in the open, hanging down and
swinging free like a cock? (No wonder little girls suffer
penis envy.)

That, I suppose, is why I was so surprised to find we all
do it: I simply assumed without thinking that I was as
alone in my discovery as I'd been alone while growing up,
with my other female thoughts about my femaleness. Logically, I accepted my similarity to other women—why
should I be different?—but emotionally I was as uncertain
as to how I stood on the subject of masturbation as I was
on whether I was oversexed. No one talked about girls
masturbating, it was not a part of the prescribed myth of
innocence, of growing up, of becoming a woman. Actually, I don't think there is a female version of that popular
myth: neither Heidi, Nancy Drew, or the Little Women
masturbated; there is no female equivalent to Studs Loni-
gan and Huck Finn.

I'll tell you some things I've learned about women and
masturbation. Despite their long training to reticence,
once you've engaged their confidence, women talk about it
easily. Once they realize they aren't the only ones, they
admit to masturbation as readily as to sex, they accept it

69

and, unlike men, seem to feel no less a woman for doing it. You could reduce this to a sign of our times, to the nature of my research or of the women who would talk to me. But it's more than that; it's the essence of what all this research boils down to: that women, once opened up and allied to other women, are indeed less ashamed, more adventurous, more accepting sexually than men. If books like mine help women to be more trusting with each other, to talk, to explore, we may find that the whole chapter on sex in our permissive age has not been written. Only half.

Here is some incidental data on the subject of fantasy and masturbation that I found interesting: Most of the women I talked to remember their first sexual fantasies and their first masturbation to have occurred at about the same time, usually between seven and eleven (for reasons I don't understand, these two ages, seven and eleven, are the specific years most often mentioned). Also, when they do masturbate they don't fantasize about the same things that they do during sex.

In fact, many fantasies during masturbation don't even concern active sex; sometimes just the fantasy of being nude on a beach is all the sexual imagery a woman wants or requires. One last thing: I think women's invention in the choice of their masturbatory tools is worth a mention —from the familiar finger, the dildo, the increasingly popular vibrators (although everyone mentions being put off by the noise of the batteries) to cucumbers, vacuum cleaner hoses, battery-operated Ronson toothbrushes, silver engraved hairbrush handles, exotic phallocrypts made by native houseboys, down to simple streams of water. Sometimes the tool is everything, appearing in both fact and fantasy in the same form—and sometimes the hairbrush becomes the desired lover's cock and the water from the bathtub faucet the pee from a very black man's cock. Shocking? Not when you think about it. ☐

Patsy

Hope this letter will be of some help to you. To give you an idea of what I am like, and maybe help in working out why I think like this, I am twenty-nine years old, married six years, no children. We have sex an average of three to four times per week, but my husband does not know I am writing to you, as there are some points I think might make him wonder about me.

First, I would like to say that I do masturbate. I use a vibrator, usually in the mornings and after I have a bath. I seem to get excited as I stroke my breasts and think of or look at some of the books we have. My breasts are not very big and when I see some of the girls with big full titties I really get excited. One of my favorite fantasies when I masturbate goes back to something that actually happened:

Once I went to a sauna bath with a friend who I thought had lesbian tendencies. What happened can still bring me on. My nipples and clitoris get firm just thinking about it. We both stripped, put towels around us, and went inside. There was one other woman there. She lay down on her back, showing all. When she left, my pal undid her towel and stretched out on her back. It was the first time I had seen her in the nude and the way she was talking soon made me feel sexy. I took my towel off and she remarked how much darker and bushier my pubic hair was than hers. She was very fair, but her bust was a lot bigger than mine. She got up and came over to me and started massaging my legs. I let her carry on. Soon her hands were all over me. She asked me to go back to her flat for tea and said if I wanted she would finish me off. When we got there I was stripped by her and given a most satisfying thrill. She licked and sucked my breasts and went down between my legs and performed cunnilingus on me (better than my husband). I could feel her sucking my clitoris, and just to feel her breasts was enough to make

71

me come at least twice. I often think of this and then give
my husband a good time. [Letter]

Norma

☐ I think of Norma's name as being just right for her; to
me it has an old-fashioned, prim ring. And so I was not surprised that Norma was reluctant to give an interview for
this book. She thinks there is nothing wrong with it, however, and believes wholeheartedly that it can have a liberating purpose. She would even like her daughter ("if
I'd had one") to read it. "I wouldn't want any girl to be
brought up the way I was."
Norma also told me that she hadn't slept with a man
since her husband, who was more homosexual than not,
left her over fifteen years ago, just after their son, Ted,
was born. ☐
I'm very brave and aggressive in my fantasies. In fact, I
take the lead. My fantasies are always about young men.
You are probably thinking there is some element of incest
there—some desire for Ted. But I don't think that's quite
right. I think the reason that I imagine that the man is always fifteen or twenty years younger than I am is that it
makes him less frightening to me. In fact, he's always
someone who is a virgin, close to it. Somebody who
doesn't really know what it—the bedroom, you understand—is all about. So it's up to me to teach him, and
nothing he's going to do can surprise or worry me. He's
just a boy.
I may as well tell you this: I always have my fantasies
in the bathtub. Whenever I feel the urge, I just go in there
and get in the bathtub. But I do it in a very special way.
The way I was trained, brought up, I can never bring myself to touch myself there. Yes, there. Or to put anything
inside myself. What I do is turn the water on to a nice
warm temperature. Then I lie down flat on my back, with
my bottom right up against the end of the tub where the
faucet is, and I position myself with my legs open, feet up

72

on the edge of the tub, directly under the running water. I usually have a towel under my head. The warm bubbling water plays over me; I can pace my fantasy by either just lying there and letting the warm pressure of the falling water find its source, or I can hold my lips apart so that the rushing water excites me immediately.

Fantasies get worn out; somehow they finally lose their erotic charge. So you have to keep making up new ones. The one I recently made up is one of this beautiful young man and me. We're completely dressed, in fact, he's in black tie, and I'm wearing something long, black, and very dramatic. We're waiting for some people to arrive; the boy and I are strangers to each other, having only been invited to this house by mutual friends. Finally they phone to say they had to take a plane, and so will not arrive till midnight. They beg us not to go, however, but to pass the time as best we can until they arrive.

I suggest to the young man that we play some cards. I tell him that while cards without risk is a boring game, I still do not like to play for money. So he laughs and asks what would I like to play for. I suggest we play poker, and that the winner can get the other person to do anything he or she wishes for five minutes after each winning hand. What I have in mind is a game of strip poker, you see, because I am a very good poker player and know that under the disguise of the game I can get him to do what I want, almost as a joke, without embarrassing myself.

The young man agrees, and in ten or fifteen minutes he finds himself sitting dressed only in his stiff shirt, black tie, and shoes. The rest is naked. Sometimes I imagine that he immediately develops an erection, other times I vary it a bit by having him so embarrassed he is unable to have one until I "carelessly" make some revealing gestures with my body. Or touch him. Then I suggest that we play for higher stakes. He asks what this means. I tell him we should play for more imaginative forfeits, and the penalty period should be increased from five to fifteen minutes or even a half hour. He becomes even more excited, and I see a gleam in his eye. He agrees. But of course I win again.

"What do you want me to do?" he asks. I tell him to lie down on the bed, half undressed as he is, and then I proceed to tie his hands and feet to the bed.

When I feel he really can't move, I go into my act. In my mind, I become the kind of sexy woman I've always wanted to be. While he's lying there, tied hand and foot, I go into the sexiest striptease you can imagine. This is the real part of the fantasy. All the rest has been a buildup. But when I get to this part, I can feel almost a flush of heat. My stomach muscles begin to cramp—but not with pain—with the feeling of approaching orgasm. I come and sit on him, but only for a second, so that before he can have an orgasm of his own I'm off him again, leaving him all the wilder, his face redder, his erection hard as a rock. I talk to him, asking him wouldn't he like to put it in me? Sometimes I pretend I'm angry with him, and say that I'd rather stick a candle up myself than him. Sometimes I imagine that I do, and I can see myself, naked, with a large red Christmas candle sticking half out of me, dancing around this beautiful young boy. I tell him that if he'll push the candle all the way in with his teeth, I may untie him and let him make love to me. Or I use that stiff erection like a ramrod, kneeling over him so that his own erection—it's now so hard he couldn't make it soft if he tried—pushes the candle all the way in for me.

And all the time I'm having these thoughts, I can feel the lovely warm water touching me, stroking me, bringing my own rush of blood there. Then suddenly my muscles do cramp, and I have an orgasm right there in the nice clean bathtub. Then I just have a real bath and get into bed and have the most refreshing nap you can imagine. [Taped interview]

Adair

Sometimes when I masturbate there is this lovely person, who is, of course, my lover, and he gathers together a bunch of darling gentlemen who want very much to fuck me . . . seems there are always these guys in my fantasies just dying to get at me. Anyway, they all have wonderful members with remarkable proportions and they tell him that they think I'm swell, and I'm really having a bit of a ball myself. But the funny thing is that my gentleman friend who has gone to the trouble of finding me all these screws gets a little angry because I start liking it a bit too much when one of the fellows in the crowd gets to propositioning me for doing other things (which aren't included in the package deal). I am tempted and my lover gets angry with both me and the other guy and gently tells us not to be so familiar. Does that sound crazy? I suppose so, but you asked for it. [Taped interview]

Mary Beth

On the rare occasions I masturbate, I use the engraved silver handle of a hairbrush, and think about my former lover, who used to let me fellatiate him . . . an act I love to do, but which my husband doesn't permit. I visualize my lover's prick getting hard in my mouth, the veins coming out on it, and then, just as I'm about to come, I love to look down and see my own juices caught between my husband's engraved initials. . . . [Letter]

Elizabeth

I imagine a variety of things when I masturbate. Sometimes it's that a man has come to the door selling something and I invite him in. While he stands there displaying his Fuller brushes or whatever, I begin to caress myself. He watches, obviously aroused, and finding it harder and harder to continue his sales spiel. Then I remove my clothes and begin to masturbate, all the while watching his efforts to control himself. He's in a real state, and of course I'm very cool—in one sense, but I'm also getting very worked up. Sometimes at this point I'll invite him to penetrate me, much to his surprise and delight. He can barely get his trousers off, his erection is so enormous. And he breaks half of whatever it is he's selling—steps all over it—in his haste to get at me. While imagining this I will insert a carrot or some similar object into my anus while I stimulate my clitoris manually or with a vibrator to enhance the fantasy.

Sometimes I change the plot: I make no attempt to entice or encourage the man. But once in the house, he is unable to withstand my quite formidable charms and he rapes me, right there in the living room—taking care not to cause any real pain or damage to me. I imagine him to be an extremely skillful lover, so that although I start out repulsed by him and trying to dissuade him, I end up begging him for more while he teases and entices me and demands that I do various things for him ... many of which I've never done before, never been asked to do before, and often wish my husband would ask me to do. [Letter]

Mary Jane

I almost never masturbate, now that I am married, but when I do, my fantasies involve only myself in most cases. I will list a few of the fantasies that I can remember. In one, I think of being alone on a beautiful white ocean beach. The sky is clear, the sun is shining, and warm breezes are softly blowing. I walk along the beach for awhile, and then I stop and take off all my clothes. When I am nude, I go for a leisurely swim in the ocean. When I come out of the water, I lie down on the soft, warm sand and feel the breezes blowing over me and the sun warming my body. In a variation of this fantasy, I think of doing similar things by a mountain waterfall. Most of my fantasies involve thoughts of my taking off all of my clothes, and often the setting is outdoors. A few times, I have begun masturbating while I was fully clothed and, as I was masturbating, I removed all of my clothes. [Letter]

Amelia

When I masturbate, I have a recurring "daydream" of a salesman approaching a lovely white cottage on a beach and finding the door partly open. He calls and, getting no answer, wanders through all the rooms looking for some sign of occupancy. Finally he comes to a closed door and hears water running within. Opening the door he finds a woman showering and he proceeds to undress, climb into the shower, and make love to the woman. By this time I usually have my climax. [Letter]

Alix

☐ "I have never cheated on my husband, even though before our marriage I was rather promiscuous," says Alix. "Even on our wedding day, I wondered if I could be happy with one man. But I am."

Alix is twenty-four, married four years, and mother of two. Her husband's frequent business journeys give her a lot of time for her fantasies. These fall into two principal categories, lesbian and masturbatory.

Alix has told her husband of the latter, and as he has his own, they often share their masturbatory fantasies together. But Alix has never mentioned her lesbian fantasies to her husband, even though, as is characteristic with many men, he thinks of a lesbian episode as essentially a frivolous matter, of less serious import than male homosexuality; for instance, he has told her he wouldn't think it "cheating" if she had sex with another woman. ☐

Most of my lesbian fantasies occur during masturbation. The most common is one in which I am watching women masturbating themselves in demonstration for me. I visualize many different positions and techniques, all under spectacular circumstances.

77

For instance, I fantasize that I am held captive by native women who dance around me in a kind of pagan rite and then make me watch them masturbate. Then there is the fantasy where I am walking through the woods and come across a woman making love to herself. These fantasies of women masturbating really stir me up. Then, while I am actually masturbating myself, I fantasize that someone, like a neighbor or my husband has walked in the room just as I am at the height and am climaxing over and over, but I can't stop—even though someone is watching —because it is so good.

My preoccupation with masturbation extends to idle daydreaming, or imaginings when I see or meet someone attractive: I invariably wonder whether that woman or that man "eats" his or her partner. and whether he or she masturbates. I don't think of these things in connection with myself, but I simply wonder whether or not they do these things.

My husband does not know of my fixation with masturbation and of my secret desire to have a woman make love to me. However, the fantasy we engage in together is very enjoyable and leads to wild times together. I love to hear him tell about masturbating himself that day (if he did that day, if not he tells the circumstances of another time, which excites me even though I've heard it before).

My husband is a carpenter and he will tell me, for instance. that during his noon hour he went to a part of the building that was finished—all the other guys were nowhere around—shut himself in a closet. took out his penis and jerked off for ten to fifteen minutes. then shot his semen on the floor. All the details of these circumstances really excite me. Sometimes he masturbates in the bathroom during his coffee break. He says he gets to thinking about me giving him a blow job and he just has to masturbate Sometimes he tells me about masturbating in the woods when he goes hunting. When I take the kids to see my mother—she lives 350 miles away—I am gone several days. He masturbates while I am away and tells me the details during our lovemaking when I get back.

Then he says, "Honey, did you do it today?" and I tell him the circumstances under which I was masturbating and where I did it. He gets very excited. He always wants to know if I took my clothes off or if I just put my hand up my panties, whether I used an object in my vagina or if I used my two hands—one to stimulate my clitoris, and the other rapidly in and out. However, I do not tell him of my lesbian fantasies during masturbation. I tell him that I was thinking about us.

All this time, while we are exchanging tales, we are engaging in serious foreplay. We also like to masturbate together and watch each other masturbate.

My orgasms during masturbation are very different from those I have during intercourse. Eventually we do have intercourse, and by this time we are wild for each other. I must tell you that before we brought this aspect into our lovemaking, that we made love infrequently and all passion on my part was fake. For three years of our marriage I never experienced an orgasm unless I masturbated.

Then one night during foreplay, I said to him, "Do it like this," and tried to guide his fingers.

Then he said, "You do it, baby," so I played with myself, but very inhibitedly because I didn't want him to know that I had done it very often before. He saw how excited I was getting, though, and said to me, "Fuck yourself, baby," and he played with his penis while I did it.

That was the start of our new great sex life. It took several more sessions before we both made full confessions, but it turned out that he had been masturbating since our marriage and long before. I never tried it until we were married one year, and I had never done it as a teen-ager. The guilt I felt was awful until I started looking into the subject and learned that it is common and natural. I still felt guilty, though, until we started doing it together.

I really think I am more intrigued with masturbation, both sexes, than with lesbianism. The latter is just part of the former. What I mean is I've always been fascinated with men and would never want to live with a woman. I remember as a child of about seven, when I saw my father and some pals of his urinating behind a barn. Penis envy was my first fantasy, and how I wanted one. I used to think that if Daddy put his penis between my legs that I would grow one too. I think men, their penises, are fascinating; sometimes I think how much I'd love to "catch" my husband masturbating, to secretly see his actions and passion when he was completely alone and uninhibited.

I find that with time, with talking about them, our fantasies and our love life get better and better. I wish we'd started talking earlier. [Taped interview]

THE LESBIANS

☐ There is nothing consistent about women and fantasy, the reasons and circumstances for it. It varies from woman to woman. And with each individual woman, from night to night and lover to lover. Even with the same lover within the same hour a woman may or may not fantasize, depending on so many things, all the uncharted tides and moons of a woman's psyche. But lesbians are different. Their whole lives contain an element of fantasy—that they are both their own sex and another. It is my belief, therefore, that lesbians fantasize more often than other women.

During sex a lesbian's fantasies have to be especially active to help make rational to herself her often wildly veering changes of identification between one sex and the other, as she switches from the male to the female role and back again. In Marion's fantasy, the first in the group that follows, she admits she has to fantasize when she's actively exciting her girl friend just so she can be excited too. And even though Marion is the butch lesbian, her favorite part of the fantasy is when Lilly grabs the Ronson dildo and becomes the man, and she, Marion becomes "just a simple cunt, being fucked by some motorcycle guy."

Most women, I have found, have what they call their "lesbian fantasies" from time to time, that is, sexual fantasies that involve other women. They have these even though their real lives are totally or predominantly hetero-sexual. Some women accept these images as naturally as their own female anatomy—"of course women think about other women"; for others they raise a question, the possibility of their own latent bisexuality, while still others ponder guiltily over whether thinking about it means they really want it. Women's secret thoughts of other women; it's like a mystery within a mystery, and a topic I'd like to save till later. For now, these fantasies are from lesbians, women who accept and/or practice their preferred attraction to women. □

Marion

□ Marion was born on a farm in North Dakota, and her first name is really Marianne; she changed it to the more sexually ambiguous Marion when she came to an under-standing of herself later in life. She has never liked men. □

Maybe it was my father's jokes that turned me off men so strong. My father wasn't really intelligent. Even as a kid, I knew he was hopeless. A big-boned, large—I don't know, *unfinished* kind of man. I remember even today the phone calls that would make my mother cry. Other women phoning him. I remember thinking about one of these other chicks—Why does my father like her over my mother? This other one sounded so stupid. Once there was a terrible fight over a letter he got from one of them. But I remember more than anything else in my childhood the phone calls, and my mother crying. I can even remember saying to myself as a kid that I never wanted to be like her. Like my mother.

You won't laugh? Fuck you if you do. What the hell do I care what you think. What I want is for a lot of cunts like you to understand how it is with people like me. Les-bians. The fuckin' word sounds so rotten. And I don't like to be called "gay." I'm no faggot. But why should the word sound so rotten? You like lettuce and I like apples.

81

You like men and I like women. So what? What the hell is so criminal about that?

Shit on the soapbox. I mean, on preaching. But it's a downer—always having to defend yourself. Okay, here's what goes through my head:

Lilly and I, we like to use an electric toothbrush. The battery-operated kind, so you don't have to worry about the electric wires, or plugging it in. [Laugh] Except that's just what you do—plug it in.

You ever go to a doctor or a dentist, and he's cut his finger, and he wears a little rubber cap on his finger? Like a little condom? Anyway, we use that—we use epoxy glue to glue the toothbrush itself onto the little metal head—otherwise the vibration'll shake the brush off. Then I use the same glue to put the rubber cap on the brush, so that it covers the bristles. Some of our friends do this, too. It's like our own "in" joke. "What are you using tonight, Jack?" we say to each other, when somebody's picked up a new girl. "A Schick?" We trade brand names. I like a Ronson. It's got four, or maybe six batteries, I forget, but it really goes.

I have a kind of strap. It goes around my waist and up over my shoulders, crossing in the back and then down under my ass and coming back up to the belt again. I had a sandal-maker make it for me. So the Ronson is really anchored right down low and in place. I mean, it's rigid. [Laugh]

Look, you talk to any guy, and the first thing he wants to know, Has he made the girl come? That's their mark of virility. That's what they're anxious about. But me and my Ronson, I can make any girl come, every time. It's simple biology. Men have this business, they don't even understand, to get deep inside. To plant the seed. That's biology. Okay, I'm butch, I'm also a woman. I understand the clit. I don't have that urge to go deep into a woman. Maybe I'm competitive with men. Or maybe I don't want to just give in to biology. But I don't care about going in deep. I know about myself and I never forget that the clit is where it's at.

So I know what Lilly's getting out of it. But there I am all alone in my head, very excited, but still somehow all alone. I know Lilly is going to be okay, but I have to make up these images in my mind so that I can get excited, too. What turns me on is that I'm raping a motorcycle rider. One of these butch studs in the polished black leather, and the big machine. I'm moving in and out of Lilly, giving her a little bit of clit, a little bit of cunt, and then a lot more of clit. But meanwhile, I can see myself in my mind, I'm still wearing that Ronson, but it isn't Lilly anymore. It's this stud, and I've got him over his bike. He's got his ass to me. He's that big, butch faggot, get it? And I'm giving him the Ronson up the ass. And he loves it. He's shoving that ass up at me. He can't get enough. And in my mind, I reach down under, to tickle his clit. As if he were really Lilly, and I was deep inside, but I knew she wanted her clit tickled too. And—I can feel it right now—I'm suddenly surprised. He doesn't have a cock at all. He *is* a cunt. He does have a clit. I have him from the back, and I reach down under his hips and push my finger through the hair and he's got a cunt. A clit. And then he flops over on his back, and I can feel the Ronson really plugged into him, and my own clit is vibrating too. He's got his legs wide open and then he puts them up over my shoulders. He's all cunt and I know the vibration is going all through Lilly, but it's going all through me, too, and sometimes at this point, Lilly grabs the Ronson out of its holder and shoves it up me and I love it.

She suddenly becomes the guy in the motorcycle leather, and I'm just a cunt, just a simple cunt, being fucked by some motorcycle guy, and I love it. I love it that Lilly is so excited that she's changed roles. Changed positions, so that suddenly I'm not the guy any more, but she is. Then I put my finger inside her cunt, and when I feel her stomach muscles begin to heave, that terrific contraction, spasm after spasm, I find myself almost screaming. I'm coming myself. [Taped interview]

Jeanne

□ Jeanne was born in Belgium, but has lived most of her twenty-five years in the USA. She had her first lesbian experience with her cousin Renee, who was a year older, and with whom she was sharing a summer at their uncle's farm.

Jeanne considers herself a lesbian still, "by choice, rather than the result of 'unhappy home-life,' economic conditions, socioeconomic factors, etc. . . ." At one time she felt ashamed of her desires, but now "a lover who really cares brought me to the realization that I'm not mentally ill simply because my sexual preference is for another woman." Jeanne has been living with this lover, Paula, for the past two years.

The incident that became imbedded in Jeanne's mind, and forms the seed from which her very elaborate fantasy grew, took place in the hayloft of her uncle's farm, where she and her cousin Renee were lying in each other's arms. The two girls were interrupted in their love play by the sight of Anjou, the cousin's young dog, mounting a bitch on the floor below. Both girls were intrigued by Anjou's "bevel-pointed maleness" entering into the bitch, and took turns describing to each other what an experience with Anjou might be like. Today, those descriptions have become ritualized into sexual fantasy, extremely detailed and lovingly elaborated. As with any work of art, it is this exactness of detail which makes the emotion of the fantasizer so real to the reader. □

Knowing that we will not be discovered, my cousin calls Anjou into the barn after he has finished with a bitch he has been mating with. Anjou's animal maleness has not receded into the sheath beneath his warm belly, and as Renee puts her arms around him she whispers to me, "Help get him on my back; I want to try, too." I am out of my mind with passion and emotion, and after closing the door, I quickly return to the rear of the barn where Renee

84

is already pulling hay down and making another "nest." I'm fascinated with Anjou's animal maleness; the enormous length of the glistening red, arrow-pointed organ is still exposed, and as Renee kneels on her hands and knees, saying, "Help me, put him up on my back," she lifts her dress up over her beautiful young hips and back, exposing her white rounded buttocks, spreading her legs apart, the moist flesh of her outer lips now totally exposed. I try several times to lift Anjou, but he growls, and then Renee reaches around and puts her hand around his organ, saying, "Jeanne, put your hand on my puss and then put it on his muzzle." All the while she is sliding her hand back and forth on the now vanishing organ of Anjou's maleness. As soon as Anjou licks my hand, his head moves at once to Renee's exposed bottom, and I become more excited as I see his long tongue flash out and he begins lapping Renee's exposed vagina.

Renee begins to moan softly, her voice comes to me from somewhere. Anjou is already mounted on her back, shifting from one leg to another as he tries unsuccessfully to introduce his bevel-tipped glistening organ into her youthful virgin vagina.

"Help him, put it in for him, hurry, Jeanne," and I put my hand around the vibrating, hot, glistening red maleness, and holding it gently I move it back and forth between the wet, fleshy, parted lips of her vaginal canal, until I direct it into the exposed mouth of her vagina.

I sit fascinated, rooted to the spot, as Anjou's red, arrow-like organ slips from its short hairy sheath and disappears into my cousin's exposed cunnie. She gasps and soon moans as Anjou begins to pump, my cousin backing her exposed bottom to meet his animal thrusts. Renee cries and moans with pleasure, and finally she begins to rotate her hips as I watch Anjou's long animal maleness move in and out of her exposed cunnie. The fleshy lips cling to his animal organ as he withdraws it and then with his forward thrusts it disappears into my cousin's belly. I can't stand it any more, and I get on my knees and crawl around my cousin, finally squatting in front of her so that she can apply her mouth to my fiery vagina even while Anjou's maleness is still pumping inside her.

Even today, I close my eyes and wish for all the world that Paula had an enormous, bevel-pointed organ stirring within me. As yet, I haven't confided to Paula that I fantasize that her elongated clitoris is Anjou's animal maleness, since I feel she might be disturbed, thinking I would prefer an animal to herself, which is quite absurd. And yet the association persists, and I like it. [Letter]

Lisa

Although I am married, most of my fantasies are about lesbians, and I continue to have occasional lesbian experiences. When my lesbian friend is making love to me, masturbating me, I climax to the thought of her having intercourse with me using a dildo.

I suppose I began having fantasies about the age of sixteen. Then, my fantasies were of going to bed with a man, having intercourse, but not having a climax. Now, when I am with my husband, my fantasies are often of animals. I imagine that he and I are lying on the bed, when a dog comes into the room and begins to lick me. I then masturbate the dog, get onto my knees, and the dog mounts me. I like to imagine that the dog ejaculates into me. I imagine that my husband mounts the dog as it mounts me.

My other fantasy is of a donkey. I imagine that my husband has sold me to an Arab, and that I am in the desert. My slave master brings his friend to watch me, their new entertainment. I am told I must entertain the animal, the donkey. I follow this through from beginning to end: the animal is led in and I masturbate and suck it. When the donkey is excited, it mounts me from behind. I like to take all of its tool and it ejaculates into me.

But my fantasies with my lesbian friend are the most exciting; it is then that the man's tool, her dildo, becomes real and totally satisfies me. [Letter]

Zizi

My name is Zizi. I am French and militant in the *"Mouvement de Libération de la Femme"* [Women's Lib]. As far as my establishment in time is concerned, I'm twenty-three years old.

I think that female sexuality is too hidden by taboos and inhibitions, that is why I don't hesitate to express some of my so-called fantasies. (In spite of my poor English, your curiosity of searching in that area excites me, I must admit.)

My first sexual experiences were the reflection of my submission to the patriarchal ideology, so I will not speak about that. My last relations with guys were more in connection with my subjectivity. What was significant for me was the overcoming of the stereotype "occidental basic position." I find my pleasure by climbing on top of the guy. I stick his penis in my cunt and I *ride* him like a horse. Then I squeeze my thighs (his penis is still inside me). His legs are spread—I have the feeling that I am a boy making a passive girl, the feeling that I have literally a phallus that is penetrating a cunt. That is a kind of revenge that I take after years of docileness. When I reach the orgasm, I feel my penis which ejaculates.

Through my love affairs with guys, I become to be conscious of my strong desires for other girls. Before I had really had sex with a girl (in Paris) I used to play some underneath "perversions." I'll summarize one: I lived in a flat in town; on the other side of the courtyard I noticed a middle-aged woman (housewife type) who was often leaning out of her window. One day, for *some reason* (!), I had the idea to walk nude in my room with the blind half down. She could not see my face. So she had the feeling that I could not see hers (no guilt). In fact, I was looking at her thanks to a subterfuge of mirror. I pretended to wash myself. She was extremely into her peeping trip. I began to masturbate my clitoris with my finger while I was

87

half cleaning myself. The more her attention seems to increase, the more I was caressing myself till I came.

Some months after that I had a love affair with a girl. We like the sixty-nine position, but we sometimes did unusual things (sort of in connection with my former fantasies). We decided to look at one another masturbating. We both sat in an armchair (we were half-dressed in order to make it more obscene). We looked at the movements of our fingers rubbing our clitorises—terribly exciting. We did not touch one another at all. The pleasure of one worked on the other and vice versa.

I could write more, but the fact that I don't know you really limits my pleasure in writing. Although it *is* a kind of trip to send some intimate sensations to an unknown girl (that I could eventually seduce? Who knows.).

Je m'aventure a te donner un baiser, ma douce inconnue. [Letter]

Kate

I have a permanent girl friend with whom I still sleep on occasion. I got married with her agreement and on the understanding that I give her detailed accounts of all that transpired when my husband did anything. Which I do in very complete detail.

Both Mary and I were virgins, as we only used our fingers vaginally with a homemade dildo which had a tube through it and a bulb on one end so that we could squeeze hand cream or something similar when used up our bums . . . which we both found *very* exciting. Apart from watching men masturbate and teasing them, neither of us was really interested in men, and I was still a virgin on my honeymoon, which Mary proved with her finger on the wedding eve. I was wondering what would happen on the first night, as I had agreed with Mary that I would stay a virgin but didn't think it would be possible. In our bedroom on that first night I waited until Fred went to the bathroom, then I quickly got into my nightie and into bed.

(We had twin beds and still always have.) He came back and undressed and walked to my bedside naked (I hadn't seen him naked before nor felt his prick outside his trousers), and I judged his prick to be about 5 inches long and it was slightly bent. He pulled the bedclothes off of me and held his prick and started rubbing it as he pulled my nightie off my shoulders, exposing my tits, which are well developed and firm with prominent teats when roused. By now he was stiff—about 6 inches long—and he just looked at me.

Then he said, "I'm going to christen you," and he knelt over my shoulders.

He kept on rubbing, with his balls swinging and touching my nipples, and suddenly he started rubbing faster and breathing hard and his spunk went all over my face and mouth. He got off, put the light out, and got in his bed.

After that night he always tossed off like that, either on my face or my tits or cunt, and left me to satisfy myself. Often at night when he thought I was asleep I watched him rub off, hearing those little squeezing noises as he rubbed his wet prick dry on my nightie. It was then I acted my fantasy as I lay in bed. I pulled my nipples and fingered my cunt with my legs wide open imagining a big dog was coming at me and watching him lick his prick and then my cunt until I was somehow compelled to open my legs wide. raised up, as he fucked me hard, stimulated by suitable action with my finger.

I was able to produce a wonderful thrill as I imagined the dog, who was always with a man who carried a whip in case I refused.

I actually bought a long, low stool, such as I imagined lying on in my dreams, and in the days when I was alone would strip naked and lie on this with a dog whip by me, legs wide apart, dreaming my fantasy as often as I wanted. I was able to place the stool in such a position that the man in the house opposite would—and often did—watch me from his bedroom window while I would watch him in a carefully placed mirror.

One day Mary came in and caught me and made me

confess everything, and later on helped me make my fantasy a fact. We had several times watched dogs and found it very exciting when they couldn't pull out of the bitch for a few minutes afterward. A new neighbor moved in and his wife had a lovely Alsatian dog, and one day when I was with Mary he came into our garden. Mary called him in and right away he put his nose to my cunt. She made me fondle him and get his prick out, and I was quite surprised how big and hard it was. She made me wash it and then lie down and actually suck it, giving me a flick with the whip to help. Finally, she made me lie on the stool with my legs open, and rubbed my now very wet cunt with her fingers and rubbed her hand over my nipples. She coaxed the dog astride me and got him to lick my nipples and she rubbed his cock and got it into my cunt. He knew what was required and obviously was experienced. It went right up me and he thrust hard and fast until I felt my cunt go wet as he squirted inside me.

This was the culmination of my fantasy, though I still dream it very often. It's lovely to be able to tell you—with Mary's consent, as you can see.

I confirm this. (Signed) Mary. [Letter]

CHAPTER THREE

THE HOUSE OF FANTASY

☐ You already know, or can easily imagine, many of the most popular themes and devices of sexual fantasy, *leitmotifs* as familiar and beloved to the medium as the toad prince and the moustached villain are to fairy tales and vaudeville (nor is the comparison accidentally chosen). And although a woman will cast and style her sexual imagery as individually as she would a dinner party, she will probably—as I have found after collecting over four hundred fantasies—select as her own one of the archetypal dozen or so constantly recurring "stock" situations to build upon; she then embellishes her chosen situation with the subjective detail which makes it most alive to her, just as a woman will use accessories to dress a basic dress up, or down, to suit her desires of the moment.

Many artists have painted the female nude, but each picture speaks to different audiences and different emotions, and in different ways. The theme is classic, or, if you like, "stock"; the details are subjective, personal, and make the difference.

Therefore, if I say there are sixteen principal themes (more or less) which run through all sexual fantasy, I don't mean this as simplistic reduction. Knowing this does not mean one knows "all" there is about fantasy, nor are these sixteen themes what fantasy is "only" about. This is how I have structured the material, letting the recognizable, the familiar, act as a frame for the unique, startling, and exotic; it gives understandable content, and hence meaning, to the most fascinating stuff of fantasy: the emotion-packed detail.

Take, for instance, a standard fantasy situation: the masked rape scene. What could be more predictable? What is new, though, and what is different each time is the way each woman will "dress" that scene—the setting, the lighting, the nuances of action and dialogue. It's almost as though she chose the obvious cardboard fixtures as a kind of diversion or cover-up for the incredible amount of sexual detail she is giving away about herself in the actual fantasy. For instance, who do those masks cover? Her stepfather? A priest? Her sister? Nine black men?

Perhaps this is why so many women don't remember more than the vague bones of their fantasies, why they keep their descriptions one level of abstraction removed from the all-revealing detail. To recollect more, not just to me but even to herself, would be too highly charged, too naked, too close to acknowledging the extent and complexities of her sexual appetite—an appetite women aren't supposed to have (or there would be a less pejorative name for it than nymphomania). Nine times out of ten, therefore, when a woman tells her fantasy, it begins and ends with something like, "I have these strange thoughts of being humiliated"; that's all, or that's all she chooses to remember. (As with recalling dreams in psychoanalysis, however having acknowledged this much. she will probably remember more the next time if encouraged.)

And so for every rich, highly stylized. and imaginatively plotted fantasy I've heard or read, there have been a dozen concise repeats of the obvious favorites, the Big Sixteen. (For a psychoanalyst's interpretation of these themes, read the afterword by Dr. Martin Shepard.) They are the old tried-and-true darlings that never really do grow old, or wear out; and no male house of prostitution should fail to take account of them. giving each female client at least a starting chance of getting what she's paid for. As Genet's characters in his play *The Balcony* come to the female bordello to live out their sexual dreams, so should women in a true House of Fantasy be encouraged to do the same by an understanding and sympathetic management.

In time, I think, women would go far beyond the obvious, building new wings beyond the Domination Room, finding new roles for the staff to play in addition to the Big Black Bully. But for now, let no House of Fantasy call itself complete unless it has rooms with the following signs above their doors. □

ROOM NUMBER ONE: ANONYMITY, OR, "TAKEN BY THE FACELESS STRANGER"

□ Anonymity is fantasy's best friend. It heightens romance and adds drama; it increases pleasure and eliminates guilt, fantasy's enemy. Whether the concealing device be simply night's darkness or a sudden power failure in the fantasy restaurant; whether the mask be an unfriendly rapist's handkerchief or the familiar hygienic face mask worn by the doctor; whether the man fucks her from behind so that she cannot see him, or is a visible total stranger ... no matter how it's achieved, a woman will try for anonymity, even in passing, for its known sure-fire power of release and lift.

With it she is Madame X, sexually free at last to do and be done to; with no relationship beyond the purely physical one of the moment, she is free for a one-night stand, free to play Sailors Ashore, with all inhibitions thousands of miles away. The not knowing—her not knowing who he is, and his not knowing who she is—reduces them both to sex objects, reduces the relationship to a purely physical one with no previous or promised commitments. While there are none of the more tender emotions, they are not what is wanted for the moment.

Anonymity frees a woman to take what she's always wanted sexually, taking it the way she's always wanted it, with no one to face; no known face, either, to account to afterward. As long as no one will ever know, since the strangers by the law of fantasy will never meet again, and while this is the first time with all its sexual excitement, it is also the last, with all the urgency that comes before farewell . . . why not try anything? ☐

Linda

☐ Linda is an old friend of mine, and in my mind she's always just come back from Paris. She is a syndicated fashion illustrator. When you see drawings in your local newspaper of the latest European collections, chances may well be that Linda did them.

She has been married twice and now lives in New York with a man who is not her second husband. He has a certain amount of money, and Linda herself makes a good salary. They live very well and quarrel constantly, not always quietly. I sometimes think their relationship is spiced by—if not based on—a certain amount of antagonism, like so many couples whose highest sexual moments follow their bitterest quarrels.

Linda is about thirty, small featured, blond-pretty in a kind of old-fashioned movie star way (which by the time you read this will probably no longer be old fashioned). I'm not surprised by her fantasy of "the hair store" (as she's always called a beauty salon). She was talking freely and imaginatively about sex before it was fashionable to do so. ☐

Gerald doesn't know this one. I can't wait until he reads it . . . I suppose that's why I'm telling you. He thinks he's such a stud that there isn't anything he hasn't done, or wouldn't do. But this fantasy . . . well, he doesn't even enter into it, does he? But I don't want to be unfair to the guy. He really is fantastic in bed. And what kind of a man—except some nut, and even I don't want that—could give me this kind of thing? But that's what fantasies are for, right? For what you don't get in life?

94

I'm at this hair store, a very posh number like Lizzy Arden's or one of the Revlon emporiums. Some fag with a very vulgar idea of elegance has decorated it with chandeliers and fountains, gold basins and shocking pink Barcalounger reclining chairs where you half lie while your hair's drying and you're having a manicure or a facial. All these chairs are in a long row, with a discreet distance between each, where green potted things grow, giving all us ladies the feeling of privacy.

I've just had a facial, so I've got this mask on, and there are cool cotton pads on my eyes. I can't see a thing. Not that I could see what's going on anyway, because there's a white silk curtain that falls from the ceiling down to my waist, then on down to the floor. No one can see me from the waist down. Neither can I. I can't see what's on the other side of the curtain. But I know. Over there, on the other side, is a young man—actually, lots of them, a row of young, big, strapping types, half nude. They're wearing a kind of loin cloth, and their bodies glisten with sweat as they go about their business. Their business is us ladies. They are there to service us. But as posh as our set-up is on our side of the curtain—with the chandeliers and fountains and privacy—these guys are over there on their side of the curtain working like galley slaves, one alongside the other, no nice lights, no pretty music, just the crack-crack of the whip as the guy in charge strides up and down making sure none of them misses a stroke—so to speak.

My particular guy is dark, good-looking in a hard, impersonal sort of way. After all, he can't see me either; to him I'm just another cunt. For all I know, he could be a fag . . . which doesn't lessen or heighten the enjoyment for me. But the important thing is that this is his job, his employment. He is a service this swell salon offers, like a masseur. He crouches there between my legs, and with the greatest expertise in the world, he goes down on me. That first moment is wildly exciting: I'm lying there, my legs in a big V, waiting for him, and I can't see him approach, I don't know he's near, until his tongue, the tip of it, suddenly flicks me with the most excruciating Zing!

So there he is, working away on me wonderfully, and me lying over there on the other side of the curtain, my expression of bliss concealed by my mask, the fountains and the Muzak playing away. His head moves from side to side as he expertly, but mechanically, builds and teases me, builds and teases . . . but mostly builds. Now, generally, he gets nothing out of this himself—except his pay. His little cock just dangles there, small as a thumb between his legs as he squats and nibbles away perfunctorily. But suddenly, with me, it's different. I'm special. The life he's aroused in my cunt communicates to him, this incredible sexuality I have . . . maybe it's the pulse in my cunt that he can feel beating. Haven't you ever felt the pulse there? With me it's like drums when it starts . . . when *I* start.

But back to my *mise en scène*. Suddenly the mean old whipmaster realizes that my guy has slowed down on the job. By that, I mean that he's giving it too much valuable time, that he's really *into* what he's doing, giving the client more than is required. He gives my guy a smart flick of the whip, but my boy doesn't even turn around. He's groaning and pressed into my cunt as though there's no tomorrow, and his cock is enormous now, his hand stroking it, bringing himself to climax as he brings me closer. The whipmaster gives him a terrible blow, but the guy is lost to everything but me . . . we're getting closer and closer, together now, and I suddenly start praying that the ogre whipmaster won't drag him away just as we're about to reach the most glorious climax of our lives. The whipmaster grabs him by the shoulder—my heart almost sinks—he can't understand it. He's never seen one of these gorgeous flunkies behaving like this, getting turned on by a client, by a client's cunt! Then, just at the crucial point, the whipmaster, dumbfounded, loses his professional cool, our excitement communicates to him. Like when the cynical stage manager hears little Judy Garland audition "Over the Rainbow" and realizes a star is born.

"I've never seen this happen before!" the whip guy yells. "Why this man is so delirious with pleasure he refuses to be paid!" (I don't know how he's managed to communicate this, with his mouth full.)

But that does it: The whipmaster is so whipped up himself, he takes out *his* cock and works feverishly to our pitch, so that when we come, he comes . . . and oh boy, it's quite a day in the old hair store! [Taped interview]

Pamela

I am on an absolutely deserted beach, lying on my back, sound asleep. I am wearing only a bikini, the bottom part fastened on each side with only a tiny bow, and the top fastened in front only with a bow, too, between my enormous breasts, which are already almost overwhelming the little bit of cloth that is the bra. I breathe deeply and evenly, shifting positions lightly as I sleep. A man's shadow falls across me; he stands looking down at me as I sleep. He's very tanned and wears only swimming trunks. He watches, and as he watches me sleeping he gets excited. He kneels beside me, very softly and gently so as not to awaken me, and very carefully unties the bow at one of my hips, then reaches over me to untie the other side. He lays the bikini back, exposing me to his gaze.

For a moment he just sits there, taking me all in. I murmur in my sleep and shift position slightly, separating my thighs somewhat, which angles my slit upwards. His erection grows enormous; he slips out of his shorts and then kneels over me with one knee on each side of my thighs. Although I don't even open my eyes, I glide one hand out to his penis and caress it gently, and then glide it, to his surprise, right into my cunt. He then fucks the bejesus out of me and I rock along with him. But I never open my eyes, just murmur as if I were sleeping and enjoying a good dream. [Taped interview]

Marie

☐ Marie has the scrubbed good looks of the other young women who live in the suburban area where she and her husband moved following the birth of their second child. She told me that she was a virgin when she and Phil married, that she's been tempted once or twice to continue one of the idle flirtations that started up at the country club or at some neighbor's party, but that she was always scared off by the consequences. ☐

I don't think I could look Phil in the eye if I ever really went to bed with another man. I'd really like to be able to do it, because I've had so little sex, and I feel so out of things, so inexperienced . . . so dull. But I just haven't got the nerve. I really envy girls a few years younger than me who've been able to cash in on all this sexual freedom. I even feel guilty about having this fantasy. but I can't keep it from popping into my mind every time we do have sex now. It makes it so much more exciting. and I try to tell myself I deserve it . . . just the fantasy, if not the reality. Who knows? If it ever happened in reality, as it does in my mind. I just might go through with it. I even find myself thinking about it if I'm standing around at someone's party outdoors. I stand there holding my gin and tonic, wishing he knew what was on my mind, the man I'm talking to.

In my imagination I picture this garden party, very much like one of the evenings that go on around here two and three times a week during the summer. I practically landscape the setting in my mind: the sloping lawns, the big trees. the rows of hedges, all very nicely kept up. I can even hear the gardeners delicately snipping away at the shrubs somewhere off in the night . . . not that gardeners work at night. except in my fantasy. It is night. because all the men are in black tie. I'm in a short dress, the only really short dress I ever bought (my concession to the mini craze). More important, I'm not wearing any stockings.

Not even panty hose, which is not at all like me. My dress
is a very pretty blue—like the real one was—and all the
waiters are in short red jackets. Is it normal to fantasize in
color? Well, I do.

I've wandered off to a rather distant corner of the garden on my own. That's typical, as I love flowers and always investigate every new garden I see. Suddenly I meet
a man, another guest, and we begin to discuss flowers and
things. I don't know him. I've never seen him before. He's
probably someone's husband; most of the men at these
parties generally are. In fact, I know in my fantasy that he
belongs to someone else . . . which both makes it easier
and more exciting.

He bends down to pick a flower for me. But he doesn't
get up; I mean, he doesn't stand up. He comes up under
my dress. I stand there, not protesting, just holding my
drink and smiling vaguely at the other distant guests, who
can only see me from the waist up because I'm standing
behind this rather high hedge. I think it's a boxwood, or a
yew. Anyway, it's very thick and sturdy, which is meaningful because it almost supports me as I lean against it in
the excitement that follows. You see, this man has discovered that I'm not wearing any underwear, which so surprises him (no woman where we live would think of going
without something) that he doesn't waste any time: He
presses his mouth right up against me, sticks his tongue
right up into me. I practically fall into the hedge, I get so
weak in the knees. There might have been a minute there,
when he first came up under my dress, when I would have
stepped away, but his mouth is too much and now I pray
for him to go on.

I look down around this point and see that he's unzipped his fly, and that he's playing with himself and has
an erection the size of which I've never seen. I keep staring at his penis, which grows as my own excitement grows.
His mouth is like nothing I've ever felt before, it's like
magic, it's tender and demanding, and his own hand on his
cock, the veins are as strained as the veins in his penis. My
legs become so weak, it's almost as if I'm poised there on

his mouth, that it's holding me up, and I feel if I take my eyes off his hand, his penis, that I'll faint. Suddenly, as I'm just about to climax, but not quite—just as I *know* I'm going to, though—these little bubbles begin to appear at the tip of his penis, bubbles, faster and faster, one after the other, and I begin to worry he'll finish before I do and that he will stop.

And then, on top of everything, the other people begin calling to us, I can even hear Phil's voice calling to me to come in to dinner. I don't know what would be worse at this point . . . if they were to find us or if he were to stop before I'd finished. For an instant I hang there in space, totally dependent on this unknown man; I couldn't move if Phil were to walk straight toward me, which he is just about to do. But then, thank goodness, everything happens at once: Just as Phil is about to be close enough to see the expression on my face, the entire garden party, all the other people, turn as a body to follow our hostess in to dinner, and at that moment, this man's bubbles turn into the most incredible jet, ejaculation, and I climax. I suppose I almost drown the poor man. [Interview]

ROOM NUMBER TWO: THE AUDIENCE

☐ We spend most of our fucking lives trying to be alone, trying to improve the privacy of our fucking with sound-proofed bedroom walls, No-Lite window blinds, and locked doors. We race miles with our lovers to "get away from everyone," and if sexual desire overcomes us at a crowded party or in a restaurant, the first impulse is to get out of there and be alone before Act One.

That is reality, and with no moral judgment intended, it's probably just as well.

But fantasy goes in the opposite direction: more often than not there are other people present. I'm not talking about orgy fantasies. They exist too, but often the other people in fantasies don't join in, in fact their presence isn't meant to imply even the possibility of an orgy. A fantasizer will indeed go out of her way to point out that the other people aren't really watching her and what she's doing with the six baldheaded waiters. The audience is simply there. Doing what? Perhaps lending their tacit approval simply by their presence. ("It's okay to fuck.") Or by adding a touch of suspense with the implication that at any minute they *could* turn, and see what's going on: "My God, look at that, Harry and Isobel are having it off and her husband's in the next room!" (Alternatively, the point of the audience's surprise could be that Harry and Isobel are not in the accepted missionary position, or that they have a second man or a dog in the act, whatever it is that makes the scene particularly exciting to the fantasizer, and so particularly "loaded" when discovered by the audience.) The *possibility* of being seen, watched, discovered, can be more exciting than the actual presence of an audience. Anyone who has ever fucked in the warm sunlight of a (seemingly) secluded beach, or within earshot but out of sight of others, must admit the added excitement which the imminence of an audience brings to an already fine fuck . . . or she's a liar.

But not all fantasy audiences are passive bystanders, inoperative in the fantasy story line. Some creative women give their fantasy audiences the active, participating role of a real audience—they have them applaud, Oh! and Ah!, and she, lucky lady, becomes not only the Sarah Bernhardt of Fucking, but also the Fellini of Fantasy, controlling both her own performance and that of the audience, her critics, pacing the one against the other so that her fantasy audience reinforces her fantasy performance, which in turn heightens the ebb and flow of her very real fucking Complicated? Read Caroline's fantasy below, keeping in mind the newspaper reports of what happened to some of the members of the cast of *Oh, Calcutta!*: they became so dependent on the excitement the audience brought to their performance in the theater, they were unable to perform sexually without an audience back home. ☐

Caroline

☐ I met Caroline, a young actress, in London through mutual friends at a party. Right off, she seemed to me to lack that narcissistic self-involvement that I had always thought of as the curse and/or blessing necessary to achieve theatrical prominence. Therefore, I was not surprised that I had never heard her name, although she said she was currently playing in a hit in the West End.

Mostly we talked about Italy, and she told me briefly about the village where she and a lover had spent six months "trying out the idea of being married." They had decided against it. She was enthusiastic to hear about my years in Rome, and my own ideas on marriage.

A few nights later, I saw Caroline's name on a theater poster on Shaftesbury Avenue, and on impulse bought seats for that night. Her role required her to spend the entire evening onstage almost totally nude, and the first curtain fell on a protracted, tumultuous scene in which she was required to have (just barely simulated?) sexual intercourse on stage, front and center. The audience loved it, and her. It made me curious about a girl who was so reticent to speak about herself privately, but was so uninhibited otherwise as to be able to perform this role on stage.

We went backstage afterward, and a group of us went on to dinner, during which the subject of this book came up. She told me she would like to contribute. Hers wasn't a typical fantasy, she said, but I might find it interesting. ☐

Ever since I had to do this love scene in the play you saw—it's been running now for six months—I've needed to feel that the same audience is there when I'm making love at home or anywhere else offstage. I suppose having to be, or at least to appear to be, so excited on the stage every night in front of so many people has really affected me. At first I tried to tell myself that it was just another role . . . you have to act so many emotions in the theater, and there's all that "Method" business of feeling yourself into the part. . . . But as I said, in the beginning I tried to keep a little "distance" between the personal *me*, and me, the actress, making love in front of all those people.

But I couldn't: As I got more and more used to the role, more comfortable in it, I found that instead of dreading the moment when I had to begin, I was looking forward to it. My nipples would become tight and erect. It was a surprisingly seductive feeling, one I enjoyed. I began wearing tighter and tighter blouses, filmier ones, more see-through, so that the audience could see my excitement, could see the excitement I felt right down—or up—to my nipples. I needed the audience's excitement for my own . . . a form of complicity was set up between them and me, a sexual conspiracy which heightened my ability, or rather, desire to play the part.

The silence, the tension in the theater during the scene communicates itself through the house—from me to them, from them to me—and at the end of the night's performance. when they clap and call me back for curtain call after curtain call, I feel it's not only the actress they're applauding, but me, Caroline, the woman, too. Acting often tends to split you off from yourself, and you don't know who you are. But in this role, the audience's applause— their approval—somehow reunites the actress in me with the private self in me. Now when I make love privately, I sometimes think, Oh, what's the use . . . it's all so dull and unstimulating. And there's this feeling of anxiety. It's as if I'm not sure I'm doing it well, you see, no matter what the man says.

Before this play, I didn't need fantasies. Or that's what I would have told you six months ago. I realize now that somewhere in the back of my mind I'd always had someone watching while I made love: me. This split between the me who is *in* the act, actually making love, and the me who is watching, this split is healed by the audience taking over the role of watcher and applauding me for my efforts. I can't tell you the feeling of satisfaction it gives me.

I remember the first time we did the love scene before an audience. The rehearsals had naturally been private, and I had been able to be professionally cool and clinical about it. But on opening night I was very nervous and apprehensive, I imagine because I was afraid that they would think I was not very good, or wouldn't give me their approval by becoming excited themselves . . . that they would just think the scene odd, and me very strange for being in it. But when they applauded . . .

Now I need an audience; without it, there's just no excitement. So even if I'm with the man I'm in love with, somehow in my mind I twist his face around so that it's the face of the actor I'm in the play with. The funny thing is, I don't even *like* the actor. Maybe that makes it even more exciting for me, I don't know. I haven't really figured this out. But I think it's because behind him, behind his back is the audience, and they're applauding him for making love to me and applauding me for responding to him in such a loving way. And as my own excitement mounts and mounts, the applause gets louder and louder . . . [Taped interview]

Elspeth

As I am sure most women do, I have had the usual exhibition-type fantasies. I especially enjoy the thought of being watched by someone who is not aware that I know he is watching me. Or I imagine that I am making love to someone, perhaps a close friend of the family, and my husband comes in and watches us, as prearranged between my husband and myself without the knowledge of the other man. It would be equally intriguing to walk in and catch my husband with another woman, also by prearrangement. I don't think about this with my husband; I only think about it for excitement. [Letter]

Mary Jo

In the first sexual fantasy that I can remember, I thought of myself undressing while a boy I liked watched me. That became one of my most common fantasies when I was a teen-age girl. [Letter]

Melanie

I am twenty-five years old and have been happily married for four years. My earliest memories of sexual sensation go back to when I was about three years old. I remember after my parents put me to bed that I would take my clothes off. I enjoyed being nude. Then I would put them back on. That is all I can remember; the exciting feelings of my own nude body.

My fantasies during masturbation are generally of my old boy friends. I never had intercourse with any of them, but when I masturbate I wonder what it would be like. Often, during the fantasy, my husband watches. He doesn't do anything, he simply is there.

My fantasies during sex with my husband are quite different. Mostly my thoughts are on what we are doing, although sometimes mentally I take it out of the bedroom and imagine we are on a quiet beach, quite nude, or lying in an open field with green grass all around us. I often think of us skinny dipping on a lonely beach. The idea of nudity, of the two of us being nude outdoors, excites me.

I have no desire to tell my husband of my fantasies, of the excitement it would give me for the two of us to be nude outside the privacy of our bedroom. I think speaking them out loud would definitely lessen their effectiveness. [Letter]

105

Celeste

☐ Celeste is a pretty, very bright-faced, red-cheeked blonde in her early thirties. She had been a legal secretary when she met Charlie, and had liked the work, but gave it up without a qualm when Charlie asked her to when they got married. They've been married twelve years. Today they live in a comfortable suburban home and have two children. Celeste works for the League of Women Voters and is an officer in the local PTA.

She describes their sex life as "very satisfactory." ☐

We still enjoy making love at unusual times, like when we're already late for a party, or an impromptu session on the living room rug, the kitchen table, etc. . . . time we can steal while the kids are away at a Boy Scout meeting or football game. I'd say we have sex most nights of the week, even when Charlie's so tired he just comes and falls asleep while he's still on top and inside me.

But something different happened the other evening when Charlie got home early and we thought we could steal some time before the kids got back. Suddenly we were interrupted—we were in the living room—by the unexpected arrival of our next-door neighbor. I just had time to pull my skirt down before Charlie let him in. He only stayed five or ten minutes, but all the time he was here, I knew something was up. I couldn't help noticing the way this guy kept fidgeting . . . and then I noticed this big bulge in the front of his trousers while he was talking to me.

It was only after he'd left that I realized that in my haste I'd forgot to put my tights back on; all during our talk, my short skirt had ridden up, leaving me totally exposed to the man. For a few minutes I was mortified, absolutely embarrassed. Then the shock wore off and I was left with this odd feeling of excitement, which is still with me when I think about it, although I consider our neighbor about as exciting as a graham cracker.

I could hardly wait for us to get to bed that night. It was

one of the most exciting sessions that I'd ever had. But I couldn't sleep, I really couldn't, until I'd told Charlie what had got me so aroused. I expected it would make him angry, just as I thought it would make me angry, too. But the idea that another man had been staring at the quim he had just enjoyed excited Charlie so much, he put out his cigarette and got on top of me again. He didn't wait the usual time it takes him on those nights we do it more than once. He wasn't in me more than a few seconds before he came again, almost like an explosion. It's as though this idea has given our sex lives a whole new dimension. Now when we're in bed together it's almost become a necessity for us.

Instead of Charlie whispering things into my ear (that really didn't excite him, they were more or less routine words to him, but he knew they excited me), I tell him of imaginary experiences. For instance, that I'm on one of those stirrup tables that gynecologists have, where they spread your legs and look deep into you. But the table is in the middle of the ring, in Madison Square Garden, and it's mounted on a revolving platform. Thousands of men have paid fifty or a hundred dollars each for tickets, and the ushers are selling binoculars so they can get a better view. I tell Charlie that the table is slowly turning around and around, with the bright lights illuminating me, and the men in the seats all around begin pushing forward, jumping out of their seats, the whole giant mob wild with excitement to see, thousands and thousands of men in a circle all around me, all wild with excitement to see me better, to fuck me, to get deep inside those wet, red lips they can see so plainly.

And all the time I'm lying on the table, I never move, except once in a while I put my two hands down, and with my fingertips just delicately open the lips so they can see the juices inside, glistening inside me, and then all the men begin to cream and some of them have unzipped themselves, and from under my closed eyelids I can see hundreds, thousands of erections just screaming to get inside me.

107

But all the time, I know that Charlie is waiting for me in a dressing room off-stage where he has a warm bed, and where in just a minute or two more, the uniformed ushers will wheel the table in, and lock the door behind them as they go out. Charlie is there, waiting for me, but it's a strange Charlie, naked, standing up, with a giant erection so big that the skin is stretched and I can see the purple veins. What's strange about him is that he doesn't speak to me, or smile at me. He's wearing the same kind of emotionless, unmoving, unmoved face that I had just been wearing when I was outside on the platform with all the men screaming around me. Charlie doesn't even wait for me to get out of the stirrups, but just pulls me to him without a word, standing up, standing between the stirrups, and sometimes at this point I imagine myself on a kind of operating table, the kind where they strap you down at the wrists and ankles so you can't fall off. And I feel the tip of that enormous hard-on just touching the lips as he pulls me onto him. He still doesn't smile, doesn't say a word, shows no pleasure, no excitement, but I can feel myself tighten my stomach muscles tighten as if anticipating some sexual blow, some sexual assault . . . but it's really my inside muscles doubling over on themselves, that intense silent moment before orgasm when your stomach and vaginal muscles almost feel as if you're having cramps and it's at that moment when instead of a blow, I feel him penetrating me, impaling me on his body, that I finally get free of the stirrups and wrap my legs around him as my cramped muscles release . . . release and release again in an ecstasy of pleasure all the greater because of the almost-pain of the tightness they had felt a moment before. Release after release after release. I sometimes finish this fantasy weeping. With just the pleasure and happiness of it, you understand?

You always hear about men exhibiting themselves on trains or on deserted beaches or somewhere. I wonder if other women have this hidden exhibitionistic desire the way I do? [Interview]

ROOM NUMBER THREE: RAPE, OR, "DON'T JUST STAND THERE, FORCE ME!"

☐ Rape does for a woman's sexual fantasy what the first martini does for her in reality: both relieve her of responsibility and guilt. By putting herself in the hands of her fantasy assailant—by *making* him an assailant—she gets him to do what she wants him to do, while seeming to be forced to do what he wants. Both ways she wins, and all the while she's blameless, at the mercy of a force stronger than herself. The pain she may suffer, the bruises and indignity, are the necessary price she pays for getting the kind of guiltless pleasure she may be unable to face or find in reality.

It's worth repeating my conviction that fantasy need have nothing to do with reality, in terms of suppressed wish-fulfillment. Women like Julietta (coming up), whose fantasy life is focused on the rape theme, invariably insist that they have no real desire to be raped, and would, in fact, run a mile from anyone who raised a finger against them, and I believe them. The message isn't in the plot—the old hackneyed rape story—but in the emotions that story releases. ☐

Julietta

☐ "I believe I can love more than one man at a time. That's not a theory. I always do. That's why I don't want to get married, and why I prefer my affairs with men who already are. They are in no position to demand monogamy from me." That's Julietta.

With strong views like these, it didn't come as any surprise to me when she told me during our conversations

109

that she is a strong believer in Women's Lib. "But it would frighten my mother to hear me say it," says Julietta. "I grew up on a little farm, but I left as soon as I was old enough to travel by myself. My mother stayed on the farm. That's the difference between women of her generation and me." ☐

It may sound freaky coming from me. but while I enjoy going to bed with some guy I dig almost any time. I especially like it if there's something in the air that lets me think I'm doing it against my will That I'm being forced by the man's overwhelming physical strength Something like that. The doctors call this kind of thing a rape fantasy, but that's as far as I want it to go. On the fantasy level, not the real thing. I don't go out by myself on dark nights, and if any horny stud threatened me, even with a gun, I'd scream my head off. All this doesn't sound like me, but you might say that the person I am today is totally at war with the girl my mother tried to make me So whatever there is left in me of the girl my mother preferred, that girl wants to think that it's not really her fault, that she's being forced into this sexual scene. That I'm really good little Julie.

So when I'm in bed with someone, I don't mind if he wants the lights on or if it's daylight. I like the look of a man . . . all of him. But when I get to a certain point, when I really become excited, I close my eyes. or bury my face in the pillow, or fling my arm or the pillow over my eyes. That way, while I can feel everything I can also be back there in the dark, having my own thoughts In fact, having something over my eyes gave me a fantasy I really dig. I imagine that I've been brought to some warehouse, or place like that, against my will. I'm stripped naked and the only thing I'm allowed to wear is a black silk mask. This is because whatever powerful person has brought me there does not want the men—yes. always more than one in this fantasy—for whom he has procured me. to know who I am. In this way, though he's brought me there against my will, he somehow wants to protect me too. I never know who he is, and he himself never fucks me. I

110

just know that he's somewhere in the background, enjoying this feeling of power he has, not only over me, but over the men, too. That's because they're so hot with desire for me that they can barely control themselves. But he can take me away from them whenever he wants to. In my mind I can imagine the men, all big and powerfully built. They're naked, too, while they wait their turn with me. I think of them watching each other as each of them performs, talking about various techniques, and what they're going to do when their turn comes with me.

Meanwhile, the guy who is really with me, every time he tries a different position, or a different idea, I pretend to myself that it's the next man in line. So it's always exciting this way, because I seemingly have an endless supply of men fucking me . . . but they never know who I am. Even if I met one of them on the street the next day, or had lunch with him, he wouldn't know.

But that's all I think of, me naked on this rough bed with just this little black mask on my face, and these five or six naked men all waiting their turn to fuck me. That picture in my mind makes me come every time. [Taped interview]

Gail

I am thirty years old, have two children, and have been married for nine and a half years.

I have a frequent sexual fantasy about being raped, by one or more men. These fantasies do not take place, however, while having sex with my husband. They take place when I am alone, and with time on my hands. I know it sounds weird or even crazy, but at times I feel as if I want to actually act my fantasy out, as if it were truly happening! I don't know why this happens, or why I should even feel this way.

At the age of seventeen I was almost raped by a boy who was my best friend's boy friend. The act was never completed . . . he was finally stopped by my crying. This all took place in his car, while he was supposed to be taking me home from a party after he'd had a quarrel with his girl friend. She left the party, and he stayed and drank pretty heavily, as did the rest of us. He volunteered to take me home, after my boy friend, who is now my husband, called me at the party from his job and told me he had to work late and couldn't make it.

I remember wondering what my girl friend actually saw in the boy, who was nothing but a rough, tough, and more or less foulmouthed bully. He had always been nice to me, but treated her like dirt. And yet she loved him, and took any kind of abuse from him, including getting pregnant by him, and then losing the baby by miscarriage in her fourth month.

Anyway, on the way home he pulled into a deserted spot in our neighborhood. I immediately sensed what was about to happen and I had mixed emotions about it. I thought to myself how awfully exciting this was in one way, and then again I was truly scared!

He immediately pulled me to him and wanted to kiss me, but I automatically refused. I really wanted to, just to find out if it was his animal charm, so to speak, that my girl friend was in love with.

He told me to relax, and that he wouldn't hurt me, and not to be afraid. He then asked what I saw in my boy friend, and whether he had really ever satisfied me sexually. I went to my boy friend's defense, of course, explaining that he was decent, kind, and a gentle person, in contrast to this fellow. He laughed and told me to cut out the "mushy stuff," in his exact words, and to relax and let him show me how it should be. I let him kiss and hold me, but when he started to explore me with his hands I panicked, and started to struggle to make him stop. He became angry and said he wasn't going to stop. We struggled for what seemed to be hours, and I was physically exhausted and by now really terrified. He kept saying that he wouldn't make me pregnant, if that was my worry, and to just let it happen and enjoy it. But I couldn't, and then just as it seemed that nothing would or could stop him, I started to cry uncontrollably. That did something to him, because he finally stopped, let me go, and started straightening my clothes, etc. He said he'd take me home now, but that I'd better not make trouble and tell anyone at all. I promised, of course.

When we got to my home, as I was getting out of the car, he suddenly took my arm and told me that he was sorry, and couldn't I please forgive him, and he started to cry, actually cry. I felt so strange then, actually sorry for him. I told him to forget it, and that everything was okay, that I wasn't angry or anything. He left, after giving me a kiss on my forehead. And that was that. Since then, we've always acted as if nothing had happened, have remained not good friends, but friends nevertheless, as he finally married my girl friend, the one who worshipped him so.

But he is still an animal, as everyone knows. He beats her, is a very heavy drinker, and is still foulmouthed.

My whole point in telling you this is that at times, even though I know it's wrong or crazy, I have fantasies that he is trying to rape me—either in his car, my home, his home, or even in his own gas station. I become awfully excited at these thoughts.

I also have fantasized that he and a couple of his rough tough friends attack me. At times, however, it's not him at all, but anyone I happen to dream up.

I don't know why I have these sexual fantasies. At other times I envision rape scenes, and actually shudder and become nauseated at the idea or thought. So, at times I enjoy my fantasies, and at other times I become almost sick.

I hope all this has helped your work in some way. I know it has helped me to finally get my experience off my chest to someone at last, after all these years. [Letter]

Dinah

Hi! I just read about your work and wanted to contribute. I am twenty-two years old, white, Latin, and a university student. And, of course, *female*. That is, bisexual. Actually. I don't fit *any* categories. I have been a lesbian, also. I thought you might want background info. But to get on with the fantasy business. I have a few really interesting ones. I fantasize not only when I masturbate, but also when I am making love. (Then I feel a little guilt, but it's such fun.)

Fantasy 1: I walk into a drugstore in a small Southern town. I am a stranger. I am dressed outlandishly, like a whore. There are several local men in the store and they all look at me with lust in their eyes. I go to the counter and order a tube of contraceptive cream The druggist gives it to me. I take it and try to leave. but the men close the door and tell me I should "try it out" (the cream). They rape me. They squeeze cream into my vagina and anus. They make me go down on all fours and come in from behind. At one point I have to get on top of a man and come down on his penis while another is coming in through my anus from behind and another is inside my mouth.

Fantasy 2: I am speeding on the New Jersey Turnpike. Two policemen stop me. I tell them I will "do *anything* not to get a ticket." They make me get in the back seat and spread my legs very wide (one of them is in the front seat. the other in the back seat). While one of them drives, the other one has me. They take turns. And then they meet a friend and he gets in on it too.

Fantasy 3: I am in a woman's prison. I tried to escape or lead a demonstration or something illegal like that. The warden is a big black woman. While two women guards hold me, she pulls up my skirt and pulls down my panties and spanks me with a ruler. Then she takes out a dildo and fucks me with it very roughly. When I get excited, she laughs. Then she tells the guards to hold me down on her desk. She looks over my cunt and says, "Mmm mmm, this is some nice pussy," and then she licks my cunt and sucks it till I come.

Fantasy 4: I am at a convention. I am the only woman

there. I have no choice: I bend over a chair and all the men are in line to fuck me. I act very nonchalant.

I *could* go on. . . . [Letter]

Sadie

I have always fantasized during intercourse and masturbation. I am being raped by one man or a group of men, while many of them watch the others "abuse" me. My attackers are always very handsome—dark hair, muscular, sexually well endowed—and brutal, in that they take what they want and the hell with what I want . . . or pretend I want. (I'm after what they are, really.)

My husband is very curious about my fantasies, will occasionally enter into them, but puts them and me down as childish and immature. He doesn't know what he's missing, in my opinion.

Other fantasies of mine include a fraternity initiation where I am tied to the bed hand and foot and all the brothers take their pleasure with me while the initiates watch. Then the new ones take their turn with me. There is always a certain "officer" in the fraternity's organization whose sole purpose is to arouse the girl chosen so that she can't help enjoying herself—although she's protesting. Or I fantasize that I am a "bottomless" waitress; every time I bend to serve a customer, someone attacks me from the rear. As waiting on tables is my sole means of support, I have no choice. Even if I do one of those "Bunny Dips" (that the Playboy Bunnies do so that they don't have to bend over), I will then be assaulted from the customer in front of me, who simply pulls me forward onto his lap, onto his prick, which is erect and exposed.

I know that they say that women aren't turned on by visual stimuli; I think it's untrue. It's another unexplored area where women are silent or ashamed. I am very aroused by hard-core pornography. If I see a picture, for example, of a black man and a white woman, I'm ready for sex almost immediately.

Incidentally, I am twenty-four, have a B.A., M.A., am white, Catholic, married six years and no children. [Letter]

ROOM NUMBER FOUR: PAIN AND MASOCHISM, OR, "OUCH, DON'T STOP!"

☐ Women are always being tied up or down in fantasy. They use "force" words liberally, almost involuntarily— "He made me do this . . ." "I then had to . . ."—in describing their fantasies, even when the fantasy has nothing to do with rape or pain. We are made to understand that even in her fantasy the fantasist doesn't have control over what's happening to her—unless, of course, control is what she is after, as in some of Barbara's fantasies (below).

But even when the force is intended, there is a clear distinction as to whether what is going on is indeed rape, or a pain-for-pain's-sake number. I would hope that whoever is in charge of the Masochist Wing of our House of Fantasy —he of the mask and heavy hand—would be familiar with the subtleties of his specialty. He must have separate rooms: the first, for the rape fantasists; the second, for the masochists. Otherwise, the "Ouch!" cries from the latter would disturb or distract the rapees, who are more intent on being forced than on feeling pain. For them, any pain felt is merely the cost of fulfilling their desire, a means to their end. For the other women like Sylvia (below), the desire is for pain itself and the pain is everything. Carried to its extreme, as in Amanda's fantasy, this desire for pain becomes genuinely disturbing and shows to what ends— imagined though they may be—a woman will go to feel something at last, to feel at least something. ☐

116

Barbara

□ We have not yet come to the difficult question of people who want to turn their fantasies into real life actualities, but while we are in this room, I think we can appropriately say that Barbara's fantasy of being spanked or caned is the type my contributors most often feel driven to experiment with. This may sound contradictory, since many of them go on to say that they in fact hate real pain. But as Barbara says, I think the explanation lies in the fact she feels she can make a bargain with the spanker about just how many strokes she will receive, and how hard—and that if the sexual experience should turn out to be more painful in fact than titillating in imagination, the proceedings can be called off at a word. □

I am not a lesbian, and I preface my letter with this comment because it may be thought that I am one when you hear about my fantasies. My particular fantasy concerns punishment with the cane, and by talking about it once, I was introduced to a woman who looked normal outwardly, but within a few minutes at her home, when I first went there, I realized that she wanted to whip me before having her usual larks in her kind of sex. I made the bargain with her that the only instrument to which I would subject myself was the school cane—not a garden cane or something about an inch thick. I cannot tell you why, but my fantasy has always been that I like to imagine myself as a naughty girl of about seventeen, hauled up in front of the headmistress for a caning, and that I am wearing the old-fashioned type of gym tunic and Directoire knickers down to my knees. From this stage I like to be told to bend over, after a lecturing, and then get caned with my gym tunic raised, the cane coming on my knickers. Therefore I told my lesbian friend just how far she could go, and the date and scene were agreed upon. Naturally I found that the whipping I got with the cane wasn't half so thrilling as the fantasy, and while I had no heart in masturbation with the lesbian woman, it came easily after the punishment.

Since then I've found a young man—much younger than I am by the way—who enjoys playing these caning games with me, and in addition allows me to flog him with the cane, on his bottom. When our bottoms are red and smarting, but not horribly marked with a real thrashing, we get down to sex. All my fantasies are concerned with various methods of being caned, and various methods of me giving the cane to someone else. For instance, I would like to be tied hand and foot, and then given twelve strokes of the birch, but if this happened, I would probably faint with the awful pain. Another of my ideas is to be strapped down on a wide seat of a swing, secured to the ceiling. As the swing comes backwards, my bottom would make a fine target for the person caning me. Another idea is that I would like to be strapped down over a flogging bench, just in knickers and bra, and the flogging bench would have handles in front which I would grip with my hands. As I pressed these bars down, by leverage there would be a rubber penis at the other end, and this would come right into me between my legs. I imagine myself being caned in this way, and enjoying masturbation via the rubber penis once the caning got going.

Yet another fantasy is that I would like a man to get on top of me, both of us naked, then gently lower himself until his enormous erect penis was resting in between my breasts. I would like to watch it as he moves up and down, then when it is getting near his time I would like him to lower himself and push it into me in the right place.

I must tell you that whenever I have sex with a man, all the time I am pretending to myself that I am wearing long knickers, bending over in the headmistress' study, and getting soundly caned on my bottom. I can only think of two possible causes of my fantasies. The first happened when I was about six or seven. I had an elder sister who was then about fourteen, and for probably a series of misdemeanors, my stepmother said she would cane her. My sister was ordered out of her frock, in front of me, and then stepmother pushed her over the settee arm. My sister Jean was wearing the usual school Directoire knickers at the time, much longer than those worn today, of course, and with her bottom in the air and her feet off the ground, the knickers tightened around her buttocks.

Stepmother then started to smack my sister's bottom with the cane, and I don't suppose it was a terrible thrashing. But it was stinging enough to make Jean yell out at every stroke of the cane. The second incident happened when I was fifteen, and getting to know a few things about sex. There was a boy next door aged about seventeen, and I used to get him to help me with my school homework. We used to cuddle and kiss. One night he said that I was so bad at math that what I needed was a good spanking, and then he pushed my face downward across his lap. After making a pretend resistance and wriggling, I had my gym frock well above my waist; I knew he could see my knickers from waist to leg. Moreover, I also knew that this had given him an erection, which I could feel. So he spanked me, good and hard, but I still enjoyed it. After that, almost each night I went to see him it ended up in me first getting spanked, and then he turned me round in the armchair and got on top of me, and we both masturbated. Later, I asked him what it was like at his school when naughty boys got the cane. It was a loaded question, and it brought the answer I wanted. He said he would give me a demonstration, and when he told me that "tonight was the night," before going in to see him I put on some very thrilling white knickers, long in the leg, and with fancy pink lace at the leg ends. His parents were out, and having the place to ourselves we lost no time in the caning demonstration. He showed me how to bend over the end of the settee with my arms stretched forward, and in that position I felt my knickers tighten up round my legs and thighs. I'd slipped out of my short frock beforehand, and we'd kissed and hugged, so that already he had a big erection. Then for the first time I got the cane on my knickers. He gave me four terrific swipes, and they certainly made me wince and yell. When he'd finished, I took hold of the

119

cane and told him that it was his turn for punishment. I found that I was terribly thrilled on seeing his trousers tight round his bottom as he bent over, and I gave him a severe caning, enjoying the feel of the cane in my hands.

Another of my fantasies is when I imagine I am secretary to the headmistress of some school for girls between the ages of fifteen and nineteen. One of my jobs, being a big strong girl, is to cane girls who have been sentenced to be caned by the headmistress. Two or three nights in the week I imagine I have about six girls waiting outside my office in a queue for the cane, and one by one they enter at my command, strip off their gym tunics, and are then ordered to bend over the whipping block, where they get the number of strokes of the cane ordered by the headmistress. Then I change the fantasy and imagine that I am one of the senior girls, aged about eighteen, caught smoking and sentenced to twelve strokes of the cane. We stand outside the door of the secretary's room and listen to the sounds of the caning going on inside. Then it is my turn. I go in, get out of my gym tunic, and stand there feeling tense in my tight knickers. The secretary points to the flogging block, says Bend over, girl, and I get across it, ready for my thrashing with the cane on my knickers. While I am pretending that I am getting caned, I masturbate.

I've read many stories of how women used to be punished in the old days, and many of these appeal to me in my fantasies. There is a lovely tale of a rich man, in the 1880's, who employed a governess for his large family of eight daughters and six sons. Frequently the children were caned, and at all such canings the master was present while the governess administered the punishment. The boys had to drop their trousers before being lashed down across a bench, and the girls had to remove outer clothing, the caning being given on their frilly long white drawers. I picture myself as the governess, first because I would enjoy giving the cane, and secondly because I fancy that after all this corporal punishment I could go to bed with the master of the house, who was widowed.

In another book of stories about the Midwest in the early days, there is a story of how girls found guilty in the courts were publicly punished. They were taken to the front of the courthouse in the one main street, and there had their wrists fastened above their heads to a whipping block, so that in their underwear, and bending forward, they were unable to move. The number of whacks with the cane varied according to their crimes, but after the sentence had been passed, the girl was left there so that passersby could pick up a cane and give her another whipping. The culprit was released after three hours.

What happened, of course, was that whenever there was a public caning of a nice young woman, practically the whole population was present, and when it was over, most of the men had erections and were ready to take their own females back to the bedrooms. Then again, in the Middle Ages, and even in later years, there were some priests who used the cane as punishment for young girls after confessions. The girl was made to undress and lie over the priest's table, where he caned her bottom, afterward getting into bed with her, so that many young girls who fancied their particular priest simply went and lied in the confession, knowing what it would lead to. [Letter]

Edith

Several years ago my parents became members of a certain religious denomination, and I began to receive religious instruction in preparation for my own acceptance. At first I was very happy about this, until a friend told me something about the man giving me this instruction.

I know you will think I must have been stupid, because at twenty-three years of age I saw nothing wrong in anything that had happened and I really thought it was all part of the instruction, even though I felt that he touched me a lot. In the end he began to undress me altogether, although I want to say that nothing else then happened ex-

121

cept that he handled me all over and did things to hurt my body, especially my busts.

The disgusting thing was that although I then knew it was very wrong, I did nothing to stop him. I even longed for him to do it to me, even though he sometimes hurt me dreadfully. Afterward I used to feel very ashamed, and eventually I told my parents what had happened. Although they, too, were disgusted, they asked me not to make a complaint in order not to upset their own position in the church.

In the end, and as a direct result of all this, I left home. Although at the time I was very unhappy about this, it seems now to have been for the best. My husband, who is a Methodist minister, is the kindest man and most sympathetic. I have no complaints, except that at the times when my husband is being very attentive to me, my thoughts return to this man and what he did to me all those times. I know this is perfectly dreadful, but it happens every time. [Letter]

Rose Ann

My husband has tried to get me to tell him about my sexual fantasies, but so far I have told him that I have none. It's almost as though he knew there was something or someone, in addition to himself, that was exciting me ... perhaps because of the cries and noises I make while he is making love to me. They are not just cries of pleasure, there are also the cries of pain that I feel in my fantasies. In fact, I wouldn't know where to draw the line between the two.

My fantasies occur whenever I am beginning to feel any real sexual arousal, and real pleasure. They don't distract from the pleasure, but on the contrary, enhance it. I am sure it is very hard for anyone to understand this, and how can I possibly tell my husband, whom I love, that I am dreaming that the most atrocious things are being done to my body while he is being so loving to me?

These fantasies or dreams usually begin with my body being stretched, one brutal man on each limb, pulling me in opposite directions, literally spreading me wide open so that some immensely huge penis—there is no one or nothing on the end of it—begins to enter me, stretching me, ripping me, my vagina, wide open as it pushes its way deeper into me. The men twist my arms painfully as well as pull them, and I can hear my bones breaking and cracking, while the sound of my skin, around my vagina, also rips audibly. I cry out in reality even as I cry out in my fantasy. But I love it, even though my intelligence and logic tell me that I am being ghoulish, that this is not a normal way to enjoy sex. And I do enjoy it. I hate what is happening to me in my fantasies, but it is inextricably involved with my very real pleasure. [Letter]

Amanda

I read your interesting letter and thought that I would like to write to you about my own experiences, which I hope are of assistance to you in your book. I am thirty-six years old, married with two children, and often indulge in fantasies, even during the day, as a relief from the pure boredom of my life.

I do not remember when I first started fantasizing, but when I was very young I used to lie stretched out on my bed and dream that I was a princess who had been captured and who was waiting to be tortured, and this made me feel pleasurably aroused. Later, as I became more sophisticated and my thoughts developed, I imagined myself being racked, impaled, flogged, branded, and every other thing that you can think of, ending with vigorous and orgasmic masturbation. I masturbated frequently and, for that matter, still do, because, although my husband is the kindest man, he is the world's worst lover.

As a girl I longed to be subjected to the most outrageous forms of abuse, and could embroider little incidents to enormous fantasies of atrocities. Toward the end of

123

school we underwent the usual examination, and in truth the doctor barely looked at me, although I hoped, and dreaded, that he would find it necessary to carry out some dreadful form of surgical mutilation. For years afterward in my dreams I imagined myself being prepared by male nurses and then voluntarily submitting myself to the most atrocious vivisection, scornfully refusing anesthetics and bravely absolving my tormentors from any guilt in my slow, lingering death (in the name of science, of course).

From all this you will think that I am masochistic, but the truth of the matter is that I am not and I just cannot stand pain. My parents never punished me and once, after stealing some money, I was threatened with the strap and this sent me into howling hysterics. In fact, you can say that I was overindulged in every way possible, and, to a degree, this has continued right up to my present circumstances.

About two years ago a friend described to me, in some detail, the lewd suggestions made to her by a man who had pierced her ears. Despite her warning, I visited him in the hope that he would make them to me, but, arriving at the door, I lost confidence and would have fled if he had not come up the garden path behind me.

I think my friend's account had been grossly elaborated, because when I warmed to the true purpose of my trip, he nearly had a fit when I insisted upon removing my dress and slip. Eventually, and not at all at his suggestion, I ended up stripped to my shoes, stockings, and garter belt, and submitted to a few half-hearted fumblings and gropings before going home with my ears pierced lopsidedly and decidedly sore.

Despite the shabbiness of the incident, in my dreams I regally and serenely present myself in front of a huge audience for the ritual piercing of my nipples with hot needles, after which huge rings are inserted. More recently this has expanded, so that in taking a simple bath I am being prepared for an elaborate ritual of circumcision, ceremonial rape, and final sacrifice (by disemboweling) to some awesome god. This is my latest and most protracted fantasy, and one which drives me to distraction whenever I indulge in it.

I hope that what I have written is of interest to you and I do assure you that every word is true. [Letter]

ROOM NUMBER FIVE: DOMINATION, OR, "HOW HUMILIATING! THANK YOU."

☐ I'd put this room next to Rape and Masochism. Not for the convenience of the clients—a woman is faithful to her favorites, and there'd be very little running about from room to room—but for the economy of the management: the costumes and props are interchangeable among the three. There, however, the sharing stops; force may be applied in all three rooms simultaneously—but to different degrees and in different directions, and the precise emotions being aroused and released will differ dramatically. Or "deliciously," as the clients themselves might say.

Whatever their reasons for wanting it, the domination fantasists long to feel low. They relish being debased and reduced by whatever means to a state of abject humiliation. How they get down there doesn't matter: Poppy (below) doesn't even bother to say how she is "made" to perform her humiliating tasks; Nathalie may get spanked into submission, but spanking is such an obvious childhood symbol of domination that we don't need Nathalie to tell us that it isn't the spanking itself that turns her on. It's the state to which that humiliating act reduces her that matters. And the more exactly specified those depths can be, the better. Heather doesn't just long to be knocked off the pristine pedestal her lover has put her on, she wants to be flat on her ass, in the lowest, most purely sexual, position; Nathalie doesn't stop at yearning to be reduced to that bane of proud and liberated women, an object—she

125

wants it all the way, to be a thoroughly, exclusively sexual object at that.

As women move more strongly into their recently won sexual freedom, and leave their historic role of second (and "silent") sex behind, I predict that they will, ironically, get into domination fantasies more and more. But the move will be in two different directions. First, the new reality of being man's equal makes them unconsciously nervous about their identity as women, and so throws them back into longing for the traditional, safe, and "known" role vis-à-vis the dominating man; but second, they will want to explore, and signal even to themselves, their new liberated age by putting themselves into the dominant position of the sexual brute. Whether as brute or brutalized, in fantasy at least the centuries of female submission are about to be avenged.

But what it all comes back to in the end is that if you're into the sado-masochistic thing it really doesn't matter, of course, which end of the stick (or whip!) you're on; turnabout can be lovely play, and as long as somebody is being debased, and you're in on it, it's great. □

Nathalie

You are so right that one tends to feel one's sexual fantasies are too "odd" to admit to or discuss. I have never heard another woman mention the topic, although I'm sure we all have some fantasy or another. I have finally been able to mention my two fantasies to my current lover, amidst much "fear and trembling" and aided by the effects of several martinis. The feeling of relief I have from just getting this out into the open has made me feel free enough to broach the subject to several of my closest women friends, who agree that we all have weird notions, but who are too reticent to share theirs with *me!*

I don't know if you want background or not—I'm assuming you do. I'm twenty-nine years old, swinging and single. I consider myself to be liberal and liberated sexually. I've had more than twenty semiserious affairs since I was relieved of my virginity seven years ago. I adore sex and will try anything to enhance my lover's pleasure. I masturbate regularly, and climax within minutes, especially if I fantasize, although I don't need to. I've always loved the whole sex thing, from the first touch to the last kiss, even though I never climaxed with a man until about three years ago.

I enjoy being sexually aggressive at times, and at times I crave to be dominated. I think about sex a lot and can get turned on easily by erotic reading material.

Now, for my fantasies, neither of which has been fulfilled—yet. The thought that my lover is now aware of them and is planning our next encounter around them is driving me wild.

My first fantasy is that of being spanked: I have always provoked the spanking, it's never unjustified. My innate female bitchiness causes my lover to say very quietly, "All right, that's enough!" I say, "Don't order me around." He says, "You're asking for a good spanking." I say, "I'd like to see you try it," in a very taunting manner.

At which point, he grabs me, grasps both hands firmly behind my back, pulls down my panties, turns me over on his knee, and traps my kicking legs between his. I am embarrassed and scared. He usually uses his hand, spanking me maybe two dozen times, very hard. Sometimes I fantasize that he uses a hairbrush or ruler. Usually his hand, though. I am sobbing and enraged. The rage turns to humiliation, which turns to submission. At the end he forces me back on the bed and enters me, not roughly, but without foreplay either. Or sometimes I like to think of myself staying at the enraged part throughout the spanking. He pushes me back on the bed, hovers over me, and shoves his erect penis into my mouth, ordering me to suck it. I refuse and bite him, which brings on another, still more painful spanking, at which point I am eager to do whatever he asks. I've never fantasized being brutalized; I don't think I'd care for whippings (although excerpts from *The Pearl* or *The Story of O* stimulate me tremendously). As a rule I hate pain, except when approaching a climax, when I find pleasure in being bitten on my inner thighs hard enough to bruise the skin. But this spanking fantasy has been with me for years and years. The thought of being spanked used to arouse sexual feelings at the age of six or seven, even though I didn't recognize them, and, of course, I didn't know about intercourse or fellatio at that age. If it matters, I have never in my conscious memory been spanked by either of my parents.

My second fantasy is as follows. Screaming and scratching and struggling, I am tied or strapped on my back to my bed. I am spread-eagled, and my arms and legs are forced just past the point of being comfortable. He has forced a pillow under my hips, and of course I am naked. The pillow has the effect of raising and exposing my vulva, and I can move only an inch or two up and down or from side to side. I am extremely panicky. I am pleading and begging and crying. He is never angry; he responds to me at all times as if I were an object, very matter of factly. He is fully clothed as he moves around checking the ropes to be sure they're secure.

ME: Please let me go.

HIM: Not yet.

ME: If you let me go, I'll suck you dry.

HIM: You'll do that anyway, honey, in a minute or two.

ME: If you don't let me go, you bastard, I swear I'll never let you in my mouth again.

HIM: Yes you will, love.

ME: But I don't want to be like this!

HIM: It really doesn't matter what you want right now, honey.

ME: (Assorted obscenities, mixed with sobs and twisting at the ropes)

HIM: That's enough. (All the time he's very cool and calm.)

ME: My legs hurt, my arms ache, my crotch is splitting. *Please!*

HIM: A little pain is good for you.

ME: (More obscenities)
HIM: Honey, stop that.
ME: (More obscenities)
He reaches out and pinches the inside of both my thighs, very hard.
HIM: You *will* be quiet now, darling, please.
ME: Yes. (Crying more from pain and rage)

He then leaves the room for what seems like hours, because of the strain on my arms and legs. When he returns he is nude and he has an enormous erection, which makes me whimper in anticipated pain. He doesn't touch me. He kneels at the foot of the bed, gazing at my exposed vulnerable pubic area. I am utterly mortified, because I have no control now. I can't shield myself or put my legs together or roll over. My whole crotch is so exposed and open to his eyes and mouth and/or penis. I'm totally at his mercy. I keep saying, "What are you going to do to me?" and he just sits there. Then the fantasy takes one of several courses. Sometimes he loves me all over with his mouth, until I beg him to enter me. Sometimes he enters me without foreplay and seemingly just takes me as if I'm nothing. Sometimes he enters my mouth, from above, which I hate because of the control he has and the gagging depth he can achieve. (In real life, I love performing fellatio, but only when I'm above him, so I can keep it shallow.) Whatever he does, the fantasy ends with him releasing me and hugging me and massaging my sore muscles and my sobbing with relief and *thanking* him—not for letting me go, but for tying me up!

This second fantasy is extremely fascinating to me, although both ideas really turn me on. I've just recently added this one to my repertoire, but it isn't quite as powerful as the other. It goes as follows: I manage to tie *him* to the bed, spread-eagled exactly as I was. This is done by some sort of "innocent" playfulness, like, "Honey, show me how to tie that knot. Oh, I see. Let *me* try . . ." and so on. When he realizes he's been tricked, he reacts with rage and fear, much as I did in my second fantasy. As a matter of fact, we pretty much change roles—he's helpless and scared, while I'm cool and matter of fact. He doesn't cry, of course, but he feels, if anything, *more* vulnerable, exposed, and helpless than I did, because of his absolute inability to protect his genitals. Usually in this fantasy I just start out kissing him ever so gently, all over, gradually working down to his pelvis, and then up inside his thighs, just tantalizing him. I avoid all contact with his penis or testicles, but just keep on caressing and licking, etc., until he begs me to touch his genitals. But I delay until he's really in a frenzy before doing so, and even then I hardly touch him—I just keep up the teasing, tantalizing, etc., until he can't take it any more. Then I either suck him till he comes in my mouth or I have him climax in my vagina. Occasionally, during the tantalizing, nongenital phase, when he seems to relax and give himself up to me, I put a little fear back into him by giving him a painful nip or pinch inside his thighs. Usually, though, I am just gentle and loving. I never threaten his genitals, nor do I hurt him there unless he asks me to bite him, which in real life he likes.

P.S. A few thoughts I've had on sexual fantasies: It seems that the more liberated I become (I'm really digging Women's Lib now) the more I fantasize about the spanking and the bondage. Since I'm fully liberated in my work situation, social life, etc., it's almost as if I'm trying to achieve some sort of counterbalance to this liberation in my sexual life. I've always had the first two fantasies, but never so intensely as since I've been involved in Women's Lib, or rather, since I've embraced the principles behind the movement. I am sure there are other women like me, who having emerged from being under male domination, crave to return to it in bed.

Another thing—the more I think of it, the more I feel an ideal male-female relationship would be one in which *both* feel free to confide their fantasies to each other and *both* care enough for each other to endeavor to make these fantasies come true. It would be great, for example, if my fantasy were to mesh with his, i.e., if he craved to spank me or tie me down while I craved to be spanked or tied down. This is not the case, but he loves me enough to be willing to try these things. Now I intend to discover *his* fantasy, and if it's at all possible, I shall attempt to fulfill that fantasy. Again, it would be too much to expect (but maybe it's true) that he fantasizes being tied down. But if he should desire to paint my body, say, or be whipped, or have me wear some kind of costume, I'll do all in my power to accommodate him. What's wrong with playing out these inner desires? Why are we so afraid to share them?

I hope you can use my experiences. I feel really turned on just writing about them! Good luck with your project. [Letter]

Poppy

I am a white Catholic American woman, 32 years old with three sons. I have been married twice. My second husband and I have been married more than eleven years.

I always entertain a sexual fantasy while having sex which results in an orgasm for me. Over the years the fantasy has changed, as we have moved about the country a great deal, and I am thus always meeting new people and finding myself in new situations.

My fantasy is about the man with whom I recently had an affair which lasted seven months. He is married and is eleven years younger than I. He has two younger college-age brothers. I fantasize that his family, he, his two brothers, his wife, and his father take my clothes off and make me wait on them, doing anything they ask. I am required to suck off all the men in front of everyone, and if the man does not feel I have done a good job, he spanks me. I receive many spankings. After I have performed fellatio on them all—including cunnilingus on the wife—I am tied to a bed spread-eagle style and they play with me, sometimes roughly, i.e., one of the men will put his anus over my mouth and request that I tongue him. His wife usually per-

131

forms cunnilingus on me, and I get very excited looking at
her and having everyone standing around and watching. I
am required to say words like "fuck" frequently and must
describe my aroused feelings to them all. Usually I come
at about this time.

Sometimes I am allowed to choose someone to degrade,
and I always choose the father, whom I didn't like. I make
him perform cunnilingus on me for hours and I always end
up whipping him for poor performance. [Letter]

Heather

I am writing in reply to your request for female sexual
fantasies.

I do fantasize, sometimes when I am having difficulty
reaching an orgasm (my boy friend always has to stimulate me manually after he has come). I pretend that I am
being humiliated in some way. Or that I am being dis-
played by a man, such as a slave owner, for the benefit of
his friends. Heaven knows why, but if I can think of this
intensely enough, I have a fantastic orgasm.

I don't think he would be jealous if I told him about
these fantasies, just angry. I think he just wouldn't be able
to understand, and would be rather disappointed in me
and disgusted. You see, we are both university graduates;
he has always been proud of my intelligence. He can't
stand girls who can't discuss a variety of topics with him
with some degree of knowledge. He likes to think of us as
being down-to-earth, sensible people. I am reserved, rather tall, dress in a fashionable but sophisticated way—he
doesn't like fluffy, giggly girls. He dominates me in ordinary things—I never get my own way when deciding when
or where to eat, what film to see, etc. But he does not
dominate me sexually, at least in the way I want him to.

He will make me massage his back or scratch it until I
am bored to tears; he expects me to fondle him and kiss
him for long periods of time without actually doing any-

thing to me. But he would never dream of forcing me to make love, or hit me or anything.

Actually, he is very good in bed. I have slept with eight other men, so I have grounds for judging him. There are times when I reach the heights of ecstasy, but there are times when I feel strongly frustrated and restless. This is when I have these strange domination-humiliation fantasies. I even have them during masturbation. (I don't actually fantasize during masturbation, I simply have to think about the threat itself.)

From what I've told you of our relationship, I suppose you are wondering why I don't tell him about my domination wish. After all, he will listen to anything I care to tell him about myself or my desires without being shocked (although he never offers up any thoughts of his own). Well, the reason is he spent a year in digs. His landlady was a nymphomaniac. She slept with any man she could lay her hands on, and she seduced him. He was young and inexperienced, and he admits she taught him everything he knows. She used to creep into his room at night, leaving her husband in bed, and make love to him. Her husband knew, but because he couldn't satisfy her, he was resigned to letting her get satisfaction elsewhere.

My boy friend enjoyed the lovemaking but felt dirty and disgusted with himself afterwards. He has always said how he enjoys our "pure" lovemaking. He loves me and says it makes him feel happy afterward. I felt very inferior when he told me. He made her sound so much sexier. Of course, she had so much more experience than I did. However, whenever I suggest extending our lovemaking, in particular to fellatio, he says he doesn't want me to do it because he's sure I won't like it. He admits he enjoyed it very much when she did it to him, however. He refuses to believe I really *want* to do it. I have done it with other men and enjoyed it, but he just won't let me. At least, he will to the point of ejaculation, then he pulls me away.

So you see, he has put me on a pedestal in a way. He sees me as pure, clean, and wholesome (even though he knows about the other men) and doesn't want that image destroyed.

My first sexual fantasy occurred soon after puberty. I was about eleven or twelve. At night I would lie in bed and imagine I was walking in the woods. A strange man followed me, and when I started to run away, he caught me and beat me. Every night I would go through varieties on this theme—the man would overpower me—take me away and force me to do things against my will. The sex part was rather hazy. I had no clear ideas on that at that age. By thinking about this before going to sleep, I could make myself dream about it, too. Later the fantasy changed to me being taken away to the East and sold as a slave. There were an infinite number of possibilities to the story, as I was bought and sold by a number of men in succession. Very occasionally I still fantasize about this. My fantasies obviously fall into the "being on exhibition" category in the humiliation sense rather than one of showing off.

My farfetched slave girl fantasies seem absurd, but there is one I will never tire of until something definite happens to end it. I went out with a boy four years ago. I was still a virgin and very green. He flirted with me, made me fall madly in love with him, and then dropped me flat. The main reason I fell for him was that he had a sense of cruelty in him—not vicious, but enough to satisfy my desires. He would grab hold of my wrists and pin me against a wall or on the bed, and force me to kiss him. I would struggle but he would always win, being extremely strong. We both enjoyed these encounters, but we never went further than that and I was still a virgin when he finished with me.

The strange thing is that we still know each other, and we are always very aware of each other's presence. When we met at a party a few months ago, we flirted with each other, and he did things that other people didn't notice, like crushing my hand when he held it, and biting my lips when we kissed until I nearly cried out in pain. He saw this and was obviously enjoying it. Then we had a serious talk, and decided we should stop messing about and be sincere friends (we didn't mention the pleasure we both got out of pain in our different ways . . . we never have and no one else knows). Since then he has been very kind to me . . . when I was upset about my boy friend, he comforted me and let me stay with him. We slept together, but I was too miserable to enjoy it and he was doing it out of concern, not desire, so it was not a success. He treats me very normally, usually, always when in front of his friends. . . . But when they're not around, there are flashes of the old treatment. He knows—I can tell by the way he looks at me—of my need for domination, and likes to tease me by sometimes cooperating and sometimes refusing to, just in little things, this is.

However, I fantasize constantly about what would happen if we were completely alone somewhere, away from all our friends, and we could let ourselves go, and not pretend to be "respectable."

I can never get him out of my mind. It is now four years, and yet when he walks in the room, I still tense up. I can never relax when he's there. Other girls, many of them, have come and gone. All of them have been hurt by him, and I am the only one who is still a friend. He has strong ambitions, he wants to travel abroad and make a success of his career, and he has no time for a steady girl friend, much less a wife who will tie him down. There has always been a bond between us, and I only wish I had met him about five years from now when he had got settled in his career, because I think he is the only person who could fulfill *all* of my needs. He has more or less said the same to me.

As it is, I am going to marry my boy friend. He will make a good husband and father, but I am afraid that I may go through the rest of my life feeling something is missing.

Well, I hope that somewhere in this long, confused letter you can find something of use to you. It has been a relief to talk about it, anyway. [Letter]

Ingrid

A few days after my wedding, I read about a young woman who on her honeymoon was taken every day to a tattooist by her husband, and during the two weeks they were staying there she had to agree to whatever her husband wanted, and she was tattooed on every part of her body.

I don't know whether it is true or not, but I thought about it a lot and I even asked my husband if he would like to have me tattooed. He thought I was kinky or something and that he had married a crazy woman, so I never dared mention it again.

Since then, whenever my husband fucks me I just think about being tattooed and I imagine myself having to strip and be tattooed without being asked if I want it or not. I think of what it would be like to have really cheeky words and pictures put on me. This gets me steamed up and really going and my husband thinks it is him that is getting me like that, and it is not at all.

At one time I used to collect pictures of tattooed people and patterns that I thought would be nice as things to have done, but then I threw them away because I got frightened that he might find them. I really would like to be tattooed, but of course it is not possible. But just to think about it gets me going. Mostly though, it only happens when I am having it off with my husband; and there is another little thing: If I get too randy, I start rolling about, and if my husband loses it out of me he gets mad at me. So I have to be a bit careful.

I have never told anyone else about this and I know you will think I am silly but it really does happen. [Letter]

136

ROOM NUMBER SIX:
THE SEXUALITY OF TERROR, OR,
"HELP! I'M OUT OF CONTROL,
THANK GOD!"

☐ I may be making work for myself, defining differences in the emotions behind fantasy where they may not exist, setting up two rooms in the House of Fantasy where there could be one. It would be easier—certainly more obvious —to relegate Johanna (below) to the Rape Room, instead of arranging for a completely separate space just to satisfy her slightly different, though none the less real, sexual desires.

But this House has no precedent, nor has my work, and therefore I choose to specify a whole separate area of fantasy that is occupied by fear. Not just ordinary fear, but the kind of total and complete terror that can be strangely sexual when you see it as leading to loss of control. It's the only way I can account for the different quality in the fantasies that follow. You don't have to be a psychiatrist to understand that for some women who never reach an orgasm, it may have to do with their fear of letting go, fear of the helplessness, the lack of control, that goes with orgasm . . . you just have to be a woman. And for some women—especially highly independent, self-contained women like Johanna and Anne (below), who manage their lives unto themselves—the loss of this control must be terrifying, the experience of orgasm impossible without, and synonymous with, the terror.

You don't have to have been "scared shitless" to know what it means. Continue the sensation of the pounding heart, the open mouth, the helpless, limp attitude of the body on to orgasm, and you're halfway to understanding the sexuality of fear for these women. ☐

137

Johanna

☐ During the time my husband and I were living just outside Mexico City, we met another couple who lived about a mile down the road, named Charles and Johanna. One day while Johanna and I were alone in their house, she opened a drawer; inside it was a gun. "Charles leaves it for me when I'm alone," she said. "I was once raped here, before we were married. Charles always makes sure I have it when he has to go away." More recently when I saw Johanna and asked if she would contribute to this book, I got more of the story. ☐

You could say that my inner sexual life still revolves around the rape I told you about. I don't think a day goes by without my remembering it. I was in this little house, where I was living alone before I met Charles. A man came in. He wasn't Mexican; I don't know what he was. He pretended that he was interested in selling me something, but I knew something was wrong. He asked if I was alone, but in such a smooth, easy way that he didn't frighten me. But maybe something in me was frightened. Because I almost knew before he did it what he was going to do next. He took a knife out with the same easy manner with which he had asked me if we were alone. He put the knife on the table, near his hand. Then he told me what he was going to do. He told me that he wasn't a pervert, and that if I did everything he said, he would not harm me. He even told me I would enjoy it. All the time he was talking, I could see the front of his trousers begin to bulge. I couldn't look him in the eyes. I kept my eyes down. He may have thought I was staring at the ground. I was watching that huge mound in the front of his trousers. I remember thinking what a cruel, powerful bulge it made.

He told me to take off my clothes. I did, with one eye on my buttons, the other on the knife that was so close to his hand. Then, when I was naked, he told me to unzip his trousers. I did. "Take it out," he said, "and kiss it." I did.

138

I didn't understand what I was doing. It all seemed so natural, it almost seemed as if I was in a hurry to help him. I did everything he told me. Then he told me to lie down on my back, on my work table, but with my feet on the floor. While I did it, he picked up the knife, and came to stand between my legs. "Spread them wider," he said, and as I did, he stepped between them even closer to me, and suddenly raising the knife above his head, plunged it point first into the table, right beside my hips. Then he knelt down in front of me, his two arms on either side of me, one hand still holding the knife that was stuck into the table, and he went down on me. I tried to think of how terrified I was, how much I hated him. But I felt myself becoming more and more excited. I closed my eyes and tried to turn from side to side, as if trying to get away from his tongue, but it was also to have that tongue touch different sides of me, inside. Once I opened my eyes. All I could see was the dark top of his head, his hair, and the hand holding the knife just beside me. Then I closed my eyes again, and I suddenly couldn't help it, I pulled his head right into me, pulled his tongue right into me as high as possible, and then I came, over and over again.

The next thing I saw was his face. He was smiling. He was on top of me, still on the table. He was on me. "Put it in," he said, and I was now eager to do anything he said. With one hand I held the lips open, with the other I guided his erection right into me. I remember he wasn't very big around, but very long and slim. I wanted to feel it all the way inside me. In just a few thrusts I could feel him coming, and I came again, too. I had forgotten to think about how much I hated him. I could only think of his long thing, long and slim, all the way up and lost inside me, and I came and came again. Then the man just went away. Just as he had promised.

I told my husband about what had happened before we were married, but I never told him how it made me feel. The time when this happened, I was going with a Mexican boy, and there was another man before I met Charles. Neither one had ever made me feel so sexually in heat the

way that man did when he raped me. Neither has Charles.
It's no good when I'm in bed with Charles, telling myself
that I love him, and that I hate that other strange man. It
just kills whatever erotic feelings I have. Other times,
Charles can bring me to the point himself, and I don't
have to think about that other man.

But sometimes when I'm not really in the mood, and I
know Charles is . . . or that funny kind of way that a really
erotic mood will overtake you and then just drift away for
no reason at all . . . that's when I deliberately think of that
man. I close my eyes and imagine myself back on that
table, with my legs hanging down from the knees over the
edge, and him in between them. I remember how much I
hated him, and the, I don't know, the fear, the *frenzy* of
the experience, and how I responded to it. Whenever I
imagine that, I still respond the same way. Every time.
[Taped interview]

Anne

☐ Anne is a widow and older than most of the other
contributors in this book, and therefore her language is
more restrained than most. But this does not mean that her
life has been in any way less adventurous.

Anne is a long-time friend of my husband's, who also
knew her husband John very well until John's sudden ac-
cidental death. She works in the fringe land of the films,
and is around movie people a great deal. She had been
married once before and figured in a Hollywood divorce
trial written up by all the newspapers in the early 1950's.
"But once I met John, he was the only man for me, ever,"
she told me. Romantic talk, if a teen-ager had said it. But
from a woman of Anne's experience and honesty, positive-
ly breathtaking. Nevertheless, she is such a vital, warm, attractive woman that I find it hard to understand why she
has never remarried. I don't doubt that she's been asked,

and I don't understand how such a sexual woman can live alone.

I have always thought of Anne as the most intelligent, good, openminded woman I know . . . of any generation. She is fun to be with and never lays her problems on you, though she's got them. Her vivid stories of her own sexual-social explorations of twenty or thirty years ago stand up to anything I've seen in the past world-changing decade. If I ever thought that *I* was alone (i.e., not like the other girls) in my 1960's explorations, how very "different" Anne must have felt back there in the thirties.

It's one thing to be the first girl on the block to smoke pot, take a lover, etc., but for all the zest that being an adventuress can bring, it can also bring, very early on, a seemingly contradictory feeling of the need for self-control. Mountain climbers have to be more careful than earth dwellers. At least, that's my explanation for my own late arrival to a *full* appreciation of sex. Anne, I am sure, has her own explanation. ☐

Now that I think of it, I find it difficult to describe. I mean what goes on in my mind during sex. I don't think I can . . . I am in the dark, but it is not just dark of night; it's a blackness of infinite space. This is probably scientifically incorrect, because I guess the astronauts, the cosmonauts, whatever they are, find light. My own blackness is a more mythological thing . . . that "outer darkness" . . . but it's not death. It's being way, way, far out somewhere in infinite space. I'm somehow in my body, but also outside of it. I'm liable at any second to fall down through infinite, unimaginable darkness, sort of like Lucifer . . . that's my second reference to *Paradise Lost;* I wonder what that means? Maybe another way to put it is that it's like falling out of a space rocket, only in absolute darkness. It's frightening and thrilling. I suppose that's what I think of men. Unless they're a little bit frightening . . . without a touch of the devil, I don't find them thrilling. There . . . that explains all the Lucifer associations. He was supposed to be the most beautiful angel of all.

I don't know why I should have this particular fantasy

141

... I certainly didn't deliberately *choose* it ... because I have that fear of heights, what's it called? ... cannot look out of a plane window or even an office window high up in Rockefeller Center, never can go near the edge of anyone's penthouse terrace ... am terrified because I want to jump. And I never had this until after I started to have really satisfactory sex relations. I suppose I never really understood that terrific loss of control, that falling down into you don't know what, that letting go of everything that orgasm brings. Before then, as a child and as a girl, I had no fear of heights, no frightening impulse to jump. I think that's it. The fear so many women have that they'll leap from the heights is some kind of desire to leap into orgasm. I suppose that's the connection ... do you? [Taped interview]

ROOM NUMBER SEVEN: THE THRILL OF THE FORBIDDEN, OR, "NO, YOU MUST NOT! ... HERE, LET ME HELP YOU."

☐ At full strength, the sensation of guilt contains an element of discovery, the possibility of being discovered ... by someone. You could say, therefore, that fantasies wherein guilt is the motivating emotion belong in the Audience Room (I even think I have one there), where the desired fuel comes from the presence, or imminent presence, of other people. But guilt is too prevalent and powerful an emotion to be carried as an addendum to another idea. It can bring, all of its own, such vitality to sexual fantasy that I give it a room of its own.

My own fantasies often ride high on the risk of doing the forbidden. I am by nature, like a lot of other women, what could be called "the faithful type," and for this type, men other than our husbands or current lovers are taboo. (This is simplistic language for defining both myself and the idea of fidelity, but I choose to be clear rather than an-

142

alytically thorough.) For us, fantasies which involve us with this or that sexually attractive man in some compromising situation give us the desired sexual kick without the real guilt; in fact, guilt, the deterrent in reality, has been transformed by harmless fantasy into guilt the exciter. We win both ways.

Some people rob banks for the sheer thrill of getting away with it. Or, to put it another way, for the excitement of maybe being caught. In every suspense-thriller the clock ticks ominously . . . it is only a matter of time. This idea of time running out on the guilty act heightens everything. It's especially so when the guilty act is sex. Whether it's the illicit affair in reality (the only sort some women enjoy) or the forbidden sex in fantasy, with both it's only a matter of time before that time runs out, before the whistle blows, the footsteps come closer, the bedroom door is opened and the discovery made. In fantasy, time is on guilt's (sex's) side, in that it adds to the thrill by threatening to run out. You only have to think of the added charge in a shipboard romance, summer love, sex in another town. To really appreciate the thrill of guilt, add the element of "stolen" love to "September Song." □

Emma

I am hiding from the others. We are playing a game of sardines and I have been given a head start to find a hiding place. At the top of the house I have found an empty room with only a bed in it. Quickly, in the dark, I slide under the bed and wait for the others to find me; their voices are very distant now. They are far away, except for one pair of footsteps, one person, who is getting closer and closer. He comes in such a direct line toward me, it's as though he knew where I was, as if I had left him a trail, a scent. As if we had planned this hiding place together. I catch my breath, my heart pounding, because I know who it is, the one person in the group I want to have find me, to find me before the others. It *has* to be him. I will it to be him.

He comes straight to the room, quietly and quickly so the others won't hear him, and slides under the bed beside me in the darkness. We lie together, hardly breathing, our hands beginning to move over one another. Hands that have never before touched me move all over me. Hands I put a face to in my mind, that face I've always found exciting but that was never mine to kiss. I hardly dare breathe as I listen for the others' voices, moving in and then away as they explore room after distant room. We both move slowly. My skin is alive, the excitement running all through me as my own hands help him to ease up my sweater, direct his mouth to my breast. I help him work the zip on the back of my pants, and then with the most incredible daring I push my buttocks up and his head down. His mouth caresses me all over. My hands, braver and braver in the dark, move over him, find his erection like a rock, and all the while we seem to move in slow motion on this bare floor, scarcely breathing, our bodies moving against the background noise of the voices on the floor below. They are calling to one another, "Have you found them?" Then calling my name, "Emma! Where are you, Emma?" With every step they move closer. The louder their approaching voices get, the more urgent our bodies grow. They laugh and call to one another, suggesting places I may have hidden; they are aware now that we are the only two missing. Then their voices fade and I pray, dear God, don't let them find us yet! Then I hear my boy friend Larry's voice, and though there is not a note of suspicion in it, the fear and anxiety I feel make me hotter, make me do the most incredible things with this man whom I hardly know. Now there is nothing I wouldn't let him do to me, even pain, even words in my ear that no man has ever said. "More." My own whisper is in my ear. "More!" I demand of him and I am wet through before he is quite in me. We are like two conspirators in the dark, breathing so hard it seems incredible they can't hear us.

Now that they know we are together, the search takes

on new urgency. "What are you two up to? Where are you?" they call, laughing, teasing now. Their urgency becomes ours, hidden, sopping wet all over now with one another's sweat, with our clothes half on and half off . . . how will we explain to the others? But it's too late for that now. There are footsteps on the stairs, someone's found the little door that leads to the attic. It's just one pair of footsteps coming. We need more time, just seconds. We hear the searcher stumble in the dark, and as the cock inside me thrusts deeper and deeper, my teeth are tearing the skin on my lower lip and our fucking is paced in double-time to the steps outside in the dark, coming closer and closer, as we get closer and closer to something we can no longer avoid. Now as I know it is beyond my control, I also know that the person coming is Larry. He calls down to the others below that he thinks he's found us. As the footsteps and voices move closer and closer, so do we, until I come. [Written down on request]

Donna

☐ I am thirty years old and have been married for twelve years.

I think my favorite fantasy is of my exciting someone to the point where they have to masturbate. I am not the sort of person who can openly or deliberately excite a stranger. I am very bashful and even somewhat backward sexually. However, accidents happen, and I have excited people in the past and I like the idea. Someday I will work up the courage to excite someone else besides my husband.

During sex with my husband I sometimes fantasize we are having sex where other men and women can watch, and they get so carried away by the sight that they begin to masturbate. I also think about other men who have made passes at me, and picture them masturbating or becoming so excited looking at me that they get carried away and even fondle their penises in full view of the public.

I was very slow developing sexually and was in my late

145

teens before I masturbated at all. Then it was in very secretive circumstances for fear of being caught with my fantasies. As I dated and would often come home aroused, I would fantasize about what could have happened while I masturbated. After marriage I again became fearful of being caught with my fantasies. However, as our experience grew and my husband became a better lover, I would fantasize that his penis became erect in a very embarrassing, compromising situation . . . and then he would climax.

I don't know how my husband would react if I told him about these fantasies. He is a very liberal man, but if put to the actual test might think differently. He has expressed his fantasies to me, and while some excite me, others disgust me. [Letter]

ROOM NUMBER EIGHT: THE TRANSFORMATION ROOM, OR, "LIFE CAN BE BEAUTIFUL."

☐ Women respond so directly to the promise of more beauty that even factories have discovered that better mirrors in the ladies' room mean higher production from the women workers. Certainly a House of Fantasy—where the most beautiful act of all relies on the promise of greater beauty—needs a room where everything can be transformed: the plain woman into the beautiful, the beautiful into the even more beautiful, a drab life into a dazzling one . . . in such a room even sex could be made to seem beautiful to those who fear their own ugliness.

We are told that some of the most beautiful women in the world have lonely doubts about their own desirability and the essential glamour of their lives; magazine sales thrive on it. So no matter what her beauty in reality, or her favorite sexual imagery, every woman who enters the House of Fantasy will want a reassuring moment in the

146

Transformation Room before going on. Illusions of greater beauty, even fantasy illusions, heighten sex by heightening the woman's own awareness of her desirability. Some women, like Betty and Monica (below), will look no further than this. The Transformation Room is all they want. Without the complete transformation of themselves and of their narrow, almost sordid view of sex itself, there could be no sex at all, imagined or real. Fantasy releases them from the dead grip of self-contempt and neurosis and into life itself. □

Monica

□ Monica is nineteen years old, short, messy looking, and about fifteen pounds overweight. She's always been overshadowed by her older sister, who was the pretty one in the family, she says. "She was the one who always got the lovely clothes, and after a time I just didn't bother."

Monica idolized her father, and in her daydreams the man was rarely a film star; he was more often her father.

"I didn't dream about him as if he were my lover," she says. "We would be a father and daughter. But I would lie in bed, or sit in school for hours, and imagine that he and I were about to go out to dinner in some fabulous place, or go dancing. Sometimes I'd imagine that we were going to do something exciting like driving to some secret place where they illegally allowed you to play roulette."

In all, a typically romantic, adolescent girl, somewhat scruffy, but with her father playing the principal idealized male role in her youthful imagination, and a pretty sister to envy.

Monica's parents belonged to a religious sect that believed very strongly that sex was a temptation to be resisted, and there was almost never an allusion to the subject in her house. "But somehow it made me admire my mother and father more," she says. "I knew that they were different from other people, purer and cleaner; even when my parents' religious ideas left me entirely unpre-

147

pared for the beginning of my menstruation, I didn't entirely blame them. Oh, maybe I did blame my mother a little for not warning me, but not my father. It was a nasty, ugly business. Why should he talk about it?

"In fact, it left me with a greater admiration for my father. His silence on the subject, I mean. I knew even then, somehow, that men were more interested in sex than women. But here was my father, this glamorous, wonderful figure who—my daydreams about him were more real to me than he himself was—only cared about the beautiful things in life, like taking me to the theater. Why should he talk to me about ugly things like my period? You see how I built him up?

"Then one day I was in my parents' bedroom. They were away, and I just couldn't resist the temptation to open my father's chest of drawers and see what I'd find there. I don't know what I expected. Some glorious symbol of that vague, secret world that men lived in, I suppose. What I found there, under the shirts, were a little pack of those nasty rubber things—even today I hate to say the word—and a copy of Henry Miller's book, *Tropic of Cancer*. I'd never heard of Henry Miller. I quickly opened the book and began to read it. Or maybe I had heard of Henry Miller. Maybe it was because the book was hidden under my father's shirts. But I knew I was doing something wrong."

The experience, Monica said, did not leave her so much disgusted or angry or, on the other hand, excited, as filled with fear. The book was a denial of all the pure and noble ideas she had formed about her father, and the description of the sexual acts in the book immediately made her realize that such performances must go on between her mother and father. "I felt I had nothing left to live for," Monica said. "My father wasn't secretly thinking about living with me some day in a world where we went to the opera, or ran a ranch together out West; he was thinking of all the things in this book. There was nothing left for me but this frightening world that Henry Miller described, filled with all these horrors. I was just a stupid kid, and I tried to commit suicide that night. I swallowed a full bottle of aspirin and all the other pills I could find in the house. Luckily or unluckily, there was nothing very lethal in the house. I just got sick and vomited all night. But even today, suicide, it's never very far from my mind." □

I began having these ideas the very first time I had sex. I'd never thought of it before in my life, and suddenly there it was in my mind. I'd met this good-looking boy at a dance, and I was very surprised that he even looked at me twice. Boys like him never did. But we got into his car and pretty soon I knew why he had singled me out after all. I usually shied away from that kind of thing, but then I suddenly thought, Well, you have to learn about this thing for yourself sooner or later. Everybody in the world knows about it except you. Why not with him? I was also very attracted to him, and maybe I was hoping against hope that if I said Yes, I would see him again.

And to tell the truth, it was very exciting. We got into the back seat of his car, and it was cozy and dark there. We were all alone. Maybe it was the first time I had ever been alone for so long with a boy in a car when he wasn't driving. I always feel that empty places are sexy. Empty rooms, especially. I think that was the feeling that took me into my parents' empty bedroom that time. There's always something about an empty room. You never know what's in there.

Anyway, this boy was an expert lover. Or maybe he had just read a lot of books and knew all the tricks. I was somewhat aware that he was doing these things to me, but all I could think of was about the moment when he would get on top of me and open my legs to push it into me. I knew somehow that it was going to hurt. But just the idea that he was going to put that thing into me was all the excitement I needed. I wanted to scream at him to forget the sex techniques and to hurry up. I remember helping him to get my underwear off, and when my panties got stuck on my ankle—we were in some awkward position, imagine!—I practically tore them off myself, I was in such a hurry.

After all that, it went in without any pain at all. I remember looking for just a second, being surprised that it grew out of his front, instead of down inside between his legs, like mine. But then when it went in, I felt almost nothing. No pain. Nothing. I just felt dead inside, with all the excitement gone. I was just lying there while he was going through all these funny motions. And then this thought came to me right out of the blue. I was suddenly not my own self. The body he was screwing was not this funny fat thing of mine, it wasn't me, it was my sister. So it all became a picture in my mind. I could see him just as he was, very handsome. But the body he was putting it in—it wasn't me. It was my beautiful sister. Part of me was glad it was her. I hated her, and I became angry and happy to think of her in this humiliating position, being fucked by a stranger in the back seat of a car. But the other half of me wanted to be like her, wanted to feel the man inside me. If it was my sister, it was all right. And right with that picture in my mind, all the excitement came back. I could feel the boy, I could feel myself moving up and back in time to him, but all the time it wasn't me, it was all happening to these two beautiful people in my mind.

Ever since then, the girl is never me. If it is, I always feel cold and lifeless and a little disgusted with both myself and the boy. But as soon as I get this picture, I feel the wildest excitement. [Interview]

Betty

During the last phase of intercourse is when I fantasize. I pretend I have changed into a very beautiful and glamorous woman (in real life I know I'm somewhat plain), and that my husband and I are in bed in very luxurious surroundings, usually in a hotel, far away from where we live. I can see the bottle of wine in a silver bucket waiting for us when we finish. I think of the people walking along outside our room in the corridor who are unaware of what we are doing only a few feet away from them, and how they'd envy us if they did know. Most of all, I like the idea that it is not our house but a hotel room, because hotels are only temporary, anything can happen. When I was a little girl I always imagined that only the most beautiful women lived in the huge marvelous hotels I'd see in the movies. There weren't any large hotels in the town where I grew up, and so I only saw them in the movies, and of course, since it was in films, all the women were beautiful.

I am quite myself before the stage mentioned above, but when I begin feeling myself to be this other woman, I usually mount my husband and give myself a good working out on his gorgeous cock. This is still part of what I think of as the "final stage," and while I am sitting there above him, moving myself up and down on him, I close my eyes and seem to be watching this other beautiful woman who is me from some other place, outside myself. I can see her so vividly that I want to shout encouragement to her . . . she loves it so much. "Go on, go on, give it to yourself," I want to say to her. "Enjoy it, you deserve it." The funny thing is that this other woman isn't me. In fact, she's not always the same woman. [Letter]

Phyllis

Hi. I am twenty-six, upper middle-class background, and had three and one-half years of college before I dropped out and bummed around the world. I have been legally married for almost four years. I am presently employed as a bartender. I am in favor of self-determination for both men and women in all areas, sexual included.

In general, I would say that my fantasies are pretty free, but my actions, though perhaps more far out than those of many people, are still conservative when compared to the possibilities of human sexuality.

I'd separate my fantasies into those I had before I had LSD and those after. Before, they included fucking everything from guys I knew (kind of tender scenes) to very repulsive or "lewd" dirty old men. Or a fantasy where I would make it with a girl, including kissing, rubbing tits, lying on top of one another. Or dreams of making it with a three-year-old girl, a priest, even an erotic kind of image of walking upstairs inside of an elephant (*very* erotic). One fantasy included my being raped by twelve black men (though I haven't any conscious prejudice against blacks when awake). And, of course, there were the general lewd fantasies of making it with my father, an uncle, or a cousin.

Other rather general fantasies I've had involve seeing myself as a kind of pin-up in a porn magazine . . . sticking out my tits, playing with my nipples, making little catlike expressions, moving my pelvis in slow circular motions while keeping my eyes just slightly open. I've thought of myself this way when I'm with guys I like, as well as guys I find distasteful. Actually, sometimes if I'm fucking a guy who fills me with disgust or anger or resentment, I think to myself, "Okay, you want to fuck, you creepy, slimy bastard, I'll fuck you all right. I'll fuck you so hard you'll die from it." Other times, I fantasize about the guy I'm with being with another guy, or a lot of other people watching us, or the guy I'm with watching me make it with another girl. Once I fantasized about lying back on the floor and having ten different people (men and women) fondling different parts of my body.

Sometimes, if I love a guy, think his body is beautiful, but hate his technique, I have a kind of "mystical" fantasy: visions of stained glass, the suffering Christ, Virgin Mary, the organ playing . . . but I haven't had this for about four years.

It's important to me how the guy talks about what we're doing: I like to hear the word "fucking," and even more, "balling" (calling it "cunting" would be absurd, wouldn't it? Whereas "intercourse" is too scientific and detached, and "making love" is too liberal and has become an offensive cliché, though if I really love somebody, "making love" is not offensive as long as both people understand that it's also fucking . . . then it really *feels* like making love). But I love to get myself worked up thinking or say-

ing things like fuck, cunt, cock, dick, tits, sucking, cocking
. . . it really makes me feel good and lewd, just so long as
it's natural and doesn't sound like we're trying too hard,
using these words.

When I'm really into a fantasy, really into fucking, I
love sucking a man—although my arm and hand and
mouth sometimes get tired and I hate getting that choking
feeling in the throat—and when I'm really aroused I like
him to come in my mouth, in my hair, in my eyes, on my
tits, on my ass, etc. When this happens I can imagine that
he is doing the same thing to me: licking my nipples, running his tongue down the middle of my stomach down to
my crotch, licking my clitoris and then right up my back.
Do you understand? In my fantasy I càn change the whole
thing around, and that's great.

As for my lesbian fantasies: girls that turn me on the
most are not usually friends but relative strangers. They
are not necessarily "pretty"; usually slender, feminine, but
not "cutesy pie"; often tomboyish; occasionally mysterious or gypsylike in appearance. Sometimes a super-bitch
appearance turns me on. (Very fascinated to *watch* super-
feminine idiotic types or super-feminine cool sexy type . . .
but I can't really fantasize this type in sexual activity with
me. Not particularly turned on by "Mother Earth" or
clean-cut cold look.) I've always fantasized about making
it with this kind of women. In high school I used to parade
around my room by myself with a very tight sweater on,
having stuffed my mother's bra with Kleenex (although I
was very modest in public). I've had three real sexual experiences with women. Usually I have to fantasize that
they are men, or I think about the time I felt up this crazy
chick in a car (I loved her tits!); I think about them when
I'm with a girl . . . those tits. The last time was with a real
lesbian, for whom I felt a kind of compassion. I tried
thinking of myself as the aggressor, but it just didn't work.

Now for my fantasies and sex since LSD. I should mention that I was a virgin until I was twenty-one. I'd had this
strong feeling that "being felt up" or screwing would make

me considered to be a whore. I really wanted to be respected. It seemed to me that all guys had this double standard: they wanted me to give in, but if I had, they'd have thought me a whore. Finally, when I was seventeen, a guy forced me to feel him up—he tore off my blouse and played with me—and I did it—jerked him off—but I felt a total disgust and hatred. Then, when I was twenty-one, I met this guy I loved (not my husband) and we took LSD and fucked. It was unlike anything that had ever happened before: I had none of those feelings of "dirtiness." My mind wasn't really thinking about the sexual organs; I lost myself in a very tangible, three-dimensional, colorful, blissful something I can't describe. For the first time I had this strong feeling that this was another human being that I loved—it was a kind of fantasy in that it all went on in my mind. It was what I was thinking more than feeling with my body that made it all so beautiful, and I felt good and not at all paranoid. For the first time I wanted to make love to *everything* in the universe (very unlike me). After that first trip, whenever I was fucking I'd remember the images in my head when I'd done it the first time, the thoughts of love, of thinking love, and I began to have orgasms. Then I had a *bad* trip on LSD, and for the next six months I had, maybe, one half an orgasm.

After that, I tried thinking my old lewd thoughts: I'd think about the guy who'd once stuck a hose up my cunt, and a wine bottle (pouring in the wine). It wasn't that I'd enjoyed these things, but thinking about it later made me feel very liberated in the sense of letting go, trying new things, and loving a relative stranger as a human, a man whom I really didn't like. I didn't think about him, but the fact that we were doing such weird things, it made me feel better, more relaxed about myself and other people. Once I had a fantasy about hitchhiking, of being picked up by a dirty old man and being raped; I thought that if I made love to him and loved him, then it wouldn't have to be rape; it was an exciting idea, and I rethought it when I was with other guys; it made me enjoy their fucking more.

I really think your book is a good idea, since nonfictional female sexual fantasies and experiences are rarely openly discussed. They are usually only in works of fiction written by men. Thank you. [Letter]

ROOM NUMBER NINE:
THE EARTH MOTHER ROOM

☐ The letters in the words above this room should be woven in wheat, or embroidered by hand onto a baby-blue sampler. They are that homey and acceptable. Images of fertility rites, even the fantasy of a matriarchal society where men are fed to satisfy women's sexual appetites, (as in Marina's fantasy below, are close enough to mythology and to "nature" to be as acceptable as, for instance, Grimm's fairy tales—which, despite fashionable psychoanalytic horror at their content, nevertheless put children to sleep.

Many women do, in fact, live the earth mother fantasy from day to day without arousing anxiety in anyone. Of all women's sexual fantasies, those that depend on the idea of woman as the symbol of fertility are probably the least threatening to both men and women. Other women—women other than the fantasist—even breathe a sigh of jealousy-free relief at such a Ceres, who is usually so all-accepting as to be almost sexless. This accounts, I suppose, for the many mothers who pray that their daughters (should they fall into such a House) would go straight to this room.

But for all its Mother's Oats cycle-of-life connotations, the image of fertility is as potent to some women as the idea of watching a girl being fucked by an Alsatian might be to the average *Playboy* reader. ☐

155

Vivian

☐ Vivian works part time as a secretary for a friend of mine who runs a theatrical production company from his home. She works for him in the evenings and has a full-time job during the day. She is saving to go to medical school, "but when I start, I want to have enough money saved so that I can concentrate entirely on medicine," she says, "and not have to hassle for money." Her mother and father died in an auto accident, and she lives with a maiden aunt. She is twenty-one, pretty in an unfashionable scrubbed kind of way, and very intense. ☐

I had this fantasy the very first time I had sex. Jimmy was the first man for me. He's still the only one, but no matter who I sleep with later on, I think I'll always have these thoughts I have with Jimmy. They just seem to automatically spring to mind whenever I open my legs.

Anyway, that first night, I don't think we slept very much. We'd had some grass, and so I can't remember just how many times. It didn't hurt a bit and there was hardly any bleeding. Maybe the second or third time that night, he put me into this position; I think it's the position that inspired this idea in the first place, the idea that I was being planted. I mean, you can't have the feeling that you're being planted unless your cunt is pointed straight up at the sky, can you? Because that's what it was: I was lying on my back, all my weight on my shoulders, really, with my legs straight up and over his shoulders. He was high above me—I remember looking up and seeing him looming large over me and coming down into me, boring down on me. Straight *down* into me. Not a frightening picture—on the contrary, I felt very large and accommodating, very wide and open, waiting for him to fill me up with his thrust. Waiting for him to plant seed like I was a large, warm, fertile hole in the earth, there just for him, just for that purpose, to be planted. I was the earth and I was the hole in the earth. In fact, I was all hole, and he, he was like some

156

great International Harvester Seed Planter moving down the field, me, moving from hole to hole with each thrust. And I was all the holes, I was the earth. I was planted again and again. It was so exciting . . . and so, well, so right, so natural. Lying there on my back with my legs up in the air, my feet facing the ceiling, it seemed, at last, the most natural position in the world. And to be fucked, to be planted by an earth planting machine, this enormous International Harvester that could plunge deeper into the earth than anything, could fill me up and leave me planted, ripe . . . that was it, I guess: not just the excitement of being planted, but of knowing that with each thrust I would be left whole, complete. Can you understand that? It wasn't the machine that was exciting—though the inexorable size of it was. What was exciting was the seed part. Or me being the earth. God, I don't know . . . but I love that feeling. [Taped interview]

Marina

☐ Marina belongs more to her nomadic social set than to any country. Now she lives in Boston. Last year it was Paris. Her current lover is an Italian banker: her former an English lord. The only thing they have in common is that each is almost three times her age. She is twenty. Her mother is French, her father Swiss, her bank balance high. For all the miles she's packed into her life, she remains incredibly naive. She speaks half a dozen languages and works for an ad agency. ☐

I had masturbated systematically from a very early age, around three, I think, and so much and so often that my parents consulted a doctor about it. As a child, I used to think of a favorite friend or playmate, or a beautiful lady neighbor of ours, whom I worshipped at the time. Around nine or ten, I started to be aware of men and think of them while masturbating. I had a vague idea of what lovemaking was, but it stopped at French kissing. My ignorance was set right by a girl friend, also aged ten

—children mature very early around the Mediterranean—whose father was a gynecologist, so she was obviously *au courant*. I remember we were munching grapes by a stream in my parents' country place on a sweltering summer day, and constantly, obsessively discussing boys, boys, boys, love, love, love, kissing, necking, petting . . . Then she said did I know what really happens between men and women, and how, and she told me, more than lucidly. Immediately I thought: "But that must be like masturbation, only instead of rolled sheets, my favorite tool, there would be juicy, moist flesh." The prospects seemed heady, and I started floating on a lovely haze of possibilities. "And if you'd really like to know what it feels like," she continued, "the thing to do is to get a kettle, fill it with warm, but not too hot, water, open your legs really wide, and slowly pour it in." There was no time to be lost. We both rushed indoors, pinched Mummy's best Russian silver teapot, locked ourselves in the bath, sat at opposite ends of the bathtub with legs wide open, and took turns at pouring the contents of the teapot all over our clitorises, while caressing our bodies with infallible, instinctive verve. I thought of myself alternately as Mother Earth, watered by fertility rain, in a lovely ritual in Eygpt, or Crete, and an autocratic empress, who sampled all the young men of her kingdom at the beginning of spring, to renew herself. (All were handsome because I'd exterminated the others.) I can't tell you what my friend thought, as I was lost in self-absorption. [Written down on request]

ROOM NUMBER TEN: INCEST

☐ Each of the remaining rooms in the House of Fantasy depends upon the presence or embodiment of a specific fantasy character or characters in order for the female client to fully enjoy her fantasies. I start with the Incest Room because, despite Dr. Freud's casual disinterest in the female equivalent of Oedipus, for women the first sexual imagery of fathers, brothers, etc., is often the most potent and lasting. It was interesting, I think, that though Freud at first accepted as fact his female hysterics' tales of rape by fathers, stepfathers, or older brothers (and became concerned should the Austro-Hungarian Empire be founded on the sick secret saga of daughter-rape), he later came to view these tales as the fantasies of women brought up under the paternal dictatorship of an age when the image of the Man of the House was so strong as to present an almost unconquerable unconscious rival for any man who came along later.

I am not qualified to discuss the psychological significance of incest, pro or con, even as fantasy. But I do think —despite the relative lack of evidence or interest in literature—that women can have as strong an incestuous preoccupation as men. Not all Sunday-mornings-in-bed-with-Mom-and-Dad have to end as traumatically as Bella's, below, but I can't help wondering how many seeds for later fantasy are sown in this kind of family romp; the adults may be satisfying some very grown-up, harmless image of their own, may have very clear and controlled ideas as to just what is going on with the whole family in their marital bed, but what about the children? ☐

Bella

I am a thirty-two-year-old registered nurse working in a London hospital. I have one son almost fourteen. I was pregnant when I was married. My husband is a doctor.

My own fantasy is so shocking to me that it has been a lifelong secret, and only because it has taken a new twist have I decided to write it down to get some of it out of my system. My fantasies revolve around incest, almost any kind of incest, and over the years I have sought out every bit of information I could about "incest," and know all the Greek myths where it occurs. To make a man sexy to myself, I just imagine him a member of my family.

159

I make friends more firmly if they happen to show interest in my subject, and one affair some years ago was almost incestuously inspired. It happened in a Midlands hospital. I was looking after a nice young man, a probation officer, who had been in a car accident. Among his cases was a father who had come out of prison after giving his daughter a baby. The law would not allow them to live in the same house, though they had recommenced sexual relations. The probation officer was happy so long as the girl remained on the pill. I talked to him at night and most of our conversation was on my favorite subject. One night, when we were both excited, he asked for a bottle. I put screens round his bed and put the bottle under the bedclothes. I took hold of his penis, which was exceptionally large, and held it for a few moments. It became such an erection that it would not enter the bottle. I began to masturbate him gently, and when I felt him go rigid, I kissed him as I felt his semen spurt along his shaft. I caught most of his semen in the bottle and our lips parted. He said, "Thank you, Sister." I replied, "Oh, Brother," and a sexual link was established. As he got better, I had intercourse with him many times and we always called each other sister and brother.

But my principal fantasies have always been about my father. I was an only child and had a good home, receiving lots of affection from my parents, especially my father. He has, since I was about eight years old, been my fantasy lover during masturbation.

Dad went to work very early, six days a week, and as a child, when I went to my parents' bed in the mornings, it was only on Sundays that both parents were in bed. This particular Sunday morning, I know I must have been eight, because the Sunday papers carried news of a hotel being bombed in Jerusalem, and this was in the summer of 1946. I was in bed only a short while with my parents when my mother decided to get up and go to a nearby farmhouse for some fresh milk. Alone in bed with Dad, I had a wrestling match with him. I remember enjoying the cuddles and embraces as Dad tried to subdue me and then he decided, I suppose, to let me win. He lay on his back, his pajamas were undone, my own nightie was up around my waist, and when I straddled and sat on my father, my naked pubic area came down on my Dad's very large and, I now know, erect penis. It was like sitting astride a broom handle. At first it lay flat against my Dad's tummy. I rocked my bottom back and forward while Dad lay very still. It was at this precise moment I learned to masturbate. Eventually Dad reached for a hankie and rolled me off him. He got out of bed and dressed in the bathroom. I continued to lie in bed and touch myself lovingly with my fingers. I then began to do this all the time in bed or when I was alone in the house, always thinking of that hard thing Daddy had, and how nice it would be to feel it between my legs again. But this was not to happen. Every other Sunday morning I went to my parents' bed, but Dad was already up and about. As I began to learn more about sex from other kids at school, I became more adventurous in my fantasies, until they settled into a set pattern when I was almost thirteen.

It was at this age that I was playing around with a slightly older girl. She talked a lot about sex and one day told me her big secret, that was having sex with a much older married brother. She told me what the word "incest" meant; part of the sex she explained was fellatio. She said how she loved to do this to her brother, and how he sometimes went down on her privates as well.

With this new information buzzing in my brain, I was out for a walk with my Dad one Sunday afternoon. Deep in the woods he decided he wanted to urinate and did so against a tree. But he turned toward me before he put his penis back in his trousers, and I gazed for a few loving seconds at my Dad's beautiful monster. It has remained the main erotic feature of my masturbatory fantasies ever since.

All I have to do is imagine myself walking in a silent woods, and I can almost *feel* that my Dad is somewhere else in that woods, and that if I can almost hold my breath long enough, we'll meet. The way I meet him is always the same. I turn a corner or come around a tree, and there he is, with his back to me, peeing against a tree. Then he turns around toward me, his penis still out and being held in his hand to guide the stream of pee. I find this too exciting to write about even now, and find myself thinking about my Dad even in real life.

Please open up the subject of incest. Is there any cure? Is there the same risk of prosecution in this permissive age? I know I can't hold out much longer. I'm certain that if I tried this experiment, the shame would kill me, but other times what frightens me even more is the idea that I would become even more deeply involved with him. [Letter]

Dominique

I'm in my apartment. I'm not really a call girl, but I am certainly someone who is experienced in the sexual arts. The doorbell rings and it is this father and his son. The father has been a lover of mine and I have given him what no other woman has: I have given him the ultimate in sexual pleasure. (I *am* a giver, I mean, I think of myself as a giver in both real life and fantasy; that's what I mean when I say I'm not a call girl in this fantasy: I don't get paid for it.) So the father comes in and says, "This is my fourteen-year-old son, and I want him to be as adept as I am, as I think I am, and I want you to teach him everything you know."

So the son and I begin, the father sitting there watching as I undress the boy, caress him, totally initiate him. But it's not the boy that excites me in this fantasy, it isn't the idea of having a young boy, it's the idea of being watched by the father. I don't know if it's voyeurism, or if having the father there, having him bring his son to me, is some kind of sexual approval. Or if it's having him watch the son, watch me with the son. Part of the excitement is that he's brought the son to *me*. That of all the women in the world, he has picked me to initiate the boy. Or maybe

162

the *real* turn-on is incest. Because I also like to fantasize family orgies. Not *my* family, but whole families, mothers, fathers, daughters, and sons, all come to this flat of mine. Yes, my husband is here, too, but a faceless husband. Everybody performs on everybody: The mothers show me what they've been doing to their daughters, and to their sons; and the fathers to the daughters . . . everybody! And it's a *very* happy scene, very happy, very sensual. The family that fucks together stays together . . . I guess that's the message. [Taped interview]

Lola

I was pregnant when I got married at seventeen. But as I'd begun fucking when I was fourteen, I'd had a good three years of fun playing around on my own . . . all of which I owe to my two brothers. One was a year older than me and the other a year younger. What happened was one day they found me messing about—quite innocently—with some boys at school. They blackmailed me, threatening all sorts of things; they said that if I didn't go all the way with those boys—and let them watch—they'd tell our parents what I'd been up to. Since what I'd been up to was far more innocent than what they wanted me to do, I don't know why I gave in to their threats. I suppose because I quite simply wanted to be fucked. I remember my brothers standing on the sidelines, instructing the other boys how to "do" me (we were all virgins at that point), and I remember to this day the combination of fear and excitement that their presence added to what was happening. Although neither of my brothers ever entered me themselves, they do in my fantasies, they always have.

After that blackmail episode I used to lie awake at nights, alone in my bed at home, and imagine that my brothers were creeping through the house toward my room. Every sound in the quiet house was like their footsteps. Often I would imagine the two of them coming for me together. They would get into the bed on either side of me. I remember one night in particular, when I was just past fourteen, when I was lying there, thinking of my oldest brother's prick—I had, of course, seen it—and imagining it going into me and growing in me. Suddenly I could not seem to control myself, and I was certain that the noise I was making—I was actually whimpering out loud—was bound to wake my parents up. But I put my hand over my mouth—imagining it was my youngest brother, while I masturbated with the other hand—imagining that was my older brother. I seemed to be flogging myself almost into a state of unconsciousness. The more I thought about how wrong the whole act was that I was imagining, the more exciting it became.

Even to this day when I'm being fucked—and I'm fifty-one—I imagine one of my brothers standing over me—just as it really happened that time they forced me—while I pretend it is the other one fucking me. The one standing has his prick exposed, and I play with it (while the other is inside me) until he comes all over my face. Then they switch positions and we continue until we are all satisfied.

Sometimes I include my brothers' wives in my fantasies, making it a larger family scene, and I imagine the pleasure my husband could give those women while I'm having it off with their husbands, my darling brothers. But usually it's just me and the boys. Are you shocked? You shouldn't be; more of this sort of thing goes on in reality than you imagine. I know. And not just in poor families, as mine was. Brothers and sisters . . . well, it happens in the best of families. [Conversation]

ROOM NUMBER ELEVEN: THE ZOO

☐ Nice friendly doggies are everywhere. Even if you don't have one, the neighbors do. And Rover is a more perfect gentleman than most: he'll never look surprised at something you may ask him to do, never make you feel ashamed, and will never, never talk. Is it surprising then

164

tha† of all animals, dogs star most frequently in female sexual fantasies, and that with good old Rover around the house all the time, dog fantasies are the ones most often acted out in reality?

Dogs bring a very important, blameless quality to fantasy: it's never your fault, or the dog's either, really; doggies have such big, naturally inquisitive noses, and before you can do anything about it, doggies' big wet tongues automatically dart out and lick anything that smells "that way." That's putting it in simple primer language, which is just where it all begins—with little girls with private parts that no one, possibly not even the little girl herself, has ever touched. The nice family bow-wow comes along, sniff-sniff, and presses the buzzer. Zing! The first sexual thrill of a lifetime has been touched off by Rover. It doesn't matter whether the little girl lets him continue (and more do than you'd think, I bet); the memory of that first lick of pleasure can stay with a woman for life. Later, hopefully, when she has discovered with a loving man or through masturbation the full potential of her clitoris, the dog with his remembered, natural expertise (if she had let him continue), or with her imaginative fantasizing of it (if she had not), can remain an exciting sexual variation, laced with all the taboo quality that only the silent complicity of an animal can bring.

As for the other popular family pet, cats, well, my research indicates that they just don't make it as sexual fantasy pets. Perhaps because they aren't sniffers, or their tongues are too small, or they don't have that very male member hanging down (oh, so visibly) between their legs —an image, especially with its aroused "red tip" that is evocative and exciting to women in reality and fantasy. As Libby put it: "My lover has suggested that we rub cod liver oil on my clitoris and let our cat lick it off. This idea does not appeal to me. A dog, maybe, but not a cat." But obvious studs like donkeys and bulls, with their not-to-be-missed pricks, are another story.

With the farmyard animals there is no licking, no clitoral stimulation either in fantasy or fact. I don't think there are many women who have actually been fucked by a bull or a donkey, either—though it is supposed to be not entirely unknown at "stag" (*ah!*) dinners. With barnyard studs, imagined or not, it's all about the visible turn-on of the prick, the incredible size of it more than anything. Imagine something *that* big—which you reacted to with such fascination, at least the first time you saw it, even if you almost immediately glanced away with embarrassment—imagine that penetrating you! How can a woman look at a prick that big and not imagine it going into her? It's like looking at a racing car and ignoring the thrill of speed. I don't think it's literally a desire to be fucked by these animals, simply an attempt to imagine what it would be like to have so much prick "filling" you up. In fantasy and reality, women repeatedly refer to "being filled"; perhaps it's a woman's way of expressing her sexual desire for *more*. But since everyone knows that unless the man is abnormally small, it isn't penis size that really matters, I think this female cry only uses size as a kind of visible metaphor to express a desire for greater sex, completer sex, the essence of sex. Advertisers have found that the public responds when they call their product "the coffee-er coffee" and "the chocolate-ier chocolate." Should it be any surprise then that women desire sexier sex? □

Jo

I often have this fantasy when I'm alone, or with time on my hands, or even when I'm making love with my husband.

I am alone in the house. My husband has left for work. I begin my housework downstairs, clearing the dishes from the dining room into the kitchen. I take off my nightgown and housecoat and work in the nude. While I work, the neighbor's dog follows me. He always comes over to visit. I take no notice of him, but his wet nose and warm breath move between my legs whenever I pause. Briefly I will let my legs part, and his tongue will dart out and lick me while I continue my chores as though he weren't even there. I keep moving about, not giving him or me too much. Slowly, as if not noticing, I let him have more: now two licks, increasing to three, four, his nose burrowing into my privates as I allow him to get at me for longer and longer periods. Suddenly he tires of the game and stops following, just as I have finished cleaning all the downstairs rooms. Except the kitchen. I always save the kitchen for last.

Quickly I call him as I go into the kitchen, and when he's in I close the door so he can't get out. Now I speed up. I don't want him to lose interest. I get down a bowl and a box of Betty Crocker chocolate cake, my husband's favorite. I mix up the batter quickly, and put half the mixture into a cake tin so we'll have at least a one-layer cake for dessert that night. The other half I smear across my breasts, and as I bend down to put the cake in the oven I let the dog lick the batter from my breasts. With my finger I scrape up batter and keep spreading it on my nipples so that he lingers on them, lapping at them until they ache, until I ache. Now I go to the refrigerator, take out the butter for the icing, and from the cupboard I take down the sugar and a small bottle of Bovril. I sit on the kitchen chair to blend the sugar and butter, right beside the kitchen table with the bowl in my lap. I smear my cunt inside and out with the Bovril, and as I stir the sugar and butter, the dog nestles between my legs and licks me. I hug the bowl to me, working on it, smoother and smoother. I am slumped in the chair now, my legs spread far apart, the large bowl obscuring the dog. The warm sweet smell of cake baking fills the kitchen. Inside the oven, through the glass partition in the oven door, I can see the cake slowly rising. My finger dips again and again into the Bovril jar, smearing my cunt so that the dog licks harder and harder, going from side to side now, excitedly working around me as he might worry a bone. The sweet smell of cake fills my head as I imagine the bright red thing of the dog's slipping in and out of his penis sheath. The cake is getting larger and larger in the oven, so that it seems about to fill the

167

oven, to push open the door and explode into the room, engulfing us in its sweet warmth. I pray that the dog will not stop and that the cake will not explode all over my nice clean kitchen before my husband gets home, before I am ready, before I have finished, before the dog has finished.... [Written down on request]

Rosie

My first sexual feeling that I can remember was one day, while playing with my dog, I suddenly wanted it to lick my cunt. But as suddenly as I thought it, I pushed the dog away and felt very guilty. Now, years later, I do rather fancy at times having sex with a dog, or letting it lick me. But only in my mind—that is, the idea of it excites me, but I would never actually do anything about it. [Letter]

Dawn

Once when I was about fifteen, I went downstairs in the morning to get breakfast completely naked. It was summer and my parents were out, and it just felt good to walk around that big empty house naked. The dog was in the kitchen and he woke up and began to bark, then he started to nuzzle up and sniff me (he was only a young dog, not very well trained and a bit stupid). I suddenly realized that the dog had this huge hard-on, and he kept trying to climb up me. I think I was fascinated and I kept stroking him. Half of me wanted to let him—let him do what? at that age I didn't really know what he'd do—and the other half was ashamed. But God, it was a strong impulse, to close my eyes and let his nose go where it would. I've always wondered what it would have been like if I hadn't got on with my breakfast. I've elaborated the picture a thousand different ways, complete with the dog's prick inside me, and my family walking in on the scene . . . you name it. [Letter]

Wanda

My fantasy begins with two men breaking into my cottage, making me dress, and carrying me off blindfolded. I end up in a big farmhouse, and my blindfold is taken off. I find myself in a room in which there are three couples, including a man and woman who put donkeys to stud. I find out that they are part of a group who hold wife-swapping, free-for-all parties every month at each house in turn. It is the responsibility of each hostess to provide sexual entertainment.

I am stood up in the middle of the room and they hold a mock court. I am accused of being a peeping Tom, of watching the man and woman manually mate two donkeys. This is a terrible offense, and I am found guilty and sentenced to be fucked by the donkey and also to be the slave girl at the party. I must do everyone's bidding or be whipped.

All the couples are high on drugs and drink and they carry me off to the stable where the donkey is; it is very well lighted. They strip me naked and make me put on long black nylons and a suspender belt and lead me over to a low table, where I am made to kneel on all fours and open my legs wide. There are straps fastened to the table, and they put these around my arms and legs so I cannot move. There have obviously been other girls here before me. To the cries and catcalls of the couples, the woman leads the donkey up behind me. She has pulled into place a wooden frame above my backside and lifts the donkey's front legs onto this. Then I feel someone spreading grease around my cunt and right up the hole. They must have played with the donkey's prick to make it stiff, as I feel the hard stiff shaft against my ass as they pull it toward me. I feel the long knob end against the lips of my cunt. It forces them apart and begins to enter my hole as the woman guides it up me. I let out a cry of pain as it stretches the walls of my cunt. Inch by inch it slowly goes

169

in and begins painfully moving up and back, in and out. The donkey's prick has been well greased, and after a few abrasive thrusts the fucking rhythm becomes easier. When they have about six inches of the donkey's prick up into me, they hold me still while the donkey pushes his massive prick up and down my cunt just like a piston: I wouldn't have believed it possible, but I am being fucked by a donkey!

Nimble fingers from the crowd feel around my cunt to feel the donkey's prick sliding up and down in me. The fingers begin massaging my hard clitoris, which is hanging down with excitement, and I am really excited now. Hands finger my vagina and breasts, squeezing and fondling them, and just as I am overcome with excitement and reaching my orgasm, the donkey gives a sound. The woman knows what is happening and holds the donkey's prick inside my cunt. I feel it throbbing in me as it begins tossing off, and she puts her hand around the entrance to my cunt. She can feel the donkey's throbbing prick pumping its hot spunk into me. The donkey has just beaten me to it, as I was just on the point of having my own climax when he did. My cunt is on fire as his juices squirt up me. After a while I feel the prick getting soft, and immediately the woman pulls the donkey's prick out of my cunt. Immediately my cunt is unplugged, the donkey's spunk pours out of my cunt in a stream. I look down between my open legs and see the juices streaming out just like a waterfall. Someone holds a basin between my legs to catch the juices. My cunt feels so big after being stretched by the donkey's prick; now it feels like my insides are dripping out. It is so sore and I feel the dripping will never stop. Then someone kneels down behind me and begins to lick my cunt dry of the donkey's spunk and quickly to drink all of my own juices which now pour out. [Letter]

ROOM NUMBER TWELVE:
BIG BLACK MEN

☐ The black man is cut out for sexual fantasy. Everything about him, real and imagined, throws fuel on the fire: He's forbidden because of his color; his cock has been endowed with mythic proportions; and the story's been around for years that his expertise at fucking comes close to black magic.

All black people are promiscuous . . . white people think. They're always fucking or they're about to. They reek of sexuality. The most loaded question in the contemporary bedroom after "What are you thinking about?" is "Have you ever made it with a black man/woman?" Most (white) women haven't, and for obvious reasons. But in their fantasies they do, and everything that worked against it ever happening in reality adds mileage to the fantasy.

The first thing a woman does in the black-man fantasy is to remove the guilt by making it a rape. Being raped allows her to throw her (helpless) self more wholeheartedly into the act, so that every determined thrust can be read as one of struggling protest. After that, the black man's rumored skill and size can go to work on her. (I can't help wondering how rough all this advance billing must be on the black man in reality; it's a great deal to live up to, whether or not his desire for the forbidden white woman is as strong as the real cases of alleged rape would have you believe. Whenever I read of a white woman yelling "Rape!" I half suspect her cry was more an accusation of disappointment than a protest against her black assailant.)

Size is the real power of the black-man fantasy. It's never just a black man, it's a *big* black man. Never just a black cock but an enormous black cock. Though size is everything, I don't think the fantasist wants to really be fucked by a black cock the size of a baseball bat . . . unless

171

pain is an added turn-on. As with the fantasies of stud animals, I think the idea of more cock, of so much cock, is an expression of the wish for more of everything sexual; the exaggerated size, the attack by something bigger than life, represent the wish to know something bigger than her life. She doesn't want to have her cunt enlarged, but to have her whole sexuality enlarged; to be filled, yes, but to be sexually fulfilled too—to know more, to feel more, to have more novelty and experience under her belt, thanks to the life-enhancing mythical prick and promise of the sexy black man.

Someone has defined a puritan as one who is plagued by the fear that someone, somewhere, is having a good time. When it comes to sex, we secretly think we may be the self-inhibited puritans ourselves, after all, and that someone, somewhere, is having a better sexual time. In fantasy, the "big" black man promises to take us to that final exploration of sex, the most absolute orgasmic time it is humanly possible to experience. And then, forever after, at least we'll have known what "it" is "all about." ☐

Margie

☐ Margie is a former model, now married and living in the suburbs. Although she loves the creature comforts her husband can easily afford to provide, I think she misses her bachelor girl days in the city. She does the usual things suburban women do to keep themselves from going crazy with boredom, but the last time we met she said, "If I had it all to do over again . . ." and shrugged. ☐

I have this fantasy usually in the bathtub, masturbating either under the faucet or using the hand shower. (I can't help having the idea that all across suburbia, at about four P.M., all us ladies—the smart ones—are lying in our tubs or on our chaise longues, playing dreamily with ourselves as we anticipate the imminent arrival of our husbands, who will probably be too tired to lay us that night anyway.)

I've never had a black man make love to me. In the days when I was single, black wasn't as chic as it is now, our eye wasn't attuned to it as a sexual turn-on yet. Now when I see an attractive black man, I look at him with as much interest as I would an attractive white man. More. But the idea that there is a black man in the fantasy probably comes more from the old myth about black men being bigger than from the current black-is-beautiful fad. Because you see, size is very important in this fantasy. The fantasy is really very simple: As I lie in my tub in the warm, Estée Lauder perfumed water, with the water from the faucet playing over my clitoris, I close my eyes and imagine that a black man, a very handsome Harry Belafonte type, is standing over me, peeing on me, directing it right on that little spot. His jet is as warm and powerful as the real jet of water, and he teases me with it, moving it around and around, up and down, just as I tease myself with the bathtub jet of water. I lie there, becoming more and more excited, and praying that he won't stop, that he won't run out of water, which I suppose is why I've made him black, because they're so big, or supposed to be, and I need a kind of black Gulliver to quench my fires. Finally, I'm begging him not to stop, which he loves, and just as I climax, somehow his jet turns to warm semen as he comes too, right on me.

Before I was married I went out with a real crazy guy, not black, but very far out. I remember once lying on the beach, there was no one else around, and I was lying on my stomach. He stood up, and the first thing I knew he was peeing on my bare back. I screamed and jumped up, but I was laughing—I was mad about him—and our tussle on the beach ended up with him inside me, needless to say. I have never wanted to be peed on in reality, before or since, but this idea of the very well-endowed black man peeing for ages onto my clitoris . . . wow, it's a winner every time. [Conversation]

Raquel

I masturbate a great deal when my husband is at sea and this is the scene I think of most:

I picture myself making love to a beautiful, large-breasted Negress. I strip her and plant kisses all over her beautiful body, bringing her to a climax by kissing her vagina. She then proceeds to make love to me. Then when we are both relaxing, she asks me if I have ever had sex with a dog. When I say no, she calls over her large dog and opens her legs and lets the dog lick her vagina. She lies back and soon has another climax. She then puts the dog between my legs, and as I am getting close to a climax with the licking, she puts her hand between the dog's legs and gives him an erection. She eases my hips over the edge of the bed and helps the dog to mount me, bringing me to another climax. At this point I usually reach a real climax. [Letter]

Lydia

I have always found sleeping with Negro men very satisfactory (even when it isn't satisfactory) because they are so sexy by virtue of their forbiddenness . . . I mean . . . wow, if your mother found out . . . so the whole Negro number is a nice fantasy when I haven't got one to sink my teeth into. I am really good at accents (this is really going to sound freaky, but I am trying to be honest), so sometimes while I am whiling away an afternoon jerking off, I think about some really fantastic black guy I know (maybe it's Melvin van Peebles or somebody like that), you know, bright and sexy and a little scary, and I talk to myself in spade talk. Doesn't that really sound stupid? I don't care . . . you're my friend, and if you must know, you must know that's all there is to it.

Let me see again . . . I really get too hopped up and

confused and can't think when I try to about these things. I shall make myself a cup of Sanka and think about it ... I think.

Just cleaned the house ... the vacuum cleaner always gives me the fantasies.

I was talking about Negroes. There's a whole number one can do on one's self about them (they are never really so good at it in person as they are in my head), which is part of our gross national guilt about black/white relations: I kind of like it when I imagine some heavenly looking black guy telling me I'm nothing but a white bitch. I feel like a perfect idiot saying that, but it's true that it's very exciting to me, probably since the black-white love affair thing is always more exciting because of the taboos connected with it. Dialogue is important anyway in love-making, and black guys can usually come up with some very exciting talk. [Letter]

ROOM NUMBER THIRTEEN:
YOUNG BOYS

☐ As there isn't much call for this room in the House of Fantasy, I'd put it in the attic at the top of the stairs. So far I haven't made any value judgments on these fantasies—a woman is entitled to her thoughts, and it's not the content of the fantasy that matters anyway, but the emotions it releases—but I do feel a certain female smugness at women's seeming lack of sexual interest in young boys. Could it mean that women, traditionally the sexual passivists, have less need of the sexual reassurance men have always sought in young girls? And if so, will all this change when women have caught up with men and find themselves sharing, along with the opportunities to explore and lead, the self-doubts that go with initiating anything, especially sex?

I don't know why so many men prefer very young girls.

I could give a dozen easy reasons, of course, but that's a man's argument to make, not mine. Mine is that I think most women prefer the experience of a knowing lover to the superficial pleasures of seducing a younger one. For a woman, even this superficial satisfaction is lessened by the fact that it is almost embarrassing to see or be an older woman with a conspicuously younger man. A woman may occasionally like to take the initiative in bed, but sexually she prefers an equal, at least.

I've been phrasing my ideas on the relative needs of men and women as speculation; if the dogmatists now raise the old excuse that it's different for men, that they need more sexual bolstering up than women because they have their constant and, above all, verifiable limp or stiff barometer of their virility, I'll yawn. I dismiss them as old fashioned. A woman can feel just as sexually inadequate as a man, or just as hot and eager and in need of a good fuck as he. But for whatever reasons, it would seem that the image of her desire, her fantasy, is seldom a young, i.e., inexperienced, boy. However, for some women, like the ones whose fantasies follow, I'm wrong, and that's okay too. ☐

Evelyn

This is the first time I have ever answered an advertisement, but I was intrigued by your request.

You ask about sexual fantasies. I was beginning to think that I was "not right in the head," because I must have my own fantasy, otherwise sexual intercourse is impossible for me to enjoy. My husband is very patient and willing to indulge in any variation we can think of, but I very rarely think of him when actually engaged in intercourse. I think of my past lovers, of whom there are many, mostly under eighteen years of age (I myself am twenty-nine). I wish myself into an erotic situation: what I want mostly is to have several young men, about sixteen years old, tied up in a row, all naked with their penises flaccid, and walk along the row playing with them until their cocks stand high. Then each one has to put his fingers inside me when I bend down in front of him. When they have done this, I suck each cock until they are nearly ready to come off. This thought gets me really wound up. Then I see them all playing with their own cocks and shooting their lot as far as they can. The one who shoots the furthest gets to fuck me first, and so on down the line. I never get a climax until the last one puts his tongue on my apex and nibbles it gently. Then I come all over him. If this fantasy were offered to me in reality, believe me I would not run from it.

This letter is quite true, and although it was hard to start I'm glad I have written it. [Letter]

Victoria

I am thirty-two, married, and have three children. I would say I am happily married, although my fantasies during sex with my husband, or during masturbation, invariably involve young boys, who are either masturbating themselves or being helped by me.

The picture in my mind is of a long line of young boys, as in a school. And I am the school matron. I order the boys to unzip themselves and take out their cocks. Then I walk down the line, stopping at each boy to masturbate him until he is thoroughly relieved. I don't know why this gives me so much pleasure. I'm sure my husband would never understand; how could he if I don't? [Letter]

ROOM NUMBER FOURTEEN:
THE FETISHISTS

☐ If the Young Boys Room goes in the attic due to a general lack of interest, then the Fetishists belong in the broken-down elevator that doesn't really get anywhere. By fetishists, I'm not referring to people who go in for black lingerie or even whips as a preamble to fucking. The fantasies of fetishists like Faith (below) are what the dream doctors call "aim inhibited," meaning the fetish is an end in itself.

While I intend this book to be an introduction to the *idea* that female sexual fantasies exist and can be talked about, I do not pretend that my research can in any way be called complete. Nevertheless it is extensive, and so I think some meaningful conclusions can be drawn from the fact that Faith's is the only fetishist fantasy among all that I've collected. This correlates closely with standard psychoanalytic findings that female fetishism is rare.

I do not know why this should be so, except for a notion I've talked about earlier: that since women were traditionally put into the passive role sexually, they never have had to have doubts about their ability. Inhibited or frigid, perhaps—but there is no word in the immense English vocabulary which is the exact female equivalent of *impotent*. On the other hand, the sexual distortions of society often force men to see every erotic encounter as a contest, in which the poor guy has to compete, at least physically, with all the woman's previous lovers and those still to come—to say nothing of the imagined demands he may feel she herself is putting on him; perhaps it is to avoid these pressures that the fetishist sighs with relief when he can substitute the symbol for the substance, and settle down with a nice pair of fluffy, scuffed mules on a cold winter's night. Are they so different from Hollywood's favorite image of our soldiers and sailors as "regular guys," who randily kiss their dream movie star good night, when it is only her photo that is present on the wall above the bed, but who would be paralyzed with embarrassment if that star should appear in the flesh *in* that bed? □

Faith

I am what is known as a urologenic. Through books and materials I have been able to more fully understand my sexual feelings, although it's rather difficult for me to explain in words just how I feel. I derive pleasure by seeing, thinking, or hearing about uncontrollable urination. Every time I think about someone (especially a man) trying to "hold back" just a little bit longer and then not being able to make it to the bathroom, I get very excited.

Although I detest violence extremely, I usually center my thoughts around "tormenting to the point of urination," but because of my dislike for violence and cruelty, I always end the scene with the tormentor having pity on the victim just as urination begins. I try not to think of things that would really hurt, because I get no pleasure out of pain.

It stimulates me sexually to see men, women, children, or animals urinating uncontrollably. Every time I see a child being spanked or a person being beaten or tormented, the first thing I think of is "I wonder if he's about to urinate?" I guess I got the feeling from childhood. I had a very rough father and we children were whipped much more than was necessary. I was very afraid of him, and it got so that every time he would go to punish me my legs would get very weak and I would wet myself.

I suppose that's why I think of tormenting scenes in my fantasies. I feel as though it's a sure way to bring on urination. [Letter]

ROOM NUMBER FIFTEEN: OTHER WOMEN

☐ Just as many a difficult truth is told in the guise of a joke, so are women more honest and revealing of themselves in their sexual fantasies of other women than they are in their real dealings with one another. Since most women are so blocked in any physical rapport with one another in ordinary life, it's no wonder that the natural warmth and tenderness that one woman may feel toward another is likely to come out only in fantasy. (For instance, take the highly stylized kiss which it is allowed for women who like each other to bestow when meeting, kisses deliberately ritualized to convey affection without physical consequences; very often their lips kiss air alone.)

I don't believe that most of these erotic thoughts of other women are highly charged fantasies of deeply buried desire, or that they should necessarily be acted out, any more than I believe that idle reveries of a New Yorker about green grass, brooks, and trees really "mean" he secretly wants to be a peasant. But the erotic imagery of women's fantasies about other women is indeed so clearly a projection of how the fantasizer really feels about herself, what she really wants from both men and women, that I was tempted to give this room an entire chapter of its own. Instead, I've saved it for the last inhabited room in the present chapter, because if I'd put Other Women fantasies in a chapter by itself, it would inevitably have come to be called "The Lesbian Chapter," and thus sensationalized beyond any hope of clarity or perspective. In my research, women's fantasies of other women are revealed as fantasies like any other—no more, no less.

If women are a mystery to men, they are even more mysterious to themselves and to one another. I'm convinced that any closer sexual understanding between men

180

and women must begin somewhere in an acceptance of the precise desires women express in their sexual thoughts of one another. These thoughts of other women are not necessarily, to my mind, lesbian thoughts, nor are all the women who visit this room lesbians. Nor should they be cheaply dismissed as "latent lesbians," which is how many of them resignedly sum themselves up: "I suppose all this means I have a secret desire to be fucked by another woman." The defeated tone itself is an indictment of the simpleminded effects of universal drugstore psychiatry on our age. Maybe she does, maybe she doesn't, maybe she *is* a lesbian, or a bisexual; and maybe not. But in the end, I don't care; that's not the point.

What interests me is that if the emotional openness women show one another in their fantasies could be extended to reality, I am sure the result would be, not a soaring increase in lesbianism, but the contrary: a broader, more meaningful heterosexuality. And yes, when we have that, more real warmth and honest affection between women, too. Who knows? In time women may come up with a new definition of what it is for a woman to have "normal" physical contact with another woman.

What is repeatedly made clear in what so many of the women themselves call their "lesbian-type" fantasies is that they are seeking from other women in their fantasies what they aren't getting from their lovers in reality. It's not the real lesbian relationship that's wanted. (Not to the exclusion of the heterosexual one, anyway; as one woman put it, "I wouldn't go out of my way to find a lesbian or female bed partner.") What they specifically find with other women in fantasy is tenderness, and complete and experienced arousal of their essentially female parts, their breasts and their clitorises. When reality is lacking, who knows more about tenderness, breasts, and clitorises than women, being women themselves? And what safer area to satisfy this need than in fantasy?

It's the most natural thing in the world that, for the same reason men do, women should turn to women for tenderness. That they should, for the most part, have to

181

resort to fantasy to do so is—life. Woman, the great giver of tenderness, has always been on the short end of the tit. Take the great Cocksman's Guide for Real Men: *Playboy.* Where in those seductive pages are men taught the values of tenderness toward women, and reassured that giving a woman this instead of a constantly hard prick makes him no less a man? One might as well impugn Hugh Hefner's heterosexuality!

The female breast, symbol of tenderness, is there for men to cry on, suck on, lie on for life. But how about women? We all begin on the breast, but little girls are soon turned from their mother's breasts into their mothers' "little sisters," and sent into a comfortless world in mother-daughter, look-alike dresses. Dad's not much help; not only has he not got a breast, but even his warm lap and hugging arms all too soon are out of bounds. No wonder young girls like Bee, whose fantasy follows, develop schoolgirl crushes on older girls and teachers. And later, when a young man becomes the acceptable outlet for these sexual needs, who then can she turn to for tenderness? Most young men are too preoccupied filling their own sexual requirements for manhood, which don't allow much room for tenderness, not necessarily virility's best friend. So, a young woman may logically come to fantasize about another woman (usually with big breasts) who holds her, perhaps lets her suck on her breasts, and may even stimulate her sexually, but always, as Tania (below) says, "with a special gentleness."

Bisexuality is in vogue these days. The best thing about it is you don't have to do it, you just have to believe it; the pressure isn't on whether you are or aren't, but on whether you put down someone who is. The popular idea is that we all have a bit of it in us. I don't know, but I wouldn't be surprised. And although I wouldn't call a man or a woman a liar who said he/she had never had a homosexual thought in his/her life, I would wonder how they managed to get around these recent years blindfolded and with cotton in their ears.

One last comment on bisexuality, inside and outside of

fantasies. Some women, like Alix, introduce a man into their fantasies of other women; the bisexuality makes it more acceptable. For the same reason, as with Celia, the other woman is sometimes made anonymous. Or the fantasist emphasizes that she is totally passive with the other woman. Or simply is watching other women and not involved herself. However they handle this "other" side of their sexual nature, in fantasy or in relating it to reality, I have found women to be remarkably candid in discussing their erotic imaginings of other women.

Conversely, as straightforward with me as women have been in discussing their sexual thoughts of other women, and as accepting of themselves for having them, their men have been just the opposite in regard to their own homosexual thoughts. Women say that their descriptions of their own erotic fantasies of other women may even bring a fond smile to their lover's lips; homoeroticism between women seems to be acceptable to men, and indeed is often a sexual turn-on. But any suggestion that the man might have these same feelings about other men is treated as an insult or a threat. It's one thing for women to have this kind of thoughts, but quite another (ugly, dirty) for a man. □

Christine

I've had this fantasy many times, as often when I'm with a man as when I'm alone, masturbating. I think the first time I had it I really was in a steam bath; afterward, I couldn't wait to get home to Ted; I was that heated up and ravenous for him. I've never told him about it. Not because I'm ashamed of it or anything; I have no real desire for another woman, would probably jump a mile if one approached me "that way." No, I simply don't tell him about it because thinking it gives me such immense pleasure when we're screwing . . . and I'd hate to take the chance of losing that by breaking the secrecy. This is it:

The steam bath is empty. I don't know this when I first

enter, wrapped in my towel that the gym supplies. The
steam is so thick I can barely find my way to one of the
tiled seats, where I sit, with my feet up, hugging my knees.
As my body begins to sweat, and my eyes become accustomed to the steam, I realize that I am alone. I begin to
fondle myself, to gently stroke myself with my finger,
reaching inside myself for the warm syrup that always
begins when I, or anyone touches me there. But I don't
need the wetness from inside my body because the sweat
and the steam run down my legs and my pubic hairs, that
whole area is drenched. I have not heard the door to the
steambath open. My eyes have been closed, my mind en-
veloped in the growing excitement, and I only realize there
is someone else with me when I hear a noise, quickly look
up and see another body on the tiled slab opposite. I am
petrified. Christ, did she see what I was doing to myself? I
am too frightened to move and I pretend that I am drows-
ing, closing my eyes again. I lie down full length on the
slab, pulling the towel up so high that it almost covers my
face. I am asleep, or so I pretend. The next thing I know,
a hand is on my thigh, slowly moving up it. I gasp, hidden
beneath my towel. The hairs on my legs bristle with excitement, part fear . . . should I run? But the towel pro-
tects me, hides me, and I remain passive. I leave the problem of another person entering and finding us to her; she
will watch. Her hands are on both my thighs now, slowly
massaging them, her fingers reaching up higher, higher,
until they gently part my legs. I wait for her mouth and
she leaves me thus for endless seconds. My lips beneath
the towel now plead silently—please, please, don't stop,
kiss me, kiss it! Her fingers have parted me, exposing my
clitoris to the warm heat, and it seems to grow, to expand
toward her, reaching for her mouth . . . and then suddenly,
softly, tenderly her lips are on me, her tongue warm
against me, moving. Half of my mind can't help but
wonder what will happen now if we are discovered, but I
have no choice. I am hers. I cannot leave those fingers,
that mouth. The sweat pours over my face, the steam
swirls all around me, I feel, have felt nothing of her but

her hands and her mouth. Otherwise she is formless. I can feel the syrup pouring from me now, and she drinks it, her saliva, her sweat, my sweat all mingling in my cunt. Her lips are so full, and her tongue so warm, slowly licking me, all the way from my ass up to my clitoris, but stopping on it, lingering on it, then her tongue moving in small circles all around it, teasing it, but always returning, and when the tongue returns, the lips too, the full kiss again and again. The heat is so intense, and my own excitement, I am afraid I will faint, that I will scream out. I bite hard on the towel, raising my buttocks suddenly so that her whole tongue is in my cunt when I come. [Written down on request]

Dolly

I have never had a homosexual experience, but I do have many lesbian fantasies. While my boy friend is making love to me I often fantasize about my best friend. We are not lesbians but we are extremely close (she is twenty-six, I am nineteen). Anyway, the fantasizing begins when my boy friend starts kissing me. I pretend it is her. She kisses me deeply and passionately. Then she gets on top of me and begins kissing my breasts and gently biting my nipples. Then I kiss her nipples and start sucking them, all the while in her arms. She tells me how much she loves me and how she wants me to love her as much. I tell her I do. Then she kisses me again. Slowly she licks my breasts all over and then, still slowly, with much help from me, she spreads my legs apart. She licks my inner thighs and then she finds my clitoris. She knows that is my extra sensitive part and she takes great care as she licks it. Her tongue is very soft. Then she spreads my legs and places her buttocks between my legs. Both our clits are protruding now from the licking and she gently rubs hers on mine until we both reach orgasm. All the while I'm imagining this, my boy friend is making love to me and I reach one orgasm after another.

At other times I fantasize that my boy friend is having intercourse with me while I lie in her arms and she kisses my breasts. With the two of them working on me, I soon come.

As you can see, lesbian fantasies play a great part in my lovemaking. Although I have never had any lesbian tendencies, perhaps deep down I'm bisexual. Who knows? It's the only answer I've been able to come up with as to why I have such fantasies.

But not all my fantasies are of the lesbian type. I masturbate fairly frequently, and when I do I fantasize. I picture a very good-looking man with a beautiful body. He is standing about six feet away from me and he has a huge throbbing penis. I am strapped to my bed and I plead with him to make love to me—but he refuses. He just stands there with his huge erection. I can't get at him because all my limbs are strapped. Gradually he comes closer to me until he is right beside me. Then he stands on the bed above my face—one leg on either side of me—and slowly squats until "it" can be touched with the tip of my tongue. But he will not let me take it in my mouth. Still squatting, he slowly backs up and rubs his penis on my huge breasts and my nipples continue to rise, hard and proud. Then he rubs his penis on my inner thighs and finally on my clitoris. Finally we have intercourse. By that time I have reached an orgasm.

Another one of my favorite fantasies is to imagine myself being the focal point in group sex. While men take their turns having intercourse with me, the women are kissing me and playing with my breasts. Everyone is telling me how much they love me and I am brimming with love for them. [Letter]

Bee

I do not now have lesbian fantasies, but for a period of time when I was a teen-age girl, I did. I had a young, pretty female teacher on whom I guess I had a crush. She

186

was very kind and nice to me, and we had many long talks after school. When she found out from me that my parents thought sex was bad and that they told me nothing about the "facts of life," she got me a little pamphlet that gave the basic information. She also answered a few of my questions about what I learned from that pamphlet. I did not learn any of the details about sex, but at least I learned where babies came from. Anyway, as I said, I had a crush on this teacher, and I would sometimes fantasize about her. I dreamed that we would undress each other, and she would hold me in her arms. Then I would kiss her breasts and suck on her nipples as though I were a baby. Other times, I would fantasize about taking a bath or a shower with her, and I would have thoughts about washing and drying her entire body. When she got married, my crush was broken, and these dreams stopped. [Letter]

Venice

I have had an occasional lesbian fantasy, but only about a girl friend feeling my breasts; nothing more than that. [Conversation]

Lilly

I don't think you would call my lesbian fantasies "suppressed wish fulfillment." I have often wondered what it would be like to be aroused by a woman, to be engaged in foreplay with her, with her kissing my breasts and sucking on my nipples, and also to have her play with my clitoris. I wouldn't want her to suck or kiss it, just play with it—and not gently. [Conversation]

Rita

I must be very selfish, but I believe it would take quite a

lot to get me involved in "swinging" or group sex. I can't stand the thought of my fiancé making love to someone else. I have, however, imagined watching another woman perform fellatio on him and later joining the two of them. However, even this culminates in him and me having intercourse. [Letter]

Mary Beth

I enjoy a full sex life with my husband. Sometimes, however, I do have lesbian fantasies, but it is difficult to describe them. I think of best friends (past girl friends) and being in bed with them, just touching and caressing. That is as far as the fantasies ever go, although I would like to meet a lesbian and experiment. [Letter]

Viv

I have thought about experimenting, finding a woman to make love with, to see if I really feel that way or not. My fantasies are rather muddled. Sometimes I think of an older attractive woman (feminine looking, not butch) seducing me. And then other times I think of a girl of my own age group, and in this case neither of us is seducing. I suppose you would call it mutual exploration. I told my boy friend about this (I can discuss everything openly and frankly with him). He said he thought it quite natural, but when I asked him if he had ever wanted to sleep with another man, he said, no, lesbian love seemed more acceptable than homosexual love. [Letter]

Lee

In my lesbian fantasies, I can never put an identity to my partner. She is no one I know and has no face or personality. In my dreams she is just a female body who takes

most of the initiative, while I am merely passive and just
lie there as she makes love to me. I fantasize that she plays
with my breasts and sucks them while masturbating herself. Then she performs cunnilingus on me. We do not
kiss, and I do not touch her genitals in these fantasies;
however, I do play with her breasts. I often engage in this
fantasy while making it with my husband, particularly
when he performs cunnilingus on me. [Letter]

Willa

Once I had a lesbian fantasy. I hardly remember it, but
it was with my very closest friend. I was the aggressor. It
was a beautiful experience. [Conversation]

Dana

I am not lesbian in any way—I enjoy men too much—
but when it is necessary for me to masturbate, I visualize
any girl with big breasts and proud nipples standing over
my face so that I can see into her cunt. My hands play
with her buttocks and while I do this she is sucking the
cock of the man. This makes her cunt wet and she drips
on my face. Another girl is opening my legs and putting a
cold bottle in my cunt while gently pushing her finger in my
behind. When the girl standing over me brings the man off,
she sits down on my face and I stick my tongue up into her
cunt and lick it, while she writhes in ecstasy. Meanwhile,
the man lifts my backside up and pushes his rock-hard prick
right up my backside, and the other girl works the bottle in
my cunt faster and faster, backward and forward, while I
put my finger up her cunt and play with her apex until she
shoots her beautiful juice out of her marvelous cunt.
[Letter]

Cara

I have occasionally fantasized about two of my friends, both of whom have very womanly figures. I do not mean "womanly" in the Raquel Welch sense. That sort of body doesn't appeal to me. Rather, they are soft-looking, buxom women. I would imagine myself as a man making love to one of these women. The breasts were very important for excitation. I should add that I've had no real experience with women, am married and prefer it this way. [Letter]

Celia

I am nineteen, a secretary, and am due to be married this year. My fiancé and I do not have sexual intercourse. We have been going out for just three years. We do, however, frequently have oral sex and are looking forward to an extremely happy and varied sex life together.

In sex, I often think of someone else (no one I know), especially if I am not finding it easy to reach orgasm. I find it particularly exciting to think of another woman and generally this "does the trick." Generally, I make up situations—strip clubs (watching or performing); slave girl (!); anything where I am *forced* to take off my clothes and make love. Sometimes I imagine there is just one other woman, other times that there are two women and a man.

I get quite turned on by female nudity or pictures (I always read erotic literature before masturbating, to give myself ideas!), and it automatically shows up in fantasies. The women in my fantasies are not friends; I just picture a faceless woman's body. I don't think I actually imagine touching her. I just enjoy the thought of the naked body. I prefer to imagine she is touching me.

When I was a little girl, about eight, I remember always bullying my best friend into playing games where we had to pretend to take off our clothes and the "wicked man" would make us walk in the street, or the inevitable school situations where we would force each other to do things. I remember when I was about ten, wanting to be a stripper . . . and there may have been some kind of intimate contact with my girl friend, but I really can't remember. I did have quite sexy ideas . . . like wanting another girl to dry me down after showering, or being forced in various ways to take my clothes off.

I would be interested to know how many women (what percentage) are bisexual, as opposed to men. I can imagine myself to be, but I suspect that my apparent interest in women, having read through my letter, is just objective and a form of extra stimulation.

I have told my fiancé about my lesbian fantasies and he is neither jealous nor angry. We discuss them regularly. He does not fantasize himself, but quite understands why I do. He considers it quite natural, in fact. We have great sexual compatibility and understanding, and I only wish every couple in the world felt the way we do about each other. [Letter]

Theresa

Although photos of male homosexuals always excited me, the thought of lesbianism did not, and was indeed repulsive to me. However, lately I have watched myself do a complete turnabout after reading some of the recent permissive literature. I was and probably still am very naive. I had never condemned homosexuality; I simply never concerned myself with it. Then an attraction to another woman developed this year. We have so far only talked, but I feel more will come of it. My husband is a very forceful and brutal man. I find her gentleness refreshing and feel as if my relationship with her would be very satisfying. So now she is in my fantasies. Just the thought of touching or holding her excites me. No lovemaking, just closeness and gentleness.

191

I must have been a strange child, because the first time I remember being aroused was when reading a marriage manual just before being married at eighteen. I married the only man I had ever dated. I have come to believe that I must be dull. It is my husband, not me, who thinks up different things to vary our sex life. Often he likes to talk dirty to me. I rather like this and wouldn't really mind being treated like a whore . . . an expensive one. But he enjoys brutality almost to the point of rape. I hate rough treatment. I like to be oh, so gentle, and won by kindness and consideration. Although he is rough, he is very controlled, and I often think how much I'd like to tease him to the point where he'd blow his cool and just do what he really wanted, instead of all the deliberate rough stuff. He is a very hard person to bring to climax.

I used to think I was strange, unlike other women. Now I am beginning to believe I'm not as bad as I thought all these years. [Letter]

Tania

I am curious to know if I have any latent homosexual tendencies; perhaps I'm just bisexual.

Most often, during sex, my thoughts drift to other women. I either imagine myself being made love to by a woman, or watching my mate made love to by another woman, or a combination of the two. He and I have discussed this and he confesses that this is often the case with him too. He encourages my fantasies by acting out his own. He very often talks to me as though he were raping me, which encourages another type of fantasy within me. I begin to fantasize that I'm tied, helpless, and at the mercy of this very aggressive man. As a result of this I begin to imagine that a woman enters the scene, dismisses my mate, and begins to make love to me in an equally aggressive manner, but with a special gentleness.

The first fantasy I can remember was about a group of people (four or six) in a large bed, all naked and caressing one another. I was never able to develop it much beyond this, but being quite young at the time it didn't seem necessary. The mere idea was quite stimulating. [Letter]

Michelle

I have been married five years, and until now have never discussed my sexual fantasies with anyone.

I don't think of someone other than the man I am with during sex unless he is performing inadequately, at which times I think of someone who *does* perform adequately. This invariably gives me enough pleasure to achieve orgasm. I think fantasies are very useful for this specific reason. Every time we have sex, it can't be perfect; the other person (and oneself) is not always in top form.

The most frequent idea that pops up in my fantasies is "being on exhibition." My fantasies vary a great deal, but this idea is usually present. People watching, not necessarily saying anything or doing anything, but just watching . . . that really turns me on.

What is interesting is that although I've never had any desire for another woman, or even looked at another woman "that way" in reality, I do often have lesbian fantasies when with a man. I don't know where this idea comes from. In my fantasies, these women and I never actually touch, no bodily contact, I simply think about them, other women, usually naked, usually large-breasted. What they seem to be doing is trying to seduce me by their erotic movements. I allow myself to get excited just watching them, but then when I have built to a pitch and have my real orgasm, the women simply smile, pleased for me, and disappear. Maybe some day I will join them in sex within my fantasy, but I don't think that is what they are building toward. I would never tell a man about these lesbian fantasies because I don't think a man would understand. [Letter]

Sandra

Often when my husband and I are making love, I think of another man (or two) and sometimes, not often, of a woman. The man I usually think of was my dentist (I say was because he moved to another state). I never had sex with him, but I would have liked to. To me, he resembles my husband. He is soft spoken, but not one to be bossed by a woman (which I like a man to be: A Man). In my fantasies we have sex in every imaginable position within reason. We even masturbate each other. However, most of the time I think of my husband during sex; he is my ideal sexual partner. He even smells sexy.

When I fantasize about the other men I find attractive, toward the point of climax, I settle on one man (or woman). So you see, I have lesbian fantasies. Usually I think of a woman who is physically similar to a man, meaning that she is heavily built but still feminine, tender, loving (motherly sometimes), compassionate. Very often she is in military uniform. She isn't beautiful, just attractive. She is assertive but open-minded, fun to be with, likes music, sports, clothes, and animals. She is well off but not rich, thrifty but not miserly. We usually masturbate, kiss (on the mouth), sleep in each other's arms (she holds me mostly). I feel secure with her. We suck each other's breasts (me hers mostly). Sometimes she and I go 69. My husband knows I have lesbian tendencies and that I could possibly be ambisexual. However, I don't go out of my way to find a lesbian or female bed partner.

I don't know what it's an indication of, but I love to think about my husband and another man having sex with me. Although my husband doesn't encourage my fantasies, he doesn't discourage them either. When I ask him if watching another man fuck me would excite him, he says probably. He knows I would like him to be with me if I am fucked by another man. We both like to watch our own fucking. Another idea that turns me on is that of

194

watching two homosexuals making love; also, I wish women got a chance to watch some of the blue films men see.

Please excuse my sloppy writing; I am usually neat, but I wanted to put this down quickly so that I wouldn't change anything. [Letter]

Patty

I have just read your advertisement and feel compelled to help you in your research. I will attempt to write as honestly as I can.

I am twenty-nine years old, have been married for eleven years to a merchant seaman, and have two children. My husband is at sea for almost six months of every year, and during one of his trips about three years ago I was introduced to lesbianism by two young girls. My first experience with these girls was so completely satisfying and wonderfully exciting that I now relive the scene almost every time I make love with my husband when he is at home.

The scene I picture is as follows: My husband is at sea and the children are at my mother's for the weekend, because I am having a night out with the girls at the office to celebrate one of the girls' coming wedding. I have invited two of the girls to spend the night at my place, as they live in the next town and they would have had to leave the party early to make the last train home. We arrive at my place, late and tired after the party. I flop down on the chair and say that I wish that I had a maid who would undress me and get me ready for bed. The girls say they will be my maids and proceed to undress me. When they take off my bra and panties they are obviously very excited by what they see, and both say they have never seen breasts as large and beautiful as mine before. They ask if they could touch them. I say they may do anything they want with them, and soon my nipples become very large and firm with their caresses. Then they take a breast each and kiss and suck my large but very sensitive nipples, and at the same time they begin to caress my tummy and thighs, and soon I am squirming all over the chair. When I start moving they release my breasts, and one of the girls sits on the arm of the chair and starts to kiss me very tenderly and lovingly and then more demandingly. Soon our tongues are deep into each other's mouths. While this is going on, the other girl is kneeling on the carpet between my legs caressing my thighs and tummy until I am about frantic with desire. I am moving all over the place trying to direct her fingers into my vagina, but she ignores my attempts. Suddenly I almost go crazy when I feel her head go between my legs and her tongue enter my vagina. I have an orgasm almost immediately, and nearly scream the house down in the process. While I am regaining my breath, the girls strip off and make love on the carpet while I watch. We then have a shower together and all three go to bed and make love all night. [Letter]

ROOM NUMBER SIXTEEN: PROSTITUTION, OR, "SADIE THOMPSON DOESN'T LIVE HERE ANYMORE."

☐ This room is empty.

When I began collecting fantasies for this book, and would talk about it to psychologists, writers, and other people who I thought had some information about the subject, they'd often smile with amusement, and tell me that of course one of women's most popular fantasies was that of being a prostitute. And from everything I've read and heard, I thought this was so myself. (For instance, who hasn't heard that old tag line again and again, that at every costume party, half the women come dressed as call girls?)

But in the hundreds of fantasies I've collected, there is

not one prostitution fantasy gone into at length; the subject is only mentioned fleetingly, glanced over *en passant*, by people hurrying to the Anonymity, Humiliation, or Masochism Rooms. This grand old theme, so beloved of Victorian women, is apparently dead. And if I'm right, and Sadie Thompson is indeed finished, it is ironically our permissive age that killed her; contrary to what her mother said, the old girl died from *lack* of shame.

In explaining what I mean, let's consider the difference between shame and guilt. Guilt concerns something about which you feel badly whether anyone knows it or not, and guilty love is still a very big fantasy of our time. It is an internalized judgment. But shame concerns something other people may or may not approve of; you yourself may feel neutral about it, or even like it; the *shame* only comes in when some outside observer catches you doing it. The woman who cheats at solitaire, for instance, will blithely go along taking cards out of turn—until someone catches her doing it, when she'll grow irritable and testy.

Shame therefore enters when your personal code of morals or behavior is felt by you to be at variance with what is generally accepted—and you feel at least a hypocritical need to pretend to go along with the majority rules. Therefore, we can see that the reason our mothers delighted so much in prostitution fantasies was their feeling that The Girls were beyond shame; they gave the fantasizer a kind of nothing-to-lose, gutter freedom. But today, why bother to be hypocritical? From every corner we are told there's nothing in sex to be ashamed about.

Good-by, Sadie. We'll keep a candle in the window of your room in case the wheel of repression takes another turn, and backlash brings you back. □

CHAPTER FOUR

"WHERE DID A NICE GIRL LIKE YOU GET AN IDEA LIKE THAT?"

CHILDHOOD

☐ People invariably ask me whether a woman's sexual fantasies reflect her background. Doesn't her education or economic class determine the nature of her fantasy? Haven't I found that my material just naturally varied and fell into these categories? By the way the question was asked—especially during my researches in England—the "Yes" answer was always implied: a woman's background will out.

But my answer is "No." Wealthy women don't necessarily fantasize about masked dukes, any more than the uneducated wife of a miner fantasizes in rough four-letter words. Nor is the reverse true. It is meaningless to discuss the class or background of the real woman behind the fantasy, except to deny that it is the primary influence on what or how she is thinking. You can never predict what is going to turn anyone on.

If you were to shuffle all the written replies to letters and advertisements requesting contributions that I've placed in various publications in the United States and England, plus all the interviews I've conducted in person in the same countries, it would be impossible to match the lady to the fantasy . . . except perhaps by nationality.

So no, Mrs. Jones, don't expect that by "birth," or by

virtue of her happy marriage to Jack Princeton, that your Abigail would be found in the relatively acceptable Earth Mother Room. With all her Foxcroft training, she is just as likely to be rolling in the mud with an Airedale, along with all the other fantasizers of sexual humiliation. She will merely talk about it more grammatically.

I suppose the language and imagery of sexual fantasy is shocking, and perhaps it has put some readers off when they first read this book. But once it is agreed that the subject is worth serious discussion, no other course is open. To try to convey the emotion, meaning, and experience of sexual fantasy through euphemism would be like giving a thirsty man a piece of paper with the word "water" written on it. It's either the real thing, or nothing.

I've had a few moments of revelation myself. I haven't gone passively and unruffled through all this material, sympathetic to fantasy as I am. I used to open my fantasy mail—the replies to letters and advertisements—in the morning, and more than one gulp of coffee went down the wrong way. Wow! Not so much at the language, or the situations . . . although they're potent stuff for nine A.M. But it was the amount of imaginative detail that amazed me, the intuitive understanding that to prettify fantasy is to take the life out of it, and above all the evocative creativity in the fantasies of women whose lives, as described in their letters, were otherwise as routine and predictable as sending the kids off to school in the morning.

Sexual fantasies are a great leveler among women. It's a shame women can't speak to one another as directly or be as honest about themselves in reality as they are in their fantasies. In fantasy, everyone speaks the same language because everyone wants the same thing. I sometimes think that's what men essentially get out of their sessions in the clubhouse locker room: there, stripped of everything, they can talk of everything without pretense or bullshit, slipping each other a little sexual identification they find nowhere else. Who knows? Through this book women may also lose some of their feelings of sexual isolation, may find some mutual identification, perhaps even a sense of female camaraderie. Sure they're "dirty" thoughts, but we all have them, men and women, and what makes them "dirty" anyway, except possibly their secretiveness? This secretiveness is one thing women do share, and it's nowhere more apparent than in their fantasies. Deprived of any real feeling of sexual identification with other women, they resort to solitary exploration within their individual fantasy worlds.

Having looked to literature for insights and answers to their own deepest desires and sexual reactions, women have found that most of literature's insightful revelations have been directed at men by men, and when the same men try to tell how it is for women, no one knows more quickly than a woman how far off the mark they are. Even the new women-for-women's books talk around it but not of it—as if the necessary vocabulary didn't exist; meanwhile, women continue to sigh and say, "No one has ever really described 'it.' " Is it so surprising that in exploring the mysterious "it" in fantasy, that they employ the strongest, crudest, most "pornographic" terms and imagery to make real, emotionally, something they've never had defined and which they *know* to be just as potent and earthshaking as every pornographic description they've ever heard or read of the male "it"? The gutsiness of female imagery may belie the beautifully turned brims on their Adolfo hats, or the pencil pleats in their Villager calico dirndls, but the images and the words are universal and classless—only incidental grammar and place names give any identity away.

But where in the world, Pretty Lady, sitting in your high rise flat surrounded by diapers, or behind the tinted glass of your Rolls Royce, did you get an idea like that? Those lips that never swore an oath, much less caressed a man's cock, and that neat little mind that "seems" to dwell on the children's education, the new job, or an even newer summer outfit, where oh where did you get the *idea*? And as often as not, should the lady deign to answer, the reply would be, "Why, from when I was a little girl and just happened to see . . ."

From such tiny seeds—a blink in childhood—springs a full-blown sexual fantasy, embellished and altered over the years perhaps, but all begun with a glance, a child's quick flash-in-the-pan peek into the secret garden. The fact that the seed grew—and to such proportions—just shows what secrecy and prohibition can do; what growth potential there is in "don't."

For instance: A young girl for the first time happens on a grown man peeing behind a tree . . . sees a bright red tip suddenly shoot from a woolly dog's prick . . . is provocatively bullied by an older boy on the way home from school . . . or forced to undergo the sexual trauma of a sadomasochistic experience at school (read Mona's letter below and weep) . . . what is she to do with this mysterious and often unsettling new information? No one wants to know, to hear, or to talk to her about it—she's "not old enough," the subject's "not nice," and she knows that hearing about it would make Mummy "nervous"—that much she does know. All this only makes the forbidden bits of knowledge more provocative. And so these thoughts join the other odds and ends of exciting, sometimes disturbing sensations, daydreams, the other secrets she's been accumulating—or repressing—while growing up. By the time she's stopped playing with dolls, during that long lull before she begins any meaningful contact with boys (I don't necessarily mean sex), she's got enough powerful imagery packed away in her head to stagger the horniest writer of the most exotic porn she ever found in her older brother's room. Not specific knowledge that she can put together with any understanding, but exciting pieces to elaborately embroider, all on her own, and all the more imaginatively for her ignorance (which the vulgar often call "innocence"). Forbidden things, locked away in tight, dark places, grow out of all proportion.

And so, in time, that tiny seed, the glimpse or idea that instantly sparked her imagination, emerges as a fantasy, clothed in more outrageous gear and language than books, TV, films, or dirty jokes can offer.

201

By the time you or I hear the fantasy—ten years or even twenty after the seed (women are incredibly faithful to their first fantasy, and often return to it after new and less potent ones have strangely lost their zap)—by the time she tells us, it is usually impossible to recognize the original seed. But she knows. Women remember important firsts. ☐

Theda

The first sexual fantasy I had was on viewing a teacher's very rotund posterior. I would have been not more than seven or eight. He wore a very short coat, was fat, and his bum filled his trousers, sharply outlining his cheeks. I remember it giving me a definite sexual feeling even at that age, also of finding an excuse for going to bed early in order to have the privacy for being able to dwell upon those inspiring orbs. This was before I masturbated, but the infantile urge to slide my hand down his bum cheeks and round to "the front" compelled me even then.

After being introduced to masturbation, my main problem was obtaining the privacy in which to indulge. I had to sleep with a younger sister who was aware of the slightest movement. The movement of my hand had to be extremely surreptitious and slow and the fingering of the clitoris would be prolonged to exquisite lengths. This would inevitably invite sexual fantasy, based on what I'd heard from other girls . . . my age could not have been more than fourteen . . . who had seen their brothers' cocks. One girl in particular, Monica, was a great source of fantasy. She allowed boys to feel her while she undid their flies and "tossed them off." The phrase still excites me, and on endless occasions I have mentally substituted myself for Monica. Monica's mother took in a lodger, and after I had been sworn to the greatest secrecy, Monica told me how she had witnessed him masturbating, and the size of his genitalia. The idea of his orgasm in truth enraptured me, and was the basis for more than fantasy: It became an ambition. I still masturbate fantasizing myself as the voyeur of this lodger's solitary pleasures. [Letter]

Lindsay

My fascination with men and the whole idea of sex began when I was about ten. I had never seen a penis before one day when I was in the woods near our home and saw a man piss. I was absolutely fascinated by his penis, but he saw me looking and whisked it out of sight. I hung around those woods every spare moment I had, hoping to see another one. If a man even stood still for any reason at all I'd think, This is it! and saunter over hoping for a glimpse. I spent hours trying to visualize just what it had looked like and thinking up words to describe a penis— proud, dominant, pulsating. I could go on. For years I would lie in my little virgin bed and think about that glimpse of my first penis. All those hours spent in the woods, hoping for another chance, it's a wonder I was never raped or murdered. [Conversation]

Fiona

When I was young, I played the usual "doctor" and "house" games, exposing my genitals and exploring my little friends. I know now that the strange, warm kind of quivery feelings I had were of a sexual nature. At that time I associated urination with these feelings, and often fantasized that I was sitting on the toilet with my legs spread far apart, while one of my little boy friends urinated into the toilet between my legs. [Letter]

Felicia

The earliest fantasies I can remember involve my parents, or my father and my older sister (which made

203

me very jealous). I cannot remember actually fantasizing about my father and myself, but I do remember that I had a strong sexual attraction to him.

I also fantasized about my parents and our boxer bitch. I suspect that some experimentation actually did take place, as they were very open-minded and at times had our dog shut in the bedroom with them when she was in heat. We also had a stud dog who would mount anything that moved when our bitch dog was in heat. Our parents never knew it, but one of my sisters and my brother and myself used to get on all fours and let him mount us for a few seconds—and then we'd turn chicken. I have since fantasized about going through with the act and being penetrated by a male dog. My husband and I had a magazine with pictures of a woman and a male German Shepherd having intercourse. When looking at these pictures I would become excited and would have my husband mount me from the rear, simulating the actions of a dog. [Letter]

Sonia

When I was about eleven or twelve I used to sit in the back seat of the car on trips and cross my legs very tightly. Our car made a very bumpy ride, and by sitting clear to one side each little bump and vibration would sexually stimulate me. The first time I experienced this I looked out of the car window and saw a horse in a field with his penis dropped way down. Every time after that I imagined the horse was entering me. I didn't have an orgasm then from this fantasy, just stimulation. But now when I masturbate and think of being penetrated by a horse, it brings on a terrific orgasm. [Letter]

Phyllis

When my husband fucks me, I often think of a former

204

employer who gave me my first view of an erect penis when I was a virgin, then sixteen. It made such an impression on me that I have always remembered it, and like to picture the scene as it happened. He opened his trousers and took out his cock and I was amazed to see it standing up, so broad and stiff. He did not fuck me, but in my fantasies I see his big prick and try to imagine what it would have felt like if he had pushed it into me.

I always fantasize when I masturbate, which is usually when my husband is at work. I picture a scene at school when I was caned. The cane made me smart so much that I pissed in my knickers, which made me feel sexually excited afterward. In my fantasies I can see the headmistress with her cane, and when I picture how she gave me those smart strokes, I soon reach a climax.

I have not discussed my fantasies with my husband, but we both use four-letter words freely during fucking, as we find that the use of such words comes naturally to us and increases our excitement. Please excuse me if my tendency to use such words has caused me to use them too much in writing to you.

I think my first sexual fantasy was on seeing a man peeing when I was about eleven years of age. I did not actually see his penis (hence my surprise when I saw one for the first time, as I said), but I could plainly see his stream of urine as he stood to urinate against a tree when I passed close by. Seeing one of the opposite sex standing to urinate instead of squatting like I did made me so excited that I have always remembered it. I take my fantasy further in imagining him deliberately exposing his prick to me and rubbing it to the point of ejaculation. [Letter]

Marlene

I am twenty-four and have been married five and a half years. I usually fantasize when my husband is making love to me, always have, and I believe he does, too. It has nothing to do with any inadequacies on either of our parts; I have always found him exciting in bed and he can never seem to get enough of me. It's just that when you're married, and always with the same man, no matter how great he is in bed, it varies the routine to think of other men. With me it used to be a guy who worked in my office; I was seducing him. Or I'm making it with a handsome black guy on TV, again with me as the seducer. Whoever it is—I've even seduced priests in my fantasies—I like to imagine that it is someone who has not had sex for a long time and is therefore ravenous.

The most important detail in my fantasies, even when I masturbate, is my breasts. As young as five or six I was fascinated by breasts and used to try to imagine what it felt like to have them. I would stare for hours at photos of film stars. Not naked breasts. My images were always of breasts with material stretched tightly across them. They strained and pushed against the fabric as if trying to burst through it. My own breasts, in reality, are fine; no one's ever complained. But in my fantasies my figure is truly fantasic; my breasts are enormous and they are my greatest weapon in my seduction scenes. I just have to close my eyes, turn on this picture of my bigger-than-Raquel-Welch breasts, and no man can resist me. [Letter]

Kay

I was a bit of a tomboy at age ten and I remember dressing up as a pirate, pulling the trousers up very tight against my crotch, and putting one of my father's old leather belts very tightly around me. I didn't know what the reason was, all I knew was that it felt good "down there," and that I ended up playing pirate a lot. When I was eleven or so, I used to get distinctly excited by "strapping" myself very tightly around my genitals and immersing myself in a cold bath more or less fully clothed. Around this age and later I had dreams about wrestling people in a pit of slushy mud, completely encased in a wet suit, and being completely buried in the mud. While thinking this

I'd rub myself against the seam of my pajama trousers. [Conversation]

Trudy

Only now as I'm writing do I remember that my sister and I used to pretend that we were making it with our dog. He cooperated quite nicely. My fantasies about dogs still continue, so that when my husband is entering me from the back, I think of dogs humping, something I remember seeing frequently since I was three or four years old. [Letter]

Mona

I hope you will keep my name confidential, as I have never told anybody this before. From what I've read, I think that I am a sadist. I may be a masochist as well, as I very often daydream about being tortured.

I developed sexually at about twelve, and as I was very wild and disobedient growing up, my parents decided to send me to a strict convent school. Corporal punishment was allowed in this school. A strap was always used. The head nun, Sister Rosario, would take an offender—which was very often me—up to the front of the class, tell her to bend down and touch her toes, and then, having lifted up her tunic, she would hit her across the buttocks.

During a holiday break I met a lovely boy whom I fell in love with. I made him promise not to write to me while I was in the convent because I could get expelled for it. One evening after P.T. class, Sister Rosario said she wanted to see me in her room. She told me that she had intercepted a letter from a boy written to me and that she had no alternative but to expel me. I pleaded on my knees to her not to expel me, and eventually she said she would not but that she would have to deal severely with me and that I was to tell nobody. I gladly agreed to this, but I can tell

207

you that if I had my choice again I would not. She told me to take off all my clothes, which I very embarrassingly did. I was nearly thirteen at this stage and I was fairly well developed. I had to kneel down in front of her while she asked numerous questions which shocked and embarrassed me, for instance:

"What is your bust measurement?"

"Do you masturbate?"

"What color is the hair between your legs?"

"What do you call it?"

She wanted to know exactly what I did with the boy and what he did. She then made me lie across a chair and gave me about twenty lashes with the leather across the buttocks. I then had to lie on my back and open my legs. She gave me six in between the legs.

After this I had to come to her room regularly and she would make me strip and would beat me with the leather each time. She would always ask me about masturbating. I tell you all this because after two weeks I definitely got a certain pleasurable sensation from the beating. It was during this time that I first started to masturbate. I still do it regularly.

Now I am a teacher and I get my pleasure from administering the punishment. The boys I teach are between ten and fourteen. I regularly take one to my room where I administer the whip and cane, having ordered him to strip naked. I enjoy punishing him but I enjoy it most when I see him getting an erection. I wear provocative clothes and I enjoy embarrassing him when he gets the erection.

I have never punished a girl, mainly because I never had the opportunity to do so. But I often daydream about it. I imagine her being strapped to a bed with only panties and a bra on. I then order one of my boy pupils to strip her and to torture her. The tortures I normally dream about are pulling the hairs from her pubic region one at a time, inserting needles into her breasts, burning her with hot candle grease, whipping her, caning her, while at the same time making her admit filthy thoughts, masturbation, etc.

I also dream about having intercourse with one of my pupils. Some of my thoughts and indeed my actions are very diverse and queer, and I find it hard to put on paper. I have never before told anyone about these things. Sometimes I feel frustrated and I would like to know if my practices are very unusual. I would be elated if you could give me some information on what other girls think. It would make me feel easier to know that others like me exist.

P.S. I find it difficult to get the type of whips that I would like here in Ireland, so I would be grateful if you could help me. [Letter]

Stella

My sexual fantasy goes back to an actual event that happened to me when I was about eleven. On the way home from school a group of girls and boys began picking on me. At one point the leader, who was very good looking, grabbed me by the arm and told me I would have to do whatever he ordered me to do. He told me that from that day on whenever he ordered me to follow him I would do so, and that he would then tell me what his wishes were. Then he let me go. Afterward, whenever I saw him my heart would leap into my mouth, but he never seemed to notice me again, never ordered me to follow him or to do any of the things I thought I would dread doing.

During my early teen-age years I used to dream about what he might have asked me to do to him. I imagined all sorts of things, and still do. This is what all my fantasies go back to, that I am forced by this good-looking man to perform all sorts of sexual acts, incredible things that no man has ever asked me to do, but which would give me a great deal of pleasure—if I were forced. This is my fantasy, even when I am with my lover.

I only began to masturbate eight months ago, although I am twenty-four. My fantasies are different during mastur-

209

bation, either imagining that I am using a dildo, which I don't have the nerve to buy, or that one or two women and I are making love with a dildo.

Oddly enough, the only other thing that turns me on is if I see a very nice male posterior. I can't help imagining how it would be uncovered. [Letter]

SOUNDS

☐ This is as good a place as any to make a parenthetic comment on noise during sex, on what it does for women. I'm not talking about Frank Sinatra in the background; I refer specifically to those words and noises and phrases that come straight from the groin and have to do with fucking. Words and noises that—if you are indeed fucking—are a more natural part of it than a gentlemanly "I love you, Helen," or no noise at all. Being fucked in silence, with the lights out, inhibits an act that's supposed to be the most liberating one in our lives. Some women, like June (below), can't even make it in silence; Nina (also below) says what dozens of other contributors have mentioned in passing . . . and would have dwelled on longer, I'm sure now, if I'd asked them directly how they felt about it: "Our lovemaking is always heightened by the use of words like 'fuck,' 'cunt,' etc., which we normally *don't* use . . . only in bed." Both these women trace the source of their fantasies back to their childhood, which is where most adults think these "dirty," "low," "vulgar" noises should be relegated, instead of including them naturally in the most adult act of all. Who said "ladies" don't use words like "fuck" and "cunt," or that one doesn't use them around "ladies"? Maybe not when you're having lunch with a lady, but when a lady's fucking, she's not having lunch. ☐

June

What I can't stand is quiet sex. It seems unnatural to me for two people to be fucking away and all you can hear, if you're lucky, is some heavy breathing. Give me a good moaner, a groaner, a real yeller any time. If I'm with a guy and he won't say anything, just breathes, and I'm too timid to start up all the heavy moaning that really turns me on, I fantasize. I remember the first time I ever heard people fucking, and remembering it, well, it releases me.

I was only about eleven when this happened. We were living in San Francisco, in a big apartment house with a center courtyard. All the bedroom windows in the building opened onto this court, and sometimes in the middle of the night in that building it sounded like a mass orgy. I may have been only eleven, but no one had to tell me what all that moaning and yelling was about. I'd lie there mesmerized—that's when I began masturbating, I think—listening to the first couple. Invariably, they'd wake up other couples, and like some kind of chain reaction within minutes the whole building was fucking. I mean, have you ever heard other people fucking, really enjoying it? It's a marvelous sound . . . not like in the movies . . . but when it's real. It's such a happy, exciting sound.

So if I'm with some silent type, just lying there noiseless with him thrusting away, I remember those noisy nights as a kid in San Francisco, and within seconds I'm moaning and groaning like crazy myself, and sure enough, the old silent type picks up on it, too . . . and we're off on a great loud fuck! [Conversation]

Nina

I am thirty-three years old, a lesbian, and have been happily, "married" for the past five years.

211

My fantasies during sex are very much a reflection of what is actually happening. Very often we will "act out" our roles as Mum and Baby, as she sucks my nipples and I sing her nursery songs. At other times she acts the male role and I describe out loud what her "cock" is like and how it is affecting me while we masturbate each other. Our lovemaking pleasure is always heightened by the use of words like "cunt," "fuck," etc., which we normally *don't* use . . . only in bed. I should add that my fantasies are always about my lover, never about some other lesbian. If I did have ideas about another woman, I would never tell her, as she is terribly jealous natured.

When I discovered the delights of masturbation, at the age of seven, even then I used to imagine it was my girl friend who was rubbing between my legs. I suppose I've always been a lesbian and it was just a matter of time before I made these early fantasies come true. Sometimes, while masturbating as a child, I would imagine her dog was licking my cunt (which it sometimes did and which excited me greatly).

However, I never fantasize about animals now. My thoughts are totally given over to my love for other women. Often, I will imagine a kind of religious orgy—lesbian, but watched by men robed as priests. There are always lots of lighted candles, vestal virgins, and a certain amount of sex on the altar with my partner. There is invariably glorious music and brilliant colors as in church. (I am a vicar's offspring and attend church regularly, but have no guilt about being homosexual.)

Every (frequent) session with my beloved partner is exciting and satisfying, all the more so because of my thoughts and our words. However, I would *never talk* about my fantasies to anyone. [Letter]

Meg

When I am with my husband, I often think of my former lover and of the time we were on a secluded, bushy beach together and he pinned me to the ground with his legs after I'd already had one climax; he just steam-rollered me and moaned and groaned when he came. That's something else I miss—my former lover's lovemaking noises and talk—my husband doesn't "talk dirty" during the act to the extent my lover used to, and he's pretty well noiseless at climax. [Taped interview]

Holly

My husband knows how much certain talk excites me, like his telling me how much he enjoys oral sex, how much he loves my big breasts; I like him to describe quite literally what we are doing when we are making love. Except then, I like him to call it "fucking." [Letter]

Evie

☐ Evie is in her late twenties, divorced, and now lives in Los Angeles with her two daughters. Her frank comments about talk during sex could be an inspiration to a lot of silent fuckers who want to be remembered. It's difficult to remember movements, to reconstruct all by yourself what happened last night or last month in bed, but a few heated groin-words can have total, orgasmic recall. Remembering just those words, a woman can keep a man erect in her mind for life. Women are the great collectors . . . love letters, roses, souvenirs, words; in a sense, women hang on to everything, almost live in the past, because we're never quite sure if "it" will ever happen again. ☐

About talking . . . that's another whole realm and I don't know if it interests you, but I think it might to know that men who talk to me can really make me cream in my jeans (just an expression) over them . . . things like "You can do it"; "You can make it"; "Come on"; etc. I won't bore you, but they really seem to make a difference in my orgasm quotient. Sometimes when I am in bed with a man and he talks to me . . . even if he just asks me what time it is while he's making love to me . . . I freak. And when I am alone with myself I often reiterate what certain men have said, or very often I allow myself the luxury of embroidering on it and inventing things that men might say to me.

You wanted some of my girl friends' fantasies, and I asked a few of them but they don't seem very imaginative. They apparently speak little in bed and they are not interested in imagining, or else they won't come clean with me, which is probable. One girl did tell me that a fellow used to send her polaroid pictures of his erected cock and she would masturbate to them while he was on business trips. [Letter]

WOMEN DO LOOK

☐ But it's too easy to say that *all* sexual fantasy, like dreams, was born of some inchoate spark in childhood. Pop psychiatry, determined to reduce the most complete aspects of life to fast, *fast*, FAST understanding, begins and ends with that premise.

All the foregoing reinforces the idea that much of our most potent sexual imagery does go back to that time in our lives when we didn't even know what it—the stimulus —was all about. Born of the innocence and ignorance of our childhood, fantasies retain their mysterious powers into our adult years of sexual exploration (even satiety). They never lose their glamour. Bluebeard's wives had all the beautiful rooms of his house to roam in, but they never could resist the one locked door.

But don't despair if you're over twelve and think you haven't had a fantasy. The most erotic fantasies I know of are ones that first came to grown women on hearing just the right word, seeing the wrong face. Sexual fantasy material is everywhere and anything, but the spark that makes it a fantasy is inside, not outside the fantasist. It's

214

not a matter of deciding "Okay, now I'm going to make up a great sexual fantasy," and then concentrating on the two young men delivering the new TV set, on the neighbor's Great Dane, or even on your husband's best friend. There are no universal fantasy symbols; what works for one woman may do nothing for another. Just as one woman may go for the classic tall, dark, and handsome type, so may another like cute blond cheerleaders. Flash a black man on the screen of one woman's mind and it will begin clicking its own rear projection, while another woman's inner voice may say "So what?" You don't will a sexual fantasy to take form and turn you on. Nevertheless, I do think a lot of women are likely to begin fantasizing after reading this book. Or rather, become aware that they have been fantasizing all along, and that those sudden odd ideas or notions they have up to now forgotten, or repressed, are indeed fantasies.

Much of the material in this book came through this kind of setting up of associations, giving a woman not a direct request for a fantasy, but giving her an idea to get her started. For example, if I simply said to a woman, "Do you have sexual fantasies?" she would usually reply "I don't know," or "What is a sexual fantasy?" or "No." But if I said, "I've found that most women's sexual fantasies have this element of anonymity, that when she's thinking about being fucked by another man, or men, that they're faceless, or strangers . . ." then the dialogue is on between me and the woman, between her and her own imagery. She has a recognizable starting point from which to take off. I don't know whether this freedom of the imagination takes place because mentioning other women's fantasies has set up a kind of competition, or because that mention freed my interviewee from isolation and guilt, or whether it was only because her up to now dormant sexual imagination simply needed that association as a springboard. I think all three contribute.

But I bring it up now, this power that association has in getting women to reveal their fantasies, because in using it as a method of collecting material, I gathered more information than I expected, in particular on the subject of where women get the ideas for their fantasies. And what especially interested me was how often these ideas had a visual basis.

I had sent a letter to several magazines describing my research and inviting contributions. Knowing how much more responsive women were if the subject was discussed as normal rather than extraordinary, and given a little personal background, I described sexual fantasies as images that could occur anywhere—during sex, while driving to work, or just walking down the street, parenthetically adding that in my own strolls, I was an inveterate crotch-watcher. Not only did I look at men's provocative fronts —as automatically as men look at mine—but I also imagined, *en passant,* the arrangement, the shape of what lay beneath. All very natural, I made it sound . . . as I think it is. No matter what else the women who replied to that article said about themselves and their fantasies, they almost all remarked on the crotch-watching: They all look. Maybe not at men's flies (though most do), maybe not even at men, but—they admitted with conspiratorial glee —whatever it was they looked at, it didn't stop there. The looking was only the beginning of the wondering, the imagining and, yes—"now that you mention it"—the fantasy.

My own feelings about women's sexuality have changed since I began researching this book. I always expected that women were far more adventurous in sex than men gave them credit for; that with the right man a woman would be game for anything. Now I've come to believe that women aren't just willing followers in sex, but given just a word, the right "starting off" association, women can be sexually original, can be an as-yet-untapped source of new sexual ideas and fun. I think women are sexually stimulated by many things; they simply aren't used to responding outwardly. But give them a clue they can relate to without guilt, get them started with an encouraging word and, as I said earlier, I think women are ready and willing to write a whole new chapter in a book that's been accepted as closed. Think about it: it usually takes two sexes for sex,

216

but after all these years of going at it we've still only heard from one. Ever since Adam, men have rolled over onto their side of the bed, lit a cigarette, and asked, "What were you thinking about?" And the woman has answered, "Nothing." Or the more outspoken, "You." How can men have really believed them all this time?

For instance, men (and their tailors) may think women look at them admiringly because of the cut of their suits, much as they would look at a fashion photo on the men's page, or that same suit on a coat hanger. And if a girl is asked directly, she will often reply something like, "I was just thinking how nice you look in gray." But in actuality, the stories women have told me indicate that when a woman looks at a man, she's seeing and wondering many things. □

Fay

When I walk down the street I constantly watch crotches. I try to imagine what the penises are like. I am especially turned on when a man's balls bulge through his pants. Often I am tempted to walk up to him, right there on the street, unzip his fly and feel his balls. [Letter]

Sukie

Looking at men, front and back, is a favorite pastime. I like to study the shapes of their asses and wonder how they use them when thrusting into a woman, or I wonder what it would be like to penetrate their anuses with a dildo. [Letter]

Constance

My husband has sort of turned me into a fly-watcher, too. He has been insisting for so long that his penis is too small (he is always measuring it when it is erect) that he has made me curious about other men's dimensions. He has even made me a little curious about his suggestion that I might be able to have more orgasms if I had sex with a man who had a larger penis than he does. So I find myself watching for crotches that indicate there might be something fairly large hidden within. [Letter]

Deana

My mind doesn't even rest when I'm outside the bedroom, as I am continually stealing looks at men, at their private areas. With trousers as tight as they are nowadays, it's not difficult to determine just what lies under those promising bulges. At least one can dream about it and try to imagine what sort of lover a man would make, what size he really is, etc. What I mean is, I think so many men arrange themselves down there in such a way that it's hard to tell whether everything's been sort of piled on top of itself, giving a vast pyramid effect, or whether he's for real. I think it's nice that men have entered the "Hey, look at me" arena where women have been parading for years. Now, while men continue to look at braless breasts under sweaters, or big bottoms under tight skirts, we women have something to look at as well. I often wonder why men stayed in those big, old-fashioned, shapeless trousers for so long. Don't they want us to look? [Letter]

Anna

I'm amused to see that your habit of being an "incurable fly-watcher" applies to me, also. Sometimes it can even be a little fun when you suddenly realize that the guy is watching *you!* Of course this all depends on who it is. I think it excites a man for him to think that you're interested in what he looks like under his clothes. [Letter]

Vera

I, too, am a "crotch-watcher." I can't help imagining the exact shape and size of a man "there" when I look at him, and I invariably compare him to my fiancé. [Letter]

Una

I myself am so unconscious of looking at men, of glancing at their crotches as they approach me on the street, that I can be thinking of what to buy for dinner while my mind is speculating on just what a guy has done to himself to achieve a particularly interesting arrangement of his genitalia. They can get the most remarkable effects! In fact, my husband says that I notice on which side a man dresses before I've even shaken hands.

A funny thing happened to me one day as I was hurrying home from work, thinking about God knows what, but also checking out the oncoming stream of men hurrying home. I suppose I wasn't even aware of how intently I stared at one particular man's well-fitting trousers until just as we passed—tweak!—he reached out and tweaked my nipple! Just like that, on Fifth Avenue! I was stunned. I stopped, turned around with my mouth gaping open, watching him disappear . . . and then I laughed. What else could I do? [Letter]

Lois

I love seeing the bulge beneath a boy's tight jeans and imagining what is underneath. I long to know whether he might or might not be circumcised. I have always preferred uncircumcised boys. [Letter]

Liz

I am also an incurable fly-watcher, and also a bottom-watcher, imagining the reality beneath the clothing. I also have an almost irresistible urge to run my fingers through a man's hair when it is well cut, reasonably long, and looks clean and soft.

I find men's naked bodies very exciting (and often wish there was the equivalent of "girlie" magazines for us women). [Letter]

Winona

Sometimes when I have been on a train or a bus I have found myself looking at men's trousers to see if I can trace the shape and size of the penis. Sometimes I have noticed a penis stiffen when the man has looked at my breasts or when he tries to get a glimpse of my thighs and then it excites me to think that I am the cause of his erection. [Letter]

Rudy

I do daydream a bit; if I have heard that a boy is particularly large, or good in bed, or something, then when I see him I undress him mentally, wondering what he looks like naked. [Letter]

Gale

I really do enjoy just looking at men. Any time I can catch a glimpse of a man's crotch I do; why shouldn't a girl like to see a crotch that's filled well and shows its shape through the trousers? It turns me on, just as watching my husband turns me on. [Letter]

Imogene

Although my husband knows I've always been faithful to him, I don't think he realizes how much I enjoy looking at other men. I do it all the time; most of the time I am almost unaware that I am looking at a man's crotch. If I see a man with a large bulge in his crotch, I just tend to stare. It is an eye-catcher. [Letter]

Francine

Of course I look at men. We're supposed to, aren't we? Why else would they squeeze themselves into tight trousers that stretch so smoothly across the front . . . except where they don't? But it's certainly a young man's game. I mean, what girl looks at an old guy in a pair of baggy trousers full of pleats and folds, just a lot of gathers hanging from the waist? It's as though they were ashamed, like women who wear dresses one size too large. You'd think they'd catch on, wouldn't you? After all, we all want to be noticed, right? [Letter]

April

I wasn't aware I looked until you asked. Sure I do, but as I've never talked to anyone about it, I guess I just wasn't aware, consciously, of how I checked a man out . . . down below. I sort of do it like a CIA agent: The eye goes blink, the man's vital statistics are recorded on my inner brain, and then the information is just stashed away. What a waste! I'll have to stop being so secretive with myself about all this now that we no longer live in the Dark Ages. [Letter]

Myrna

Naturally I look. Doesn't everyone? But I'm very canny about it. You see, I have this wandering eye—an eye that *really* wanders due to poor muscular control. What I do is focus my good eye on something or someone legit, then I half-mast my eyes in this seductive, lowered-lidded manner I've developed, and then my wandering eye "looks." I really dig looking at men. Even when I was in school I was very aware of how a guy's pants fitted him, the way they'd hang low on his hips, the tight fit across the ass. I've always felt very sorry for guys who don't have an ass, just the way I guess guys feel sorry about poor flat-chested girls. [Letter]

Laurie

When I see an attractive guy, I find myself imagining what his penis is like. I see it in my mind as I'm sitting there talking to him, or when I think about him I see his penis erect. I imagine my hand on it, I imagine it touching me, I see every little groove and detail of it enlarged in great erection. I can even feel the heat of it in my hand or in me. [Letter]

Jeanie

I have developed an unusual fascination about men's buttocks. When I see an attractive man from the back, and he is wearing close-fitting pants, I often try to imagine what his buttocks would look like with his pants off. Sometimes, I even try to imagine what it would be like if he were bent over my lap and I were spanking his bare buttocks. To a *much lesser* degree, if I see an attractive man from the front, and he is wearing close-fitting pants, I

222

try to guess whether his penis is larger, smaller, or the same size as my husband's. [Letter]

SEEING AND READING

☐ I know popular theory has it that women are not as sexually aroused by what they see and read as men. Men are supposed to have this trigger response to the sight of a breast or a bottom; whole segments of our economy depend on it. Whereas women, they say, feel nothing at the sight of a cock, except perhaps a sense of embarrassed amusement, or even distaste. Several years ago, the essential humor of a successful Broadway play *(You Know I Can't Hear You When the Water's Running)* depended on this idea. On the other hand, some people will concede that the *erect* cock does arouse some women . . . but even there the debate goes on.

Certainly if it were reduced to a contest of who responds quickest to what, men would have the edge on women. Their minds have been freer since childhood to respond to just the outline of a breast, the mention of a word, the scent of a woman; they were even encouraged, in this way, to be "little men." But women . . . In the girl's school where I went, there was a pale gray fig leaf even on the dark bronze reproduction of Michelangelo's *David* (thought to have been added by the spinster librarian). It was years before I got my first really good look at a really good picture of a cock. And let no male expert tell me I wasn't stimulated. Even if I'd still not seen an erect one, my child's imagination graphically made up for what was missing, raising that cock to uneasily exciting (if anatomically incorrect) erect proportions. By the time I'd grown up, there still wasn't (and isn't) a garden of sexual stimuli for women in the world around us; but to go so far as to say that a grown woman—a woman who's not only seen but caused a few erections—requires the already erect cock, the male sex symbol in full totality before she can

223

feel anything . . . it's ludicrous. Who *more* than a woman should feel aroused at the sight of a limp cock, at the provocative thought of what she might do to it?

It's exactly because a woman has been taught not to look, and has been deprived of real outlets for what real visual and verbal stimuli there are, that she's more talented than anyone at making pictures do for the real thing— in short, it's why she's so good at fantasizing.

Of course, there's less to make up nowadays: men's trousers have never been tighter, their shirts more body-hugging, their own awareness of their visual sexuality keener. Are we all playing "The Emperor's New Clothes"? I'm not surprised that so many women say they're sometimes (secretly) tempted to "just reach out and touch it." Who's it meant for anyway? The new visual turn-ons have done worlds for fantasy, and now that we're all having a good look at it, fantasy can get on with the story development.

With all this happening, I find it baffling that sexually informed writers and psychologists as generous and liberating as Robert Chartham—who book *The Sensuous Couple* begins by saying that no couple is sensuous unless both parties are equal, equal to initiate, lead or follow— that even such a man as this argues that women are not as readily aroused sexually as men. Given a pornographic book, Chartham told me, a man would be more fully and quickly aroused than a woman. "A man would have an erection in seconds," he said, as if it is only man's outward barometer that is to be considered, the cock's signal readiness for use the only measure of a person's depth and quality of sexuality. When I staunchly replied that I, too, could be aroused very quickly by just the right printed page, he looked at me kindly, paused and said, "Then you are unusual. Women take much longer."

What makes this entire argument difficult to discuss sensibly is that buried within it—and usually given as proof of the male's more immediate sexuality—is the undeniable fact that he comes more quickly. But what has that to do with how quickly and to what depth either sex is aroused? While a man can come quicker than a woman, she can continue to have one orgasm after another in immediate, rapid-fire succession. Really, it's all a silly argument. We're not in a race, and even if we were, supposedly we're in it together, men and women, running after the same thing.

The closest I can come—especially after this book—to agreeing with Dr. Chartham and others who say that women do not respond quickly, or even respond at all, to reading or seeing sexual stimuli is to say that if they respond more slowly than men do, this is not nature's decree; it is the way they've been trained to respond. Women do respond immediately at times, but the response is not the male's socially accepted smile, come-on, and erection. With the woman, it will more often mean the retreat into a secret fantasy, with or without deliberately chosen stimuli. Here are a few examples. ☐

Mary Jane

I am a little hestitant to respond because I do not think I have as many sexual fantasies as many other women. I will try to tell you about those I do have, anyway.

I feel ashamed to admit it, but my mind sometimes does wander when I am having intercourse with my husband. Usually I think about other men I find sexually exciting. Sometimes I think about Paul Newman, the actor, because I think he is the most attractive man I have ever seen. I close my eyes and imagine that he is making love to me rather than my husband. Also, I feel guilty about it.

I once dreamed I was making love to my father-in-law while I was having sexual intercourse with my husband. My husband's father is one of the most handsome and attractive men that I know personally, and I have often wished that my husband were more like his father.

Several times, a really strange idea has come into my head for no reason at all. In my mind, I will see myself kneeling in front of Paul Newman, and I am sucking on his penis. I put those kind of thoughts out of my head very quickly, though, because I have never done that to any man, not even my husband.

A little while before I was married, I started to have fantasies about statues of nude men that I had seen. Some had such beautiful bodies that I could not resist thinking about making love to them. My favorite was a statue of Hermes, the Greek god. In particular, I was fascinated by its small, delicate-looking penis. I have an aversion to large or gross-looking penises, although I have only seen my husband's and those on nudes in paintings or on statues. Even now, I sometimes fantasize about making love to that statue of Hermes, since it has become something of an ideal of male beauty to me (especially after I discovered on my wedding night that my husband's penis is as small as the one on that statue). [Letter]

Miranda

During sex I occasionally think of a man other than the man I am with. He is never someone known to me. Physically he is an image of the "ideal" man. If I am in reality with someone young, who has a beautiful and exciting body, I may change him in my imagination into someone unknown that I have just met on the street.

If I told my lover, he would be jealous and would think it was something lacking in his sexual performance that caused fantasies such as this. (Not true; I think of things like the above just as the mood takes me.)

The thought of two men having sex together really excites me and I would love to see this. (Recently, the man I have been living with for three years was "felt up" by a homosexual when we were at a party where everyone had had a lot to drink. He was horrified and felt "disgusted," to quote him, but I found it made me immensely excited.)

Sometimes I imagine an audience watching me have sex with my boss; sometimes young boys being given an intimate anatomy lesson with me as the model. (Ridiculous,

226

really, because I have done art school modeling in the nude and merely felt bored.)

I also get pleasure imagining I am an empress who has unlimited supplies of men and who lines them up to choose. I imagine giving banquets where the servants are naked men, and afterward accommodating the women guests with any male they desire, all having been tested as to performance by myself previously. This and variations of this theme I particularly like, as the men can be erotically clothed or decorated if necessary.

I have many erotic dreams, often of transparently clothed men, or Greek god types, usually nude. Sometimes at night I dream I am having sex, but in my dreams it is always with someone familiar, never a stranger. My fantasy men are always beautiful and blond and unknown.

One of my favorite fantasies is being invisible among crowds of naked men, and being fascinated by the way they move. In reality and fantasy I simply love to look at men, their bodies, and have had such imaginings, of which these are an example, since I was about twelve. [Letter]

Margaret

I am twenty-six, unmarried, and living in the country by myself. I have never written to a magazine before. I was determined, however, to reply to this letter.

Some years ago I was about to become a nun. I was at a convent for a year and began to hate the environment, for I was convinced that a vast number of the novices were indeed sex-repressed. I certainly was from the outset and just had to give it up. I had slight lesbian tendencies prior to going to the convent, but they then enlarged. I masturbated frequently before I went there, but this increased enormously. I just had to get relief somehow. Fortunately, I grew fond of a novice older than myself and secretly we masturbated together quite often. Then it was that I started having fantasies. I would grow fond of a nun, and while playing with myself I would think of her. I would imagine that it was her fingers that titillated my clitoris. I would try hard to imagine her standing by the bedside stark naked with hairs on her pubic region. I also tried to think of her being played with by another nun. This brought me to a climax speedily.

When I left the convent, I went in for teaching at a girls' school. I would enjoy being present when the girls went for showers each morning en masse. My thoughts would always veer toward a particular girl whose body was fairly well developed. Then, in the seclusion of my own room, I would strip, lie on the bed, and think of the girl as I had seen her in the showers.

Then I met a man who seemed exciting. I have met three of his male friends, and I might add that we are broad-minded and at times have a small sex party at which we are all nude. Here again I have fantasies. I am not in love with any of them, but enjoy being fucked by them while the others watch. While I am actually being penetrated, I think of one of the other men present. One is dark-skinned, as he is Italian, and has a large penis. When another man is inside me I pretend it is the Italian. I seldom come when I am fucked. I come when I play with myself or use a vibrator alone in my apartment. Yet I simulate a climax just to make the man feel happy and often use obscene language. I buy many sex books, and I even have an album of girlie pictures. When I want to feel naughty I place this on a bedside table and with my vibrator and tape recorder I actually speak out loud and think of some man or maybe some girl whose body I long to play with. I am not crackers. I am very normal but sex interests me enormously. I will never marry. I would be faithless, I know. I like my own body far too much and like other people playing with it! [Letter]

Alexandra

I am seventeen and have had one intimate affair with a man. Once, when we were making love in the car, we had stopped in front of the public school that I attended as a child. I remember now that I secretly laughed at the thought of how ironic it was. I tried to imagine myself as a child looking upon this situation. Perhaps because I was now doing something forbidden as a child, it excited me.

My first masturbating experience was after I had read *Candy*. I still remember because I pretended that I was the girl in that book and for the first time I had an orgasm. I didn't know what it was then, but I soon found out. For a while there I was reaching an orgasm at least once a day. I would read a "dirty" book and then reread the lines in my head as I masturbated. After reading an uncounted number of books, I began putting together my own stories, or fantasies.

Off the cuff, I'll describe some situations that used to turn me on: being picked up on the corner while hitchhiking at night and being raped by three guys; same situation, only intercourse willingly with all three; call girl with a good reputation; being seduced while under the influence of drugs; subject of sexual experiments such as in the Nazi war camps; intercourse with a dog with a friend looking on; intercourse with my brothers; sex play with my father, sisters (in the fantasies involving a mother or father, they were not my own parents; likewise the faces of siblings were changed—a point which I find interesting because I do it unconsciously); intercourse with my favorite teacher . . . the list goes on.

Many of my early fantasies involved some sort of sadism or masochism, but after I experienced the emotional side of lovemaking these fantasies very quickly wore off. I found them really distasteful. Now I have just as many "favorite" fantasies to choose from, but they all involve emotion, whether it be love or hate. Usually gentleness surrounds the feelings of my fantasies now: being accepted in a coven of witches through their love ritual (I read that somewhere); making love with someone I've just met, with whom I've instantly gotten along really well; having an affair with my high-school teacher, which I'm sure would not be a fantasy if I gave him a little encouragement. All these fantasies are very close to reality.

I've also had occasional lesbian fantasies. In them I am never a part of the action, but an onlooker. In the past I also had fantasies of orgies, and again I was always the passive partner. But I don't use those anymore. Now I'm into emotion. [Letter]

Stephanie

When first thinking about your request for sexual fantasies, I said to myself, "But this doesn't apply to me, as far as I can remember I have never fantasized." But upon reflection, I realized that I had disciplined myself to forget them. Upon wracking my brains, I realize I have fantasized but never realized I was getting a sensual thrill from it until now.

After reading a book about Roman orgies, I imagined I was having intercourse with a donkey, having read an account of just such a happening. But it quickly grew distasteful. Another fantasy I've had several times, and usually when I'm afraid of having sexual intercourse, say after having a baby or during times of stress (am I rationalizing?), is this: I imagine myself in the jungle with a primitive tribe. I am forced to watch punishments being inflicted upon some of their tribe members for various sexual misdemeanors. I go into great detail over the tortures. The men have their penises or scrotum cut off, or red-hot liquid forced up their urethra. The women have red-hot pokers thrust up them slowly. As the only civilized person there I am duly horrified by these events.

Just now in recounting this fantasy to you, another upon similar lines has entered my consciousness. In this one we are in a Nazi camp. There is a fiendish woman torturing the men. She makes them hold their urine until they burst. She has a machine into which she inserts their penises. This machine keeps on stimulating them so that they have constant orgasms. I remember trying to con-

clude that particular torture, and couldn't think of anything except that their organs became flaccid and so another torture had to be devised to follow that one--which I
can't remember. The women in the camp were all very
young girls and were being raped by a mad professor.
Their sexual apparatus was very immature and he always
managed to kill them. He adopted all sorts of techniques,
but I only remember this ward full of girls, each tied into a
position whereby he could examine their sexual apparatus
and choose which one was going to be his that day. By the
way, most of these fantasies are things I have read about
and very little is invented. Other events take place in these
fantasies, but all along those same sadistic lines.

I told my husband of the jungle one and I think he was
a little taken aback, but it made me laugh when bringing it
out into the open. I certainly didn't feel guilty about it, for
although I might be a perverted sadist somewhere down
deep, it doesn't seem to show in my daily life; in fact, I am
a gentle person, so I could afford to laugh, feeling secure
in the fact that I have disciplined this part of myself.

As I say, I had difficulty remembering these fantasies,
mainly because I felt them to be a threat, and so I only indulged in them two or three times and quickly suppressed
them. Never because I felt guilty about them, but because
I feel it a lack of self-discipline to overindulge oneself in
anything. [Letter]

RANDOM ASSOCIATIONS

☐ Things women see turn them on. It's a simple propo-
sition, but I've spent a lot of time on it because it is so often
denied. Even a magazine as comparatively uninhibited as
Cosmopolitan, when it recently published its female reply
to *Playboy*'s naked "Playmate of the Month," went along
with the myth that women think the sight of the male body
ugly or frightening; the male model was nude all right—
but his oh-so-casually-placed hand and wrist masked what

231

one would have assumed was the very point of the proceedings. This simple denial of the sources of women's
fantasies is almost as endless as the fantasies themselves,
even though these sources are so obvious that just to name
them is to recognize how easily they can serve as the start
of a fantasy.

Women fantasize about their former lovers, their first
orgasm, their first "different" sexual scene, say, with another woman or several people. There are the fantasies
that are continuations of a real or remembered sexual moment—a stolen kiss, the pressed hand, last night's first
dinner in an as-yet-unconsummated but sure-fire affair—
sexual sparks that haven't yet, or never will get off the
ground, but do in fantasy. There's the totally fictional fantasy sprung from the fantasizer's imagination inspired by
an attractive face at a dinner party, or the hero of a TV
play, or a pop music or film star. If this last possibility for
fantasy hasn't struck you as endless, just think of the mil-
lions of women—perhaps one sitting next to you right
now—whose eyes glaze, palms moisten, and lips part in
half-smiles of anticipation at the sight of Tom Jones or
Paul Newman. Do you really think their minds are blank
or that they turn off when the TV does?

Less obvious are those fantasies that spring from a
woman's effort to deal with emotions and desires too
frightening or destructive to be played out in reality. In
much the same way that dreams act as a healthy outlet for
the violent emotions we would not want to experience in
reality, so sexual fantasy can give a woman a chance to
explore and thus lessen the anxiety of jealousy and the
conflict she feels when she has desires for other men.
That's why I've included Gelda's fantasy here; if her fantasy, touched off by her jealousy of her lover's former girl
friend, takes the form of a lesbian relationship with that
other woman, at least she doesn't take her destructive feelings of jealousy out on her lover during the day. ☐

232

Susie

I have been married for over three years and last year
finished a year-long affair with a fellow executive civil ser-
vant (G.), who is twice my age. Frequently, when my husband makes love to me, I imagine it is G. on top of me
again (difficult, as G. is heavier, taller, and much hairier-
chested than my husband) and find my own climax is in-
tensified if I am thinking of my lover. Sometimes when I
come I even call his name out, but stifle it a bit. (Fortunately in this respect, my husband is deaf in one ear!) I
had a much more passionate relationship with my lover
than with my husband, even while we were engaged. G.
and I only had to look at one another and he would have
an erection and I would become wet. It even helps me to
think that the bedclothes my husband and I sleep under
are the same ones G. and I lay under while my husband
was away in another city on business.

Since my affair, I have tried to rebuild my husband's
shattered ego by telling him what a good lover he is. (It
helps now that I have regular orgasms with my husband,
whereas before my affair I only came in the "superior" position.) Sometimes I have to keep my husband convinced
with a few white lies. I think he'd walk out of the house if
he knew what I was really thinking about.

When my husband fucks me I dream about G.'s favorite
game: for me to be dressed all in black with garter belt
and stockings under a long black skirt that buttons up the
side. After stripping down to his trousers, he would kiss
me, then bend down and stroke my leg where the skirt was
split and bring his hand up under my skirt until he felt my
stocking tops and garters, which would make him catch
his breath. Then he would undo the skirt buttons from the
bottom. By this time we would both be pretty worked up
and I would "climb" him, swishing my nylons against his
trousers. Sometimes at this stage of my fantasy, having
taken my top off and unzipped his fly, we would start in-

233

tercourse standing up, with my legs around his waist and G. holding me under my back, but more usually he insisted on sucking my left breast and then we would undress each other completely. Then we would admire each other in the dressing table mirror and tease each other, and I would admire his erect organ and very frequently go down on him, which he loved. (No other woman had ever done that ... at first he thought it was perverted!)

My fantasies, as you can see, are all mixed up with what actually happened. In the mornings G. would pick me up in his car and fantasize on what positions he was going to take me in that night, often petting and kissing me to such an extent that once or twice I ended up impaled on his prick at 8:15 A.M. in the front seat, while his bosses wondered what had happened to old reliable G! His particular ritual was to tease me so that I would plead with him to enter and "quench my fire." This was okay so long as he could control himself, but very often he couldn't, especially in front of the mirror, and we would fuck ourselves silly all over the floor. One night in particular he waltzed me around the front room carpet on my back while I was having multiple orgasms, and it wasn't until half an hour later that we saw that the skin had come off my back in about five places. I told my husband I'd been doing floor gymnastics. All this, the real and the imagined, gets confused in my mind during fantasy.

Also, G. and I used to share a fantasy of what it would be like, when we were making love in his car in a secluded spot on a promontory with bushes all around, if the two hundred men on his staff would suddenly appear from behind the bushes and see us at it. In fact, I think I would have really enjoyed it, and have since wondered about seeing all that lot masturbating when they saw that their boss was pretty good at things apart from work. I would have liked to watch their reactions when I toyed with my lover's penis in my mouth—that would shock a good many of them, old women that a lot of them are, especially when they saw me bring him to climax that way and swallow his seed, or when I made G. come simply by flexing my vaginal muscles (tricks my mother taught me—ha!—I can't do that with my husband though; he's not sensitive enough).

My husband never seems to really take the initiative in bed, and a climax for him seems to be more of a relief than a release. (Incidentally, we've been married three years and he's twenty-four.) What I miss most is my lover's manipulation of me during intercourse, and his more or less mastery of the situation. Most of all I remember when I'm with my husband how G., when his climax came, used to grunt and groan with the pleasure and kiss me fiercely, making me feel a complete woman, completely possessed. I haven't really felt like that for months now.

Thank you for giving me the opportunity to get something off my chest which has been weighing me down for almost two years. Very often I've longed to tell my husband the details of my adultery—it would heighten my opinion of my husband if he could take joy in what my lover has experienced. But I know it's just not possible. After all, my fantasies are based on the real thing. [Letter]

Adrienne

☐ Adrienne is one of those lively, gregarious types who are easy to get to know. I met her on the QE2 trip from New York to Southampton. Although the voyage is only five days, a ship has a way of bringing people together in terms of intimacy so quickly that it seems incredible when remembered back on shore.

This was the case with Adrienne and me. We were introduced at the Captain's cocktail party. (The two of us being practically the only unattached women under sixty on board, we were naturally asked.) Nicknames, very quickly invented and bestowed, are another part of shipboard life, and there was a man on board whom Adrienne almost immediately named "The Gambler." She had already met him by the time I got to know her, and the three of us would often have a drink together before dinner. The

235

Gambler was one of those men who like to talk about sex a great deal, and with astonishing perseverance would want to know more about the slightest detail ever mentioned. It was after the Gambler had gone off on his own one night that Adrienne and I had our talk.

Adrienne is a plump, almost professionally social thirty-two or thirty-three; as I said, I doubt if we'd ever have exchanged more than first names on land, we had so little in common. But she loved to talk and I listened. □

When you asked me the other day if I ever had sexual fantasies, my first reaction was that I really didn't think I ever had. What had I been missing? Maybe the Gambler has something to do with my "second-thinking." What I mean is, he reminds me of this guy I used to know. Now, on reflection, I realize that on more than one occasion my thoughts have run wild and that I do have a vivid imagination. It's just that I wasn't used to calling these ideas and images "fantasies."

Several years ago, I was going out with a man called Ted. He was tall (like the Gambler), handsome, and I found him very attractive but elusive. When I first met him we were at a dinner party, which was held outdoors on a lovely terrace overgrown with pink and white petunias. It was a warm night and we were sipping buck fizzes—a drink which always makes me feel very romantic and rather sexy. We had really only just been introduced, but there we were, off alone on that terrace, and I found myself telling him that I had a giant teddy bear back home at my apartment, and he immediately replied that now I could have another "Teddy, bare" that night. He said it so easily, and with such a spirit of fun, that I thought to myself, "Well, why not?"

He was a wonderful lover. You know how some people always have to have a record player going when they make love? With me, all I have to do to get into a sexy mood is remember the conversation that first night. Time and time again I would imagine him as a large teddy bear and me as a honey pot. He was a very hungry bear and would suck and scrape as much as he could out of that pot

236

and I kept wishing and wishing that my pot could always
be full. Just thinking of it right now . . . I can feel myself
getting all excited . . . Hey! Where did the Gambler go?
[Conversation]

Doris

☐ "Here was this experience that was supposed to be the
climax of a girl's life, and it was like a form of calisthenics,"
says Doris, talking about her sexual initiation with Jim,
then her fiancé. "My reactions were always the same. I'd
find myself heated up by the preliminaries, but then just
waiting for what's called 'the real thing' to be over."

Doris felt obscurely cheated, and resentful of Jim. In
the end, it ended their engagement. But before it did,
Doris told Jim of her feelings. His response was to buy
"something special." "It was like a little fat rubber band,"
says Doris, "maybe an inch wide, but on one side it had
this funny little upward thing. I remember thinking it
looked like some kind of shark's fin, sticking up from the
middle of the rubber band." Jim slipped the rubber band
around the shaft of his erect penis, and with every thrust
"the little fin rubbed my clitoris both going in and coming
out in a way that Jim's shaft never could. I never had felt
anything like it. I never had an orgasm like it in my life."

A year after the engagement was over, Doris married
someone else. Her husband refuses to buy "one of those
little upward things" like Jim used to have, but has
learned to bring her to orgasm with his finger. ☐

It's dark—maybe that's because I have my eyes closed
so I can see the picture better. I just think of that big shaft
of Jim's, going in and out of me, like a great pink shark. I
rarely imagine that the man is my husband. Usually, it's
my old boy friend, or sometimes some other man I've recently met. I picture it very clearly, the man's big shaft
parting the hair, parting the lips, sinking into me, with that
little tip riding toward the clitoris as if it's hungry to touch
it. I concentrate on that little rubber shark's fin, just

touching me in the right place with each stroke. Rubbing as it goes in, rubbing as it goes out. I've never mentioned it to my husband again ever since he refused to buy one. But it's one of the nicest wedding presents my old boy friend could have given us . . . this picture of it I have in my mind.

I like to imagine that we're making love in some tropical sea or a warm swimming pool. And I can just see this pink shark swimming toward me, and I open my legs wider and wider. The shark knows me, and he likes the warm feeling inside. He likes to wriggle around just at the lips. Sometimes even when my husband's not inside me, I only have to think about that shark's fin and I start climbing the walls. I can see the picture in my mind's eye. That's all I ever have to think about. Just the pink fin rubbing me. [Taped interview]

Lulu

Any lesbian fantasies I have go back to the time my husband and I experimented in bed with another girl. It was the only time this had ever happened—not for my husband, but for me. I must admit I enjoyed it. It was my husband's idea, and although he asked me to make the advances toward the girl, I didn't really mind. Since that time I have sometimes wondered what it would be like to pick up a girl all on my own somewhere and seduce her, or to be completely seduced by a dominant woman, especially as my own experience so far has been as the initiator. When I am in bed with my husband I'll go over this scene again and again, imagining how that first girl really was with me, the things I might have tried had I only known. If I like I can even imagine that my finger is her tongue, as I remember it. That's a lot of memory from just one experience, don't you think? [Conversation]

Daisy

I've been having sexy fantasies ever since I got married three years ago. I imagine that I am walking down the street when suddenly a fantastic car screeches up beside me and sitting at the wheel is Robert Redford. Beside him, of course, is Paul Newman. They take me to an elegant dress shop where mannequins model the most incredible clothes (just like in the old films from the forties on TV). They buy me the most elegant, sexy clothes imaginable. Then they take me to a ball.

Everyone is there, film stars and the most divine-looking men any woman could want to meet. Naturally, everyone wants to dance with me: Tom Jones, for one, whom I refuse, just to see his face . . . Engelbert . . . Franco Nero is incredibly jealous . . . The one and only Elvis asks to take me home, but I refuse them all and end my fantastic night by going home and making passionate love to Marc Bolan of T. Rex. [Letter]

Kit

I am a happily married woman of thirty-five, and often think about other men and imagine how they would make love to me. My most vivid imagery is of Tom Jones. Just the other day, as we were driving along, my mind drifted off. Suddenly my husband looked at me and said, "What are you smiling about?" I replied, "I was in bed with Tom Jones." "What happened?" he asked. "Everything!" I said. "And it was smashing!" We both had a good laugh. [Letter]

Flossie

I'm a James Bond fan, and often imagine ordinary

tradesmen have done fantastic things to me before sweeping me off to bed. I was picturing the milkman that way recently when he asked how many pints I wanted. "Oh, oh seven," I whispered dreamily! [Letter]

Josie

I used to imagine in bed that my husband was Mick Jagger, until the night when at the height of our sexual crescendo I moaned, "Oh, Mick!" I *still* haven't convinced him that Mick isn't the mailman, or the man who reads the gas meter, or a brush salesman! [Letter]

Brett

I wonder what making love would be like with the couldn't-care-less Tony Curtis, or the sexy Roger Moore. I'm a great-grandmother of sixty—36" 29" 38"—which I'm afraid is not terribly sexy. When I see my fantasy lovers, I'm practically in the TV scene with them; then the program is over and I have to go to bed with my husband. [Letter]

Sarah

It has always been my fantasy just to tell someone that I dream of very young men. My favorite of the moment is Richard Benjamin. I do feel so ashamed, as I am going to be fifty next May. I also admit to having sexual fantasies whenever I see well-dressed men with *no tummies!* I can't tell you how exciting I find a flat stomach. [Letter]

Maud

Thank goodness for your article. I was beginning to

think I was the only one with certain fantasies when indulging in sex.

I've never dared discuss my thoughts with anyone because of being considered indecent. Even now I feel rather shy in writing to you.

My first fantasy, I remember, was on the occasion when, as is normal on most evenings, our love play started in front of the fire with me between my husband's legs fellatiating him. But on this occasion the television was on with the sound turned down, and I suddenly imagined myself doing it to the man on the screen instead of my husband. The thrill I got was trying to imagine whether the man I was watching had a penis to compare with my husband's. This certainly heightened my eagerness to please hubby, and although he had no idea what I was thinking, he certainly enjoyed my increased intensity because in no time at all he arrived at a delightful climax.

The other occasion was inspired by the first: again, with the television on, I was on my knees watching a play when he mounted me from the rear, and while he was thrusting home I was imagining that it was not him but the handsome brute in the play. The effect on me was indescribable and I was putting up such a performance that my husband did, I am sure, suspect something, because he reached over and turned the set off, much to my annoyance.

On other occasions, when he sometimes performs cunnilingus on me, I lie back and imagine him to be a young fresh teen-age girl (I've longed for that to happen). But alas, I never get the chance to meet one, as I cannot get out on my own. He is far too possessive to allow me out. [Letter]

Gelda

Until I knew Sam, my current lover, I'd never had a fantasy like this, that is, one that involved me with another woman. Lots of fantasies, but nothing like this. And I've never even thought of a woman that way in real life, just wouldn't ever want a woman sexually. It's just that ever since Sam told me about her, the girl he used to live with, I can't help thinking about it, about them together. I know how she changed Sam's life sexually, made him a better lover. I also know he's through with her, that he loves me; I am as convinced of it as one could rationally be. But jealousy isn't rational, is it? And I hate it, jealousy; I hate what it does to people, and I'm not going to let it ruin things for me and Sam. Sometimes I feel that if I ever met that girl I'd scratch her eyes out, at least I'd want to. But in my fantasies it's all different. This is more or less how they go:

The bed is one of those wrought-iron antique beds you see in Italy. The Italians hang religious medals and ornaments on them, and they make a chiming noise with the up and back motion of fucking. The bed is painted red and there are gold balls all along the spikes at the head and foot. The bed is in this girl's room, in her apartment. I can see the apartment just from Sam's description of it, complete with the little dog, small, with long gray and brown hair. The dog is on the bed with us, licking the asshole of the girl. who is between my legs. I can't see the dog but I know it's there, that the girl has trained the dog to do this. I feel the girl's long hair on my thighs and against my lower stomach, as she slowly kisses me, parting my lips with her fingers, her tongue going straight to that delicate spot. touching it gently, and then her lips, full and lingering against me, pressing warm against me, and then the tongue, slowly, very slowly at first—and not just the tip of the tongue, which would be too hard, but the whole length and breadth of it, soft, warm, licking me in slow, great, warm, repeated kisses. The blunt feel of her teeth as her mouth presses against me. Sam is there, standing across the room, watching us, watching me, my face. He is leaning against the wall, cool, detached, interested. knowing how I am. He is wearing his old khakis, the red Banlon shirt, the old blue sneakers. His eyes never leave my face, he is fascinated, he waits for the flush to start in my cheeks, as he knows it will, as I know his cool look of detachment will change. My lips part, and as my breathing becomes heavier, faster, so does his. I can see the bulge in his trousers growing larger and larger and his hand moves to it. Something in me fights letting this girl give me pleasure, any pleasure, but she is so good at it, she knows every little trick, just the rhythm, the right rhythm, slowly at first, with the full tongue spread warm and lingering against me. Now the idea of her hair, of all that long silky hair—the idea that she *is* a girl, the idea that she is Rosie, Sam's old girl friend, excites me. I watch Sam unzip his fly, still standing there, still watching my face, but needing my excitement now for his own. He takes out his cock and his long thin hand begins to stroke it, the foreskin slipping, slipping slowly up and down over the pink smooth end. His rhythm is slow at first, like the girl with me. I watch his cock, I know it so well, I watch it, the veins in it strained like the veins in his hand, and I gear myself, pace myself to him. My hands feel for the girl's hair, the beautiful soft feel of it—Christ! is it another woman doing this to me?—and with the slightest pressure I keep her head, the movement of her tongue, paced to Sam and me. I don't have to guide her though, she knows; she has always wanted me. We don't need Sam. Now Sam needs us. I relax; I give myself to her. Push myself against her mouth so that her lips are pressed against her teeth and her tongue slips into me, wanting me. My face is hot, my cunt aches with wanting her. I watch Sam's hand moving faster, faster, he is bent over, his body barely able to hold him up, his mouth open, his hand moving up and down, up and down the way he has taught me to jerk him off, his eyes glued to mine, pleading, begging me not to stop. The girl moans, her tongue moves faster and faster. She is ready to come, but she holds it back, waiting for me. The scream is in Sam's throat, I am almost there, but I poise at the height, not wanting it to end, wait Sam, wait, not yet, not just yet? The little dog is on his back now, under the girl, so that he can lick her cunt which drips, but still she waits, her sucking lips pleading, her tongue never stopping until *now!* [Written down on request]

CHAPTER FIVE

GUILT AND FANTASY, OR, WHY THE FIG LEAF?

WOMEN'S GUILT

☐ Do women dress for men or women? I've always wondered why that eternally provocative question is put in terms of approval—as if the heart of the matter, the answer, were indeed a question of approval by either sex. But the question is never satisfactorily answered because it is incorrectly posed. It's disapproval, the fear of it, that motivates most women, and with disapproval it doesn't matter where it comes from.

It's no different with sexual fantasy; the question is not for whom do women select their sexual imagery, but out of fear of whose disapproval do they suppress it? And the answer's the same as above. Nor is the parallel especially contrived between what a woman chooses to put on her body and what sexual imagery it is that goes into her head.

In the marvelous climactic scene of an early Bette Davis film, *Jezebel,* when she appears at the traditionally all-white-dress cotillion in a flaming red torch of a dress, whose hearts stop (along with the music) in shocked disapproval and anxiety at what she's dared to wear? Absolutely everyone's, *both men and women.* Everyone, that is, except handsome gambler George Brent, who suddenly sees that his own private fantasy of a woman is also Bette's. And ours in the audience, too, of course. For an instant there, we share the fantasy of being the most daringly beautiful woman at the ball, who, rather than being rejected for her daring, is chosen because of it by the manliest man, the Hero.

Then the lights go up; we sigh and go home to reality, where we would no more think of actually buying a dress like that than we would think of responding to the next "George Brent" who comes along. Not because a red sheath doesn't suit us; there's an equivalent on the market for what that dress *does,* for every woman, just as there's an equivalent George Brent somewhere who could do for every woman what George did for Bette. But we don't dress "out of character" (and *in* to fantasy) for the same reason we don't act unpredictably; it would arouse too much anxiety. Anxiety in other women, in our men, and in ourselves.

What happens, instead, is that the guilt we feel in advance at what we might have done—in our wildest fantasies—doesn't merely restrain us from doing it, it suppresses the fantasy as well. That is guilt in its most repressive sense. You've seen what the end result is: Women walking past shop windows of clothes ("Oh, that's just not me") with the kind of indulgent smiles that convince you they haven't even *seen* the clothes, any more than they really sexually *look* at "other" men. Having turned off their fantasy like a light, they become blind to reality as well; it's safer that way. Repression is a defense line that is ever moving forward, ever seeing threats further and further afield, and in the end, even the fantasy itself, no matter how far removed it is from being acted out, has become so sexually loaded that most women who would not dream of "experimenting" in reality, won't experiment in their conscious dreams either.

To be fair, women have had little training for thinking about sex (except in their almost unconscious reveries). Doing it maybe, but not thinking about it. It's why men's burning bedroom question, "Tell me what you are thinking about," usually goes unanswered, or he gets an honest, but right off the top of the head "I wasn't thinking about anything." Women's conscious minds, like the bodies of virgins, just don't spontaneously progress from the most obvious sexual possibility to the next. It's a matter of exercise, or lack of it, like learning the scales. When the occasional sexual reverie does occur, it's generally on a straight line and short-lived. It's like thinking in a foreign language. It has nothing to do with intelligence or even "liberation." Interested and unabashed as we all are getting to be in this age where one can no longer be shocked, when it's all been written and filmed and become so socially accepted that the only rule left is "let the sun shine in," women I know still grow tongue-tied when the topic of sexual fantasy comes up.

While I was putting this book together, I met women who were instantly in tune to what I was doing, who so intuitively knew what it was all about that they were saying my words before I could get them out of my mouth. They were encouraging and enthusiastic and fantasizers, too— except suddenly, as they were talking all over the subject, they couldn't remember the heart of it, their own specific fantasies. "But that's ridiculous," one would say, perplexed. "I know I fantasize, I just can't remember . . ." Then, as often as not, after a lapse of days—during which they would adjust to the idea, or perhaps have the fantasy again but this time remember it—they would triumphantly tell it to me.

I expect most women to say they don't have sexual fantasies. (Contributors to this book, aware of their fantasies, are the exception, not the rule.) I even expect the same women who say they don't fantasize to be the ones who most want to discuss the topic, to be interested and eager to pursue the idea. But what I'm not prepared for (or at least wasn't when I began) is the inarticulate stumbling for words, the sometimes near-hysterical half giggle, half groping for sentences, and the almost universal disclaimer which tries to deny everything by admitting all: "There must be something wrong with me; I never have fantasies at all." Listening to an intelligent woman trying to put one word in front of another in an effort to describe what sexual fantasy means to her is like watching a healthy normal child who has suddenly developed dystrophy trying to put one large block on top of another.

I mentioned in an earlier chapter that I think a woman's divorce from sex begins with her childhood exclusion from adventure and exploration, both physical and mental, and those limited, limiting toys and games allowed her. It's as if it were a crime for a young female body to get knocked about and bruised in play, as if the crime were in the contact of anyone or anything with her body. And the feeling that it's a crime to be touched, even by herself, increases in her teens, so that if she stumbles upon it by accident, the ground for guilt has already been prepared.

If her own hands are hesitant to touch what's obviously and tangibly hers, how much chance does her mind have of exploring the possibilities of that body? And where would she get the rudimentary material her imagination needs to build with? What books or magazines offer any more than her childhood toys, incentive or ideas for sexual fantasy concerning this body that's so out of bounds? By the time she's twelve they've got her senses all tied up: Nice Little Girls don't do "those things"; Nice Little Girls also don't look—thus the fig leaf, just in case they do. And as Nice Little Girls don't even think about "those things," even the fig leaf become a mystery.

Later, when the mystery is solved and the fig leaf removed, women look (at least some do), but they still don't speak. The conspiracy of silence that began with her mother, and which makes each woman her own jailer, keeps women verbally tongue-tied and as securely blocked off from their minds as their minds are from their bodies. To me, the saddest part of this is not that a woman feels guilty in her fantasy about what she's doing (that guilt is usually as buried and unconscious as the fantasy itself), but the guilt a woman feels for having a fantasy at all. To feel guilt, not for something you've done, but for something you've only been thinking about—that *is* sad. □

247

Christiana

I suppose my sex life is as normal as any twenty-eight-year-old woman's. It's happy, it exists, and I've never felt frustrated. Ted and I've been going together for two years now and we'll probably get married, when and if we feel like it . . . and if it doesn't mean I'll have to give up my job, which I love. I have to travel a lot for the company, and Ted knows I probably sleep with another guy now and then. But jealousy's not one of our problems. We don't really have any—sexual problems. We hardly ever go to sleep without making love first. It's just natural. The only thing that isn't natural is this recurring thought of mine, what you would probably call a fantasy. If this is a fantasy it's the only one I've ever had, and I have it almost every time I make love. It's the only unnatural thing about me. Invariably, when a man is on top of me, inside me, I have this desire, this image that he is having me from behind. He's not really, but it's what I want—yes, to be fucked from behind, again and again. It's what I always dream of. Perhaps if it happened, just once, I wouldn't feel so guilty thinking of it. [Letter]

Hope

Are you going to publish the results of this work? I really hope so. I used to feel so guilty about my sexual thoughts, my fantasies, about everything to do with sex, I guess, including masturbation. But I didn't stop, not the sex or the fantasies . . . I couldn't in a way, it all seemed so natural. But the guilt, that seemed natural too, until I met my husband. He's helped me out so much.

First, let me say that I'm a married woman of three and a half years. I am twenty years old. And though I say that my husband has done a great deal to lessen my feelings of guilt about sex, I must admit that I've never told him about my fantasies. I've never told anyone. I've just had them and then felt awful about it. I'm telling you now because deep down inside I believe it's the guilt that's wrong and not the fantasy. Here's how some of my thoughts go.

It gives me an extra thrill to imagine that one of our friends, another man, is making love to me while my husband is actually doing it. I don't really have any desire to have any relations with another person, but I get this added excitement just thinking about it. Is that so wrong? I'd never dream of telling my husband. We are very liberal about our sex practices, but I wouldn't hurt his masculine ego for the world, and telling him these things might.

Sometimes when my husband is going down on me I imagine that this woman, whom I knew long ago but had no physical relationship with, begs me to let her eat me. I imagine she does it whenever I wish, which is often. This increases my ability to have giant orgasms. Then, after orgasm my fantasy completely dissolves until next time. It's not that my husband doesn't perform well—he's great—but thinking of her makes it even greater. Except later. I sometimes feel like I'm cheating him.

Now I remember an even earlier fantasy . . . I'd almost forgotten about it. When I was six or seven I can remember masturbating and imagining my father inserting the handle of a large screwdriver inside me and masturbating me. There never was any other contact but this. It's strange because I'd never experienced being penetrated yet, and my father and I have never gotten along at all. I had that one for a couple of years.

I think you're going to find that all men are really going to get upset about this book of yours. So many of them still think that women are for their enjoyment only. Some won't admit that women (if handled properly) have strong sexual desires and feelings, just as they do. Most men that I ran into before marriage didn't even know what foreplay was. If it becomes more open and publicly known that foreplay is usually necessary to get the ball rolling for the woman, I'll bet there'll be a lot more sexually satisfied women than there are right now. I had sex with thirty or so men before my husband and never had an orgasm; I always got the ones who jumped on, then jumped right off and took me home, and of course I told them they were fantastic lovers and all, but I felt nothing but frustration.

I told you that my husband has done a great deal to make me feel less guilty about sex, about what we *really* do, which is anything that gives us pleasure. I don't know why I feel so hesitant to tell him about my fantasies; I don't know why I feel so guilty about having them. I don't always fantasize while we are having sex. Just as often my husband is enough. But other times, even when he has his fingers as well as his penis in me and you'd think there was nothing else he could do to stimulate me, still I fantasize that I am being fucked by many different penises, that I am a nymphomaniac who can't get enough of different men. I would like to feel easier about my thoughts. I already do just writing them down and hearing that I am not the only one in the world with these ideas. I sometimes think many women would be ashamed to admit they have *any* sexual feelings.

I don't pretend to know what makes people work, but I'd be willing to bet that if more people were more open and let themselves go during sex, their brains as well as their bodies, the world would be a better place. I doubt that so many people would be so aggressive and power-crazy if they found a suitable sex partner who would accept all of them. If people could free themselves of deep-rooted sex guilts they'd spend more time becoming good lovers and wouldn't have so much time for revenge and wars. Good sex makes my husband and me very mellow. Who would think of hating and fighting and plotting to get someone else if they'd just been very sexually satisfied . . . no matter what means they employed to reach that happy goal? Not many, I'll bet. So I'm ending up defending my "dirty" thoughts! Believing in them, I guess is what I mean. [Letter]

Lil

I only fantasize when I masturbate, and I suppose what I think about is typical. I imagine it is a man making love to me, that he kisses me passionately all over my body, concentrating most of his ardor on my cunt, teasing the outer lips, loving me totally and expertly. I simply lie there in ecstasy, which makes me feel a little guilty later at having such a selfish fantasy, since I never even imagine touching *him*. [Letter]

Alison

When I was fourteen, I had the usual relationship with a close girl friend (I think most girls have them). In my bedroom she would pretend to be the madam of a house and I would be a virgin girl. She would dress me in a sort of sexy bikini made of chiffon scarves. She would then be the customer, a rowdy seaman who would take me against my will. She would lie on me and rub her vagina against mine. I experienced very intense orgasms (more intense than from any man). After she moved away I never had the chance of another relationship like ours. Now when I masturbate I usually think that I am being seduced by a pretty female. However, if it ever should occur again in reality, I would need to be seduced by the woman in order to control my embarrassment.

I have spoken to my lover about my lesbian fantasies. He knows I feel guilty about them. He has tried to enter into them by talking to me during sex, telling me that he is a woman, and so on. This does excite me to an extent, but I'm not sure if he does it for me or for homosexual feelings of his own, although he says he has none. He does like me to lie on top of him (my back to his chest) so that he can feel my breasts. From things he says, I think he wishes they *were* his. It's an exciting thought to me and I don't

251

understand why he won't admit to the slightest interest in homosexuality—after all, I have. As he sees no shame in my lesbian fantasies, why should he feel shame at his homosexual fantasies?

Not all my fantasies are in the lesbian category. The man I live with has a good-looking cousin, a man; I used to fantasize that he would come to the house and find me naked, and I would make love to him, or sometimes he would arrive with friends and they would all touch me, trying to arouse me; I would then make love with the one I fancied most. I rarely have this fantasy now. The men in my fantasies nowadays always take me by force and are older than I am (usually about thirty-five). Sometimes my lover will encourage me to think that lots of men are making love to me; he will paw me, touching me all over very quickly, as though his hands were many hands. This excites me very much at the time, but later I can't help feeling ashamed. I sometimes think he enjoys my fantasies, that they excite him when we are making love, but that later he looks down on me because of them, that he blames me for them.

Am I a suppressed lesbian? I just don't know. Perhaps I could be less two-faced about my fantasies if my lover were. [Letter]

Clare

I am trying very hard to free myself of sexual guilts and frustrations. Thanks to my husband, I'm hoping to soon be totally sexually free—but I must admit I'm afraid to take the chance of telling him about my fantasies. When we first met, he was jealous of other men. (I never flirted, I just liked to look at men, just as men like to look over a woman.) However, we are now more broadminded, and he may not be jealous at all of my fantasies. I suppose it's not really that I want to tell him, I would just like to feel that it's all right that I think these things, that he thinks it's all right.

252

I don't think that he would like to know that sometimes during intercourse with him I think of someone else. It is usually of another man whom I have just met, who was extremely attractive, and who I would like to make love with. I love my husband completely—he's the greatest—but I think we're capable of loving others sexually, also. I wouldn't tell him this, I just wish he knew and could accept it without my telling him.

I do however think he might be ready to hear about my fantasies during masturbation. Most of the time I imagine someone very slowly approaching me and moving closer to me to kiss my genitals. As I imagine the person getting nearer, I become more excited, and as I imagine the kiss I have an orgasm. Sometimes this imaginary person is female—which makes me feel guilty. These lesbian feelings do worry me, and I want to be open with my husband about it, but I am afraid. Also, when I see the excitement my husband gets from performing cunnilingus on me, I sometimes wonder if my doing the same to another woman would excite me also. All my lesbian feelings are imaginary; I would probably be disgusted if I were approached by a lesbian in reality.

My other sexual fantasies involve a certain amount of voyeurism or exhibitionism. One particular one concerns someone—no particular person—who walks into the room and watches me masturbate, then possibly joins me. At other times, while masturbating, just as I reach an orgasm I imagine I am licked by a huge dog. During lovemaking I even fantasize that people are watching us, and that possibly the man with me is black.

Even during the day my mind wanders. If I am extremely attracted to a man, I can fantasize an entire affair, just as if I am writing a book or a play about the relationship.

I think my husband might encourage these fantasies, especially as our relationship has changed so for the better. I have told him that as a child my earliest sexual thoughts were not of intercourse, but more of nudity, naked people, many people walking around naked at a pool or in a park. I, of course, was one of the nudists, and being nude and seeing others nude would turn me on.

We have only been married three years. For a while there things were quite boring during our lovemaking. But we've overcome that by falling more deeply in love and by throwing off our many sexual hang-ups.

Thanks for wanting to know. [Letter]

Penelope

I wanted to contribute to your work, even though my sexual life is probably lacking and will add very little to your research. But even that fact alone will tell you something, and I do want to feel more in touch with the world, with other women. I say my own sexual life is lacking even though I don't know what is normal or average. I am sure there is something more to sex than what I've felt.

We've been married seven years, and our sexual life is no different now than it was when we were first married, except that there's less of it. You would think, or hope, that as people lived together longer they would discover new and interesting things about one another that would help them to give one another more happiness in sex. But it's only when I imagine that someone is performing cunnilingus on me, which my husband will not do, that sex becomes exciting, and I've always felt too guilty to discuss this with anyone. [Letter]

MEN'S ANXIETY

☐ Women waste so much time and emotion on guilt, meaningless guilt; fingers of shame imagined in isolation and ignorance. I sometimes think each woman goes through life secretly pursued by her own particular demon, representing her own particular brand of shame; a frenzy after her, not for anything real, but everything imagined. Shame and self-incrimination grow like mad in the dark. If nothing else, I hope this book helps women who fantasize to feel less guilty by letting them know that they aren't alone . . . they aren't the only people in the world with these odd, often unbidden thoughts or ideas; that thinking something "awful" doesn't mean you are awful or really want something awful; and in the end you shouldn't be found guilty for what you think. (No Virginia, thought police didn't go out with the Nazis; they're very much with us still.)

But not all the guilt that surrounds the subject of female fantasy is imagined. The tension and anxiety the topic arouses in men is very real indeed, and a woman can't help but pick up on it; if he feels the anxiety, *she's* guilty.

I can understand a man not wanting to hear about other men in his woman's life—especially hearing that they are in her mind while he's making love to her. I also understand why some women feel they want to tell their men everything—but can't understand why they do. Telling all isn't necessarily the way to overcome guilt feelings; sometimes it only spreads the anxiety. (Though I don't think one can make a hard-and-fast rule about this; only you yourself, knowing the man, can decide how much you feel he really wants to know.) But more about sharing your fantasies— is it a good idea or not?— in another chapter.

I mentioned earlier that I gave up talking about their fantasies with women when their men were present because, despite the initial interest the topic aroused in everyone, a more detailed discussion always clearly brought on tension in the men. Exactly why they feel threatened by the subject is no mystery.

A woman's fantasy brings up in him the spectre of the unconquerable rival, with magical abilities and unimaginable proportions, and, above all, a rival over whom he has no control. Some men don't react with anger or panic, but with simple denial. I was discussing this subject over drinks one evening with a man friend, when he said, "You really have to talk to my friend Harry. He'll be here in a minute. Harry will be fascinated with what you're doing.

Why, that man's the original beast in the jungle. There's not a sexual experience he hasn't had, and the number of women he's been to bed with is like a telephone book." Fair enough, I thought, I'll meet a man of such vast experience, who'll be so expansive and broadminded, that at last I'll be able to discuss women's fantasies with a man without making him feel nervous. And so I smiled warmly at the Beast in the Jungle when he arrived, and he smiled right back, until my friend started telling him of my work. The Beast's expression toward me changed as he drew himself up to his full psychological attack position and lit a cigar. "No woman *I've* ever fucked," he said, "has needed sexual fantasies."

This book isn't about men or *their* fantasies, but I do want to print just this one letter from a man who not only tells me what his wife thinks, but also writes the letter for her, even signing her name.

Tina's husband

My modest wife has asked me to write for her. So I am telling you herewith that I don't think she has any peculiar fantasies.

Her fantasy, if any, and she expresses it to me (we have been married thirty-five years), is that she gets a great loving feeling whenever we have sex. She has a right like anyone to her secret feelings or desires, which we discuss frankly. She is offended to read of women who might fantasize about other women or animals. She doesn't have to tell me this, as I know.

She has told me that she could—as would I—be aroused to see large animals like horses or elephants having sex. We would very much like to visit a stud farm and see this sort of sexual activity. But I am sure this is not in her mind when we have sex.

As for myself, I have no fantasies during sex. I enjoy thinking of my wife as a healthy, clean woman, and her one preoccupation, or fantasy, is of herself wearing nice clean clothes, which she knows pleases me. She has never masturbated, and although she used to share a bedroom with her sister, I am sure she has never had a lesbian thought.

Her fantasy, I repeat, is the feeling of love for me she gets when we have sex and she is giving me all the enjoyment she can.

I would, however, like to see more written on fantasies, although I do not think the average woman has the sexual desires and fantasies that many men apparently have.

Thank you for letting me write to you for my wife. [*He* signs *her* name.]

CHAPTER SIX

FANTASY ACCEPTED

☐ Some women feel no guilt at all about their sexual fantasies. They accept them, act them out, share them with their lovers, even live them on a day-to-day basis, as does Sophie (below). A few have gotten this far on their own; more of them have needed the encouragement of an accepting lover. And a very few, I think, are just lucky; they were born guilt-free.

As you've read, most of the women who contributed to this book did so with a feeling of anxiety, almost in a tone of self-reproach or even disgust—though many ended on the relieved note of, "Well, thank God, I've finally told someone who understands; I thought I was the only freak with these thoughts. . . ."

This relief from the anxiety of being alone with their thoughts, and the greater reality which sharing them can bring, was sometimes such a powerful sexual stimulus in itself that it excited several of my correspondents to interrupt themselves in midletter to masturbate. Carried along on the euphoria of the release, they even told me about this—so, more therapeutic relief from guilt. For example: ☐

Please excuse me if this is rather disjointed, but I am sure you will understand that I could not write this without masturbating, which I am doing at this moment . . .

The only fantasies that I speak out loud are the ones I make up to please my husband. I always keep my real fan-

tasies locked up in my mind. I have found it a little exciting to tell you about my fantasies, and a few times I have
stopped and manipulated my nipples with my fingertips
while I was typing this letter. (The more I did that, the
better I felt about telling you these things.) In fact, while I
am typing this sentence with one hand, I am manipulating
my nipples with my thumb and first finger on the other
hand.

Excuse me, I have got myself quite carried away, and so I
must go and bring myself off if I can . . .

After reading through this letter I am wet through to my
panties . . .

This has been a difficult letter to write. My recollections
have been so arousing that I have had to stop twice to
masturbate with a "phallocrypt" made by my houseboy.
This is rather like a dildo and is used by some native
women when their men are away to satisfy themselves. My
particular one is made exactly to the size of my husband in
erection. My thoughts when I use it are that the native boy
who made it is standing in for my husband. But this does
not matter when I close my eyes and cannot see the boy,
just feel the delightful weapon working exactly as my husband does. If only it could spurt semen or cream into me
. . . right now. [From a correspondent in the Pacific]

"OF COURSE I FANTASIZE, DOESN'T EVERYONE?"

☐ A guiltless minority never seem to have any hesita-
tions at all about the subject. They contribute as readily as
if I'd invited them to a party where they know they'll have
a good time because they already know the guests. "Fantasies? Of course I have fantasies, doesn't everyone?" In

fact, Gloria (below) was convinced that no fantasy anthology could be complete without hers, which she uses daily in her work as a model. For women like her, there's no wall between fantasy and reality; what you *think* and what you *do* needn't be the same, but they don't have to be separated as though they were at war with one another. A woman who lives this close to her fantasy isn't dragging out the dirty laundry from the bottom of the pit when she talks to you; the material is easily available to her. What's significant isn't whether her real and fantasy lives coexist, or even whether she acts out her fantasies, but that each does exist and is accepted. Her fantasies are part of her self-awareness; there is no threat, no anxiety. That's how she is.

For women like Hannah, there are no secrets or shame in fantasy: she keeps a photo of her fantasy lover in her mirror as she would that of a real lover, and enjoys slipping into her fantasy routine any night she happens to be alone and in the mood. To Sophie, her fantasy is barely a fantasy at all—just a desirable way to live, and she proceeds with no hesitation at all to put her desire to live with two different, equally exciting men immediately into practice. As I said, some people live so close to their fantasies that they live inside them.

I don't know how significant it is that the four women in the fantasies that follow are young, but I suspect it is. I've included my youngest contributor here—fifteen years old and technically still a virgin—because of her simple candor and self-acceptance. Maybe it says something for fantasy's future. ☐

Gloria

I really don't think any anthology of sex fantasies would be complete without mine. It's got to be the greatest one there is.

I should tell you I use it professionally, when I model. Let's say I'm in a studio, standing there waiting for the photographer to finish fussing with the lights and everything. I look bored, because I am bored. Then, when he's ready and we begin, I deliberately "go to market"—that's how I think of it, and as I get more and more into my fantasy, even though I'm following his directions (I am a genuine professional at this) *I become more and more interesting to look at.* Every photographer I've ever worked with has remarked on it. I don't tell them how I do it (that's my business), but I have enjoyed great commercial success with it. Of course I amplify it and change it all the time, but this is what it is basically:

I am strolling with my flunkies through a market, an enormous place with high vaulted glass ceilings, up one aisle and down another, looking at the merchandise to decide what I want. All the merchandise on display in all the booths is simply naked young men, all sorts but all strong looking. I am the only customer in the whole place, and dancing attendance on me are all sorts of salesmen or hawkers or press agents, all trying to sell me on one or another of these studs. Sometimes, if I feel like it, I listen to them as they tell me fantastic stories of what these men are capable of, and this is in itself exciting; at other times I brush them off and stroll on. At some point my attention is caught by one particular young man, then another two or three, or more, depending on how I feel. When I've a few candidates, the flunkies assemble them on one platform, while other flunkies get the screen ready. The screen is gigantic, filling one whole side of the hall, fifty times the size of the usual movie screen. All the others in the market, except my own people, are now sent away temporarily, and then the film begins. The film is of me, in glorious Technicolor, stripped and reclining, with the camera at my level at the foot of the bed. As my knees, which are together at the start, move apart, I start writhing on the bed and the camera moves in. The head in the distance thrashes on the pillow, the breasts in the middle distance roll from side to side as the hips churn, and the zoom shot —but slow—gets to the slit, which becomes more and more gigantic as the thighs widen completely and the feet go in the air. As all this goes on on-screen, the studs are watching it and I'm watching them. I walk around to see each of them from all angles, up on the platform above me, and as their erections grow and grow I make my choice.

So I motion to the crew that this one will do, and as they get cameras set for the next filming, I conduct this by-now wildly horny stud to a giant bed which is set up in a curtained studio in a corner of the market, all arranged for this. I get my clothes off, which weren't much anyway, and get the stud on his back on the bed, and I get on top. With my knees one on each side of his waist, more or less, I raise my ass high in the air and get poised right at the top of his cock, and tease it a little. The poor bastard is panting and heaving at this, but we have to get the cameras angled just right: one camera is behind me, one above, others all around. When everything is right, and with all my teasing his erection has become even more gigantic and hard, we begin. First I ease down on his shaft slowly, then up again, down again, up again, now with a little swiveling, then it gets faster and rougher until I'm riding him like a cowboy and he's bucking and we're really fucking up a storm. As we do, up on the giant screen is the multiple-image, split-screen picture of what we're doing, or what we were doing a second or two before, and everybody in the market is back now, all watching the giant screen, and we see it, too, out of the corners of our eyes, and that contributes to the climax, too, when it comes, and when it does the audience applauds. Sometimes we draw it out for a long time, sometimes we come once and then go down on each other to get started again. But in any case it builds up and up, with variations, until, as we race each other to a fantastic finish, the applause builds up and at the end the whole hall is roaring even louder than I am. [Written down on request]

262

Hannah

□ My introduction to Hannah was a letter in which she described what she felt were the most important facts about herself. "I am twenty-three, married (separated), have a baby daughter, and am *bisexual*—love both men and girls!"

When we met, I learned the rest: She is from Wales, as is her husband; both their fathers were coal miners. But they met in London and decided to marry when they learned Hannah was pregnant. She had half wanted to have an abortion, but Harry had strong feelings against it. "He never knew I was bisexual before we were married," says Hannah. "In fact, I never knew it myself, except that I knew I had these kinky thoughts now and then. About other girls." After they were married, Harry and Hannah fell in with a group of young London people who regularly went to parties where sexual partners were exchanged. ("Wife-swapping" would be a provincial description of these parties, since most of the participants, living together or not, were not married.)

"It was at one of these parties that I discovered I was bisexual," Hannah said. "While Harry would only get excited when we'd get home and he'd make me tell him about what other men were like, when he opened a bedroom door once and found me with another girl, he blew up. The idea of other men never made him jealous, only excited. But the idea of competing with a woman drove him up the wall." She left him, and they've been separated for several months. □

I mostly have these daydreams when I'm alone. It puts me off even to have the baby in the room with me. I discovered this when I used to leave her with my mum when I wanted to go away for a week-end. When I got back home, suddenly my whole little flat was different. Just being alone in it made it all so sexy. It's strange, isn't it? After all, what can an infant only a few months old know

263

or see? They don't understand anything yet. But there it was. When I'm alone in the flat is almost my favorite time in the world. I sometimes think I like it so much that I never want to live with a man again. With anyone.

What I like to do is when I come home at night from work, I pull the curtains so that I feel really alone. I turn the radio on to Radio One—the pop station—and I imagine it's a man in the other room, talking to me while he's putting different records on my machine. When I found photos of the best-looking disc jockey in magazines, I'd cut them out and put them in the edge of my mirror. This helps me imagine the man in the next room.

Then I begin taking my clothes off. I even talk back to the man in the other room. I put on a G-string, suspender belt, black stockings, fluffy garters (no bra), a frilly, or see-through, blouse or transparent negligee, no skirt, and a blond wig. First of all, I like to put a Tampax in. Putting in a Tampax is thrilling at any time, but I get an especial thrill when I don't really need it.

I like to walk around the bedroom while I'm getting dressed this way, and imagine the man in the other room. He sounds very cool, just putting these records on and chatting me up as he does through the half-open door, talking away as if he had nothing on his mind but the Beatles or Blood, Sweat and Tears, but all the time I know that he's there, having a fantasy about me in here getting ready for him. I like the idea of his voice sounding so cool and friendly, so relaxed, while all the time I know he's growing an erection like a battleship underneath his trousers, for me. I like to imagine his face—that's when I like to look at the photo—as he walks about the other room, trying to control himself. I like to think that little beads of sweat are breaking out on his face and rolling down his cheeks—he's so impatient, you see, but he knows that if he lets me know how hot he's getting waiting for me, that I'll enjoy it so much I'll just let him wait even longer. I just reach down and give the Tampax a little shove further up when I think of his sweating face.

What gives me another kind of satisfaction is practicing

WOMEN'S SEXUAL FANTASIES

a certain kind of walk when I'm alone and dressed like that. It makes me laugh when I go to the films and see the way they make the girls walk in one of those sexy movies. Girls don't walk like that. But it excites me to see it, even in films—I suppose that's why they do it. So when I'm alone, I practice it. Do you know the way that Maurice Chevalier used to walk—with his arse jutting out just that little bit? I practice that. I imagine that I'm a teen-age girl walking like that—I peer at myself in the mirror; that's when I most like to see myself in a frilly blouse, as if I were in the street, not at home. I think that I'm a young girl, walking past myself, just to turn me on. And I imagine taking this girl home with me. The first thing I do is take off her G-string. (I act this out, while I think about it.) And I find that she's clean-shaven there. (That's how I like to be—white all over.) It makes me very excited, and I imagine myself kissing her on her tiny little white triangle. The girl in this dream is always younger than me, and she half doesn't know what she's doing. She just likes to walk around with her arse stuck out like that because she knows it excites other people, and excites herself. But she doesn't know what to do with the excitement, you understand, until I teach her. So her little white thing is so fragile looking, so vulnerable. I'm dark, you see, and I can imagine my dark hand on that white piece of skin . . . my dark fingers slowly disappearing into all that white flesh . . . just disappearing inside her as if into a white cream jelly. It gives me goose bumps to think about it.

My husband left some of his clothes behind when he was last here, and the other thing I like to do is dress up in them. I especially like to put on his underwear. The fly front just fascinates me. That's when I like to put another Tampax in, through the slit opening, and I try to get it so that it hangs out . . . not all the way in, you know? But the angle is wrong, isn't it? I mean, men have it coming out in front, but the Tampax just points down, and you can't sit down naturally. But it's very exciting, and I imagine that I'm Harry, just dressed in these slit-front shorts, and there's a black man with me. I like the idea of the contrast

265

of color. The black man is really black, and he's covered with sweat, so that he almost shines. It makes my own skin even whiter. I like to imagine that the black man has an enormous prick, and that he's secretly waiting for me to tire of walking around in this special way. He's having a fantasy of his own, you see, of putting that giant prick up my little white arse, but I feel him, and come up behind him while I'm walking around and shove my Tampax right up him, and grab him around the waist, by the balls, so that he can't move without me doing him an injury. Every time he tries to wiggle away, I just give his balls a twist, and finally, he has to give in, and in goes this giant white prick I have, and in the middle, he begins to love it, and he drops down on his hands and knees so that I can get in easier. "Shake it!" I yell at him, and he begins to wiggle his arse in little circular motions to feel it better.

I always enjoy these little games the most because I know that I still have the whole evening and night ahead of me. I don't really have an orgasm when I have these thoughts, but I get very excited and my breathing changes. So I usually have a bath and turn on the telly. It makes me feel so peaceful. I'll tell you something—all this business about orgasms must be a lot of twaddle. I've had orgasms with men—and with girls. But they always leave me feeling a bit on edge, anyway. Exhausted perhaps, but still ready to have another go. But when I have my fantasies, and I take a bath after they're over, I can just drift off into the most peaceful sleep of my life. So somehow they must be more satisfying than the real thing. At least, that's how it seems to me sometimes. [Taped interview]

Sophie

☐ Sophie is eighteen but already has a full and varied sex life. When she was sixteen her parents found out about it and she left home after the subsequent quarrel. She took a bus to Chicago and lives there now on the Near North Side, which is the Chicago equivalent, more or less, of

New York's Greenwich Village. She holds no steady job but finds various things to do when she—or the friends with whom she lives—are out of money. Her job at the moment is shampooing in one of the fashionable new barber shops where both young men and women come to have their hair trimmed and shaped, where loud music plays, coffee is served, and waiting customers may even be dancing. She likes this job and says she has no plans for leaving it at the moment.

Sophie lives communally, as she puts it. An older generation would call it living with two men. It is also typical, I think, of Sophie's generation that she is very aware of her fantasies, and is not only unembarrassed to admit having them or talking about them, but indeed tries to live them out in her life. □

I never had any hang-ups about sex; it was something people did when they felt like it, and so I didn't like it when my family came down on me so heavy about it. I told them they had their scene, I had mine, we didn't have to quarrel. But they insisted that I only make their scene —two-by-two, married—so I split.

It wasn't sex that was my hang-up, but the kind of man I wanted it with. What chick wants to be alone? But all my life, I've always dug two different kinds of guys. The first was always tall and dark and I was never sure that he really liked me. Or anybody else, if you stop to think about it. A hard kind of guy who never took crap from anybody. Naturally, a guy like that, all the girls were after him. Which was all right with him. I remember one. Practically any chick who wasn't a horror could ball him for a night or two, but after that it was all over, and if she cried or told him she loved him, that was tough titty, he just laughed and took a walk.

My other type, Type B, is just the opposite. He's mostly small, and maybe with kind of washed-out blond hair. But good-looking and sad, as if he had TB and wasn't going to live very long. Type A, the rough one, was a school dropout, but Type B was very hipped on books and reading and had all sorts of theories about philosophy . . . about the way the world really is. He has this kind of appeal, you see, he could talk to you, and explain why certain things were happening. He made you feel calm. But his main appeal, of course, was that you wanted to take care of him.

So ever since I started going out with guys, I'm like a grandfather clock, tick tock swinging between these two opposite types, thinking about the one type when I was with the other. But it wasn't ever that clear to me. Until some movie house had a Clark Gable festival and I dug right away that this chick in the picture, *Gone With the Wind*, she was hung-up between Type A and Type B, too. Clark Gable and Leslie Howard. Leslie Howard, Jesus, what a Type B he was, perfect. So when you ask about fantasy, I knew right away that my fantasy wasn't some story I made up myself to get it off better with some guy. Some of the guys I know, they're always reading to you from these books, about lesbians, and eight people going down on each other. But that's all in the mind, it doesn't affect me much. Anyway, it doesn't get me all turned on the way it turns on the men. I don't know what you'd call my own story. It's just the way I live and that's what I think is so exciting for me in the bed scenes.

And the scenes we have! Like, when I'm in the sack with Type A, he'll order B to bring our big portable mirror closer so we can see ourselves better. Or else he tells him to roll some joints for us while we finish, and then the three of us light up and have a friendly smoke afterwards. But all the time I'm making it with A, I know B is there in the room, too, and he's thinking about me, watching out for me, digging that I'm enjoying it, and I'm digging that B is enjoying it, too.

A lot of times I make it with B, too, of course, but it's always different with him. He's not so freaky as A. He likes it when I take the lead. Sometimes, with him, I get the feeling that it's almost like having a baby in bed with me. Once A got mad at something I'd done, and slapped me across the face so hard that I fell down. Then A took whatever loot we had in the house at the moment and split. But B stayed with me, and he was so tender, even trying to explain A's psychology to me, so that I wouldn't hate him so much. He's so cool that he dug it that down beneath, I really liked A so much it would be bad for me to hate him.

Sometimes I get the feeling that B is in love with A. Maybe A thinks so, too. He often calls him "sweetie" or "dearie" or some other faggoty name. In fact, I think the reason B gets so excited when I'm screwing A is because he doesn't know which of us he'd rather be fucking himself, A or me. Or both. In fact, we've tried that, too, a few times. Talk about a chick living in a dream, having the two of them in me at the same time and groping each other, too, all at once. But we don't do it often, because after one of those scenes A gets mad and disappears for a day or two, and I hear that he's balling some other chick somewhere.

So you see, I don't have to make up any stories to turn myself on. I'm really living in one. I don't like the word "fantasy." It sounds like some neurotic thing you're into, and the next thing they're coming for you with the psycho nets. So I wouldn't say I have a fantasy about sex. Or if I do, it's my whole life. [Letter]

Bobbie

I am only fifteen years old, so I don't want to tell you my name, so that I can be sure that my parents won't find out any of this. I saw your questionnaire in one of my big brother's magazines, and I just felt like replying to it because I guess I think about sex quite a bit of the time. I pet with boys a lot, but the only guy I ever tried to go all the way with came before he was able to get his penis into me. I thought you ought to know that so it would help you understand my answers better.

Most of the guys that I have had sex with wouldn't get uptight about knowing that I was thinking about someone else when I was having sex with them. I'm sure that sexy girls who turn them on come into their thoughts, too. Besides, a guy has no right to get angry about what I'm thinking about as long as I'm giving him what he wants.

I masturbate almost every day, and I almost always fantasize when I do. One of my favorites is to think about having a boy who turns me on tied up. He is helpless, and I take down his pants and play with his penis. When he is almost ready to come I stop and just watch him suffer. Then I make him do what I guess is called cunnilingus to me before I finally play with his penis until he comes.

When I pet with boys I like to have them do cunnilingus (I usually just call it eating my pie) to me, and when I masturbate I like to think about guys doing that to me.

Sometimes when I masturbate I play with my nipples and then I like to imagine that a boy is sucking on them.

Lots of the time, I just imagine that a guy is fucking me and that my finger is his penis going in and out of me. I keep doing it until I'm worn out from coming.

One of my weirdest fantasies is about being spanked. I imagine that some guy who really turns me on grabs me, lifts my skirt, takes down my panties, and spanks my bottom until it really hurts. Then when I cry he kisses my bottom all over and does cunnilingus to me.

I have sucked some guys' penises when I've petted with them, and every once in a while I'll think about that when I masturbate. I sometimes suck on my thumb when I try to imagine that.

I guess that the most common thing in all of my fantasies is to think about having the boy under my control and being able to make him do whatever I want him to do to please me. I think about myself sitting on a big chair like a throne with my skirt pulled up and my panties off and the boy is kneeling between my legs doing cunnilingus to me. Sometimes if I really feel devilish I imagine that I pee in his mouth and he has to swallow it. In the fantasies like this the boy's hands are tied so that he cannot touch me except with his mouth. Usually he is naked and sometimes I imagine that I am whipping him when he is kneeling in front of me like that. I usually add to these fantasies in whatever way I feel like at the time.

I have other fantasies, but these are my favorites right now.

A couple of years ago, an older girl and I did mess around together some. Mostly we masturbated each other and I sucked on her nipples some. She was the one who first taught me about cunnilingus, too. When I masturbated myself then I would think about the things she and I did, and I still think about them once in a while now when I masturbate. Mostly I think about the way she used to get so turned on and come so much when I played around with her. Sometimes I like to imagine what it would be like if I did those same things with a younger girl. Also, I like to imagine what it would be like to have a penis like a guy and have sex with a girl.

When I see a guy who turns me on I like to try to imagine in my mind what he would look like standing there naked with his penis erect. It is the thought of his erect penis that stands out in my mind. If a guy like that is looking at me, I imagine that he can see me naked, too. Once in a while, I have the same thoughts about a girl. Sometimes at school when I pass by the boys' rest room I imagine the boys in there with their penises hanging out of their pants. That makes me laugh to myself instead of feeling sexy.

The guys I have sex with don't know my fantasies, but sometimes without them knowing about it I get them to do things that I have fantasized about before then. I enjoy making them kneel in front of me and do cunnilingus to me before I will do anything to them.

I like to imagine myself going all the way with some guy who really turns me on with all my girl friends watching us. I imagine that they get so turned on that they start masturbating themselves and plead for him to have sex with them, but he stays with me. I also like to masturbate while I am listening to rock music. I sometimes imagine that one of the singers is having sex with me in front of a big audience.

I like horses and I sometimes imagine that I am naked and riding bareback on a beautiful thoroughbred horse. I feel bad about thinking such a thing, but I once tried to imagine what it would be like to try to get a horse's big penis into me. That was more like devilish curiosity though.

The only time that I've spoken any of my fantasies out loud was a few times with that older girl that I told you about. Then it got us more turned on.

I am sure that there are other things that I could have told you about if I had remembered them, but I hope that this much will be some help to you.

Peace. [Letter]

Paula

☐ Paula is a lovely, black Haitian, whom I met in Rome. Her current lover, Tony, is a white Englishman. I would say she's in her early twenties. I've left my dialogue with her unedited to illustrate how these interviews generally developed and took form. Paula, as you can see, is no sexual shrinking violet, but she originally refused to contribute to the book, saying she didn't have any sexual fantasies. It was only when I gave her several to read that she exclaimed, "Oh, *that's* a sexual fantasy! Something that makes you feel good."

It's interesting, too, and typical of women when they begin to talk of their fantasies, that they find they have much more to say than they thought. As Paula warms to the subject, she begins to release information, new even to herself, as if she is verbally getting in touch for the first time with up-till-now untapped realms of her self. I don't mean she deliberately withheld information at the start of the interview——having decided to talk, she was genuinely eager to tell all and, in fact, insisted that I use her real name—but I think the depth of her fantasies and their involvement with her real life only became more conscious as she discussed them. As for myself, it wasn't until I was halfway through the interview and beginning to get confused as to what was fantasy and what was fact, that I realized how much Paula's fantasy and real worlds over-lapped; that she, in fact, totally and happily accepted and lived her fantasies. ☐

Q: Have you thought some more about your fantasies since we last talked?

A: Can I read some other people's fantasies, just to see what they're like? What I'm thinking of may not even be a fantasy.

Q: Remember the one you read about the girl fantasizing that a guy is going down on her in a restaurant?

A: When I'm making love I love to think that the guy is fucking another chick, not me.

Q: Where are you, are you in the fantasy, too?

A: I'm in my mind, I mean I know I'm being fucked but I like to think the guy is fucking somebody else.

Q: Anyone in particular, a girl friend . . . ?

A: No. Sometimes girls I used to go to school with, they're the other girls, and I love it so much, what's happening, I know they'd love it too.

Q: They're fucking the guy you're really with? That excites you?

A: That's amazing, you know? To think, when you're making love, that somebody else is getting it, not you. I like sometimes to have another girl in bed with me, I like to get it together, with me and my boy friend, and to have him make love to her, and make love to me. I get extremely jealous, but it turns me on like crazy. The jealousy turns me on . . . how it's being done, just to look at it is fantastic, to look at him fucking someone else.

Q: In your imagination, or in reality?

A: No, in my imagination. I really love it. I think about it when I'm making love. What happens is I get the kinky feeling that I know what *she's* getting. I get really excited, thinking about all the things that she may be thinking about as well . . . like, oh, what a great fuck he is . . . even if she *isn't* having a great fuck, I think, Oh wow, that's really . . . strong.

Q: Do you see yourself in your imagination watching them?

273

A: Oh, yes. When I'm making love my eyes have to be open, even if I'm not really looking at anything. My imagination is so strong, I have to be looking, I have to have my eyes really open. If my eyes are closed, it's no good.

Q: Most people do fuck with their eyes closed.

A: Not me. My eyes have to be open, staring at *that* object *there*. It's really real, it's amazing.

Q: Do you ever feel any jealousy in reality?

A: I get jealous if I think I would be there and just looking . . . but no, I am not jealous, basically. Because I know I'm really getting what she's getting in my mind, and that's such an enjoyment that it helps to stop the big jealous thing. I m jealous, but happily so, because it's so exciting for me to know that she's being fucked, and going crazy; that it's so strong.

Q: What's nice is that you have your eyes open. It shows how close you are to the whole thing.

A: And I actually can see it. The woman can be anyone. Everyone I know comes into my mind. They come and then disappear. I imagine everyone being fucked, everyone I know . . . acquaintances, friends . . .

Q: How about men . . . do you sometimes think of Tony with other men?

A: Yes. When I'm making love I love to see another guy making love to him.

Q: Does that bother Tony?

A: It doesn t bother him, no. I hate a guy to say they don't like me thinking that. I know most guys say they wouldn't really go with another guy. But to say they hate the idea of it, thinking of it . . . I hate a guy to be that way. "Oh," a guy should say, "that's a wild idea, that turns me on like crazy." A guy shouldn't put you down for what you think.

Q: I think many guys feel threatened if you talk about their making it with another guy; they say, "It's one thing for a woman, but quite different for a man" to get into some homosexual number.

A: I know. But if you say it to someone who's really groovy—that you're thinking about him with another guy

—he'll like it, he won't put it down. Which is nice. I love saying it to a guy I really dig, "Oh baby, I'd love to see you with another guy." I always say it if I'm really enjoying myself when we're making love. Even if it never happens, him and the other guy, still it's nice to say it, and if it does happen . . .

Q: Thinking it doesn't mean you want it to happen, or that it has to happen. It's just the thought that it could happen . . .

A: Right. Whenever we make love I like to think that everything can happen, it doesn't matter how dirty or how nasty. It just blows my mind to think that it's possible to do anything. For instance, I wouldn't mind being fucked on a horse. I like to think that it could happen . . . that I was in the front, and someone I really fancied was behind me, and he could just slip it in as we rode off, slip it in and out. It's something I'd love to try. I know it sounds ridiculous.

Q: Nothing sounds ridiculous.

A: But these things do go through my mind. When I go to the polo grounds to watch Tony play, I think, Oh boy, I'd really dig being taken right now, right there on that horse.

Q: Guys on horses, they're a very sexy sight.

A: Very. I asked him once, do you come sometimes when you're riding? And he said, "Nearly."

Q: Do you ever get into any group scenes in your fantasies . . . I mean more than, say, just three of you?

A: Not really. I usually have this major thing about the other girl, the girl in my fantasy, and when she's going to come. This picture's always in my head when I'm making love. It doesn't matter which guy it is, it's not necessarily Tony, but I just like to think that this other girl is feeling what I'm feeling, is getting what I'm getting.

Q: Why do you think this makes you feel more excited?

A: Because the excitement is something I want to share, because I know that some girls would love that kind of excitement, and I like to think that they're having it at the same time. Even if I'm really tired, I just have to open

275

my eyes to watch what's going on in my head. It's like looking at your own imagination.

Q: When you meet an attractive guy, does your mind start to wander?

A: Oh, yes. But I would think that's the most natural thing, to think: I wonder if he's a good lay. Even if it doesn't happen, or couldn't, I think it. Later, maybe that night when I'm with Tony, I'll think about that guy, think that it's him I'm fucking. But that's natural. I'm sure guys do it all the time, fantasize about other chicks when they're making it with their chick.

Q: Are the girls you think about always people you know?

A: It's much more exciting if I know the chick. Say, I haven't seen her for a few days, then when I think about her, wow, it all comes back, the performance. It goes on for days in my mind.

Q: You remember the scene with this girl, a real scene?

A: Right.

Q: I suppose these fantasies of other girls especially happen when the guy's going down on you.

A: Oh, yes. Because then I can open my eyes and see his head, imagine everything, pretend everything. Seeing his head, there, I can see his mouth, too, everything . . . and imagine he's doing this to some other lucky chick, as well as me.

Q: You're a very generous girl, Paula.

A: I never just think about myself when I fantasize. I like to think of lots of people getting what I'm getting, I like to imagine a roomful of people, lots of color, and voices . . .

Q: So many people like to make love with the lights out, under the sheets . . .

A: Oh, no. I like the lights on, my eyes open. I get some of my wildest fantasies when I'm driving.

Q: So that's why you like driving so much.

A: Always, when I'm driving a car, I feel sexy.

Q: I think lots of women feel that. Why do you think it is, women, driving, get that feeling?

A: There's like a whole scene going on sometimes when I'm driving. It's all happening. Most girls when they're driving . . . look at their faces next time you see one. They look very . . . proud. They never look bored, never. A kind of look they have when they're making love, thinking of sex.

Q: Does Tony like to hear about these fantasies? Do you tell him?

A: Oh, yeah. When we're fucking he loves to know what I'm thinking, he'll ask me and say, "Oh, that's beautiful; go on, tell me more."

Q: Many people seem to fuck silently. So many women tell me they wish their guys would talk to them more.

A: It's beautiful when you get someone to talk to you. I love that. Fantastic. I can really lose my mind. It's only half a fuck when you do it silently, it's like you're by yourself. But when a guy's inside you and saying, "Oh baby, I love to fuck you like this," and telling you about how it feels and then I tell him how it feels and what I'm thinking and when he hears that, oh wow, he just fucks me all the wilder. Oh, yes, I love to chat while I'm fucking. It gives me encouragement, makes me want to do even wilder things. If a guy doesn't talk to you while he's fucking you, you don't dare to do certain things. It's like he's cheering you on when he talks. Guys spend a lot of time wondering what chicks are thinking about when they're fucking them . . . I think it worries some of them. But the only way fucking can get better is when you tell them, and they like it. And you've got to say it right, you've got to use the exciting words, you've got to be vulgar, or it doesn't mean anything. Because when you're fucking, you should use fucking words. You've got to be vulgar, really vulgar.

Q: Fucking is not about vaginas and other medical terms, it's about cunts and cocks . . .

A: You're not going to the doctor, are you? You're being fucked. I love to say, "Oh, I'd love to be naughty, darling, I'm thinking such naughty things . . ."

Q: When you think of him fucking another guy, where

are you in your fantasies? Watching? Are you fucking, too?

A: My favorite is that he's fucking me while another guy is fucking him. That way I can imagine what he's feeling, too. It's also like I'm sharing in what he's feeling, like the cock going into him is also going into me, so like there's extra pressure from above. I'm getting two cocks.

Q: When you think about other girls are you in the active role or the passive role?

A: I like to be the aggressive one. Maybe because that way I'm like a guy fucking a chick. I like to be able to think what he's feeling, because what he does to me makes me feel so good. So I think about me doing wild things with these other chicks.

Q: Most women I've talked to say they have had thoughts about other women. They seem to accept this; they don't feel guilty about it.

A: When I see a girl naked, I usually get excited. Then I think, wow.

Q: Wow, you'd like to fuck her, or see her being fucked?

A: Mostly that I'd like to see her legs apart, see her being fucked by some guy.

Q: Your guy?

A: Any guy, mostly my guy. It's exciting. It's the way most girls react to being fucked that excites me. Because my mind is so . . . I can imagine it being so strong, I can almost feel it for them. I think, Oh wow, they're really enjoying it.

Q: And no guilt feelings?

A: Oh, no. When I'm making love I'm not ashamed of anything. If you're ashamed, then your mind's not free to create, and your body's not free either. I think maybe I wouldn't do the things I do when I'm making love if my mind weren't really free to create.

Q: I don't think women *always* fantasize during sex, but to deny that it ever happens, to deny it altogether . . .

A: Oh, you've got to fantasize when the time's right. When I'm fucking, I don't fantasize about the guy I'm

278

with. I know he's doing it. I mean, if I didn't like a guy I wouldn't be fucking him, but the guy in my mind is always someone else. I know it's him inside me, but making it in my mind with another guy at the same time, it's fantastic.

Q: Tell me, what comes first, the fact or the fantasy?

A: The fantasies have always been there, very strong. That's how I knew I would really dig that sort of thing. Ever since I was . . . eleven or twelve.

Q: That's the magic age all right. Did the fantasies change, say, the ones of you and another girl, after you started *really* doing it?

A: No. When I was young I used to sometimes see people making love, and it used to make me feel quite good. I wasn't involved, I was much too young. Well, where I grew up, sometimes people would get careless, forget to close a window or a door, and I'd walk by.

Q: Gee, I wish I'd grown up in a place like that! When you tell Tony your fantasies now, do the two of you sometimes think of making them come true? Like another guy fucking him while he's fucking you?

A: Yes. Anything I tell him, my fantasies, are all things I'd really like to have happen. Like, say we're at a party and feeling very good. Suddenly we both begin thinking this is the night we will get it together. I'll say, "Oh Tony, I'd love to have a scene with that chick." He'll automatically say, "Why don't you get it together?" Recently there was this American girl staying with me, and Tony and I came home very late one night. I'd never had any kind of scene with this girl before, and Tony really didn't fancy her, but he was enjoying our scene, him and me, so much, and I said, "Come on, darling, let's get it together," so I called to this chick to come join us. He enjoyed himself like crazy that night. I don't think she'd ever been in a scene like that before, but she really enjoyed it, she never stopped talking about it. She wanted it every day after that. But Tony didn't want it again. He didn't really fancy her, it was just that that night he was already excited and he'd got so turned on listening to me talking about my fantasies.

Q: How about with another guy?

A: Only recently. Once I got him so excited one day talking about it, that the following night, there was a guy who was always trying to get him, that we actually had a scene with him. I don't think Tony was very pleased in the end, because it's not his scene, he likes chicks too much. But he said I'd turned him on so much about it, he thought he should try it.

Q. Are you more turned on with guys?

A: Oh, yes. Guys more than chicks . . . but it all depends.

Q: Generally, I think women can handle both sexual scenes, even just thinking about them, with much less anxiety than men. They don't seem to be threatened by their fantasies of other women.

A: No, I don't think chicks feel threatened by it. Girls . . . there's something sort of innocent and beautiful for them in that sort of scene. They think of it as beauty rather than vulgar, or disgusting. And if they really do get into a sexual scene together, they are very natural about it.

Q: Do you still fantasize about Tony and that guy he made it with?

A: Oh yeah, but I don't talk to him about it, because I know he really doesn't want to do it again. But I think about it. I go back through recent scenes all the time when we're making love, even if he wasn't with me at that particular scene. I love going back over the particulars of a scene even while I'm in a new scene. It makes it all so fantastic. I even fantasize when I'm in bed alone. I love it. I get excited all over again.

Q: Did any guy ever put you down for your fantasies, for telling him?

A: Oh, no. I've never found any guy who doesn't like someone being as naughty as I am. The way I say it, tell my fantasies, they're so beautiful, no one in his right mind would put me down for them.

Q: When you were talking about jealousy earlier, you said it excited you. What did you mean by that?

A: For instance, if there's a girl in the room who I

think Tony would like to make it with, a girl I'm jealous of, then I start thinking about making it with her. I'd like to say to him the next day, "I fucked that girl." It would annoy him, but it would satisfy me. Even if he went with her after that, I wouldn't feel too bad because the conquest would really have been mine to start with. But that's only because of jealousy; if it weren't for the fact that he wanted to fuck her, the thought wouldn't have occurred to me.

Q: Do you sometimes want these jealousy fantasies of making it with the other girl to come true?

A: Oh, yes. Sometimes I'll really get it together, me, the other chick, the one I'm jealous of, and Tony. These scenes, I really enjoy them, but even during them I still feel jealous. But the jealousy excites me, too. I mean, if I've been jealous earlier in the evening, and then Tony and I are in bed, I get excited because of the jealousy . . . even though I hate being jealous. Maybe I'll fantasize that the chick is also with us. I know most chicks, normal people, get very aggressive when they're jealous, but me, I just become quiet, almost passive, and wildly sexy.

Q: If you know Tony is fucking some other girl, and you're not in on it, you're not there, how do you feel about it?

A: I fantasize what's going on. If you know the person very well, you can imagine everything. I get an almost satisfaction thinking of their movements, it excites me, and I think, Oh, wow. I feel jealous, but I know he'd like me to be there, too . . . and I imagine myself with them. I imagine him thinking of me while he's fucking her and in a way I am there. Can you understand that?

Q: Are your fantasies of black girls as well as white girls?

A: No, I never fantasize about black girls. They don't come into my mind at all. If you're going to fantasize, it's always the opposite you think about. Except when I was at home, of course, because there weren't any white girls there.

Q: Do people in your fantasies dress strangely, wear

281

masks, or do the fantasies take place in strange surroundings?

A: No, I always just think of them nude. And it's always in bed. A bed that I know. And my fantasies are always in color, never black and white.

Q: Some people, if they want to really do something wild while they're fucking, they have to fantasize about it first.

A: Sometimes, not always, I really *need* my fantasies to get me started, I can't get turned on without them. Maybe some people, they only have to be touched and they get sexy. But I really doubt that most people can think about absolutely nothing and get sexy.

Q: If it's somebody totally new, maybe then you get instantly turned on.

A: But if it's somebody you've fucked a lot though, even if he is the greatest fuck in the world, I still think it helps to fantasize . . . in the beginning, you understand, just to get you started. Sometimes I get turned on thinking about the wild things *he* must be thinking while he's fucking me.

Q: Do you think men fantasize as much as women do, especially in bed?

A: No, I think men often depend on the woman to start things going. If a woman, for example, can just relax and confide in her man and tell him about her fantasies, it really turns him on. The other night, we were in bed, and I knew he was still thinking about his work, that he wanted to fuck, but his mind was preoccupied. He even said, "I'm too tired." I said, "You're not tired." And he just had to look at me to know what was going through my mind, because I'd told him of my fantasies so often. He could tell from a look that I was into one of them and suddenly he was into it, too. That's why women really should tell their guys what goes on in their minds. It could change their lives. [Taped interview]

FANTASIES THAT SHOULD
BE REALITY

☐ The content of a fantasy, what happens, is not the clue to whether or not it should be acted out. (Always excepting, of course, obviously dangerous or physically damaging notions like playing Russian Roulette in bed, etc.) What may sound ugly, even horrific, to you or me may mean sexual satisfaction to the woman who thought it up. In the end, she's the only one who knows whether a fantasy should stay where it is—in her mind—or whether living it would add something to her life. Where women seem to get confused is in thinking that accepting their fantasies means putting them into action, and that unless they do, they're sexual hypocrites.

But accepting your fantasies can mean just that, and end right there; there's nothing that says you've only gone halfway if you don't act them out. Fantasy has no *Hoyle's Book of Rules*.

What must be clear, however, to anyone who's read this book is how many of the fantasies in it *should* be part of a woman's real life. How many fantasies are sexual desires for things any woman has a natural right to. And this right may go beyond the satisfactions ordinarily understood by saying a woman is married, or has a lover, or even that she is sexually satisfied. Because, after all, what they want is so simple that it is a mystery to me why a woman is afraid to ask. What it means, I suppose, is that women just don't talk, not even to their lovers, don't express their desires, whether through shyness or fear. This fantasy is typical, except that its surprise ending makes it even more poignant. ☐

Martha

I am a married woman of thirty-four. I would like to tell you about my sexual fantasy. My own fantasy has a true base on which I build. About eleven years ago, before I was married, but was engaged, I went out a number of times with a married man with whom I worked. This was no "love" affair. It was purely sexual.

Although I made it regularly with my boy friend, this man really excited me. We were lucky that we had a room to go to and didn't have to make it in the back of a car. First we would undress completely. He would always have the most incredible erection. He would fondle, kiss, and suck my breasts. He would caress my bottom and smack it. He would play with my clitoris and insert his fingers up me. Then he would suck my clitoris and insert his tongue in me. During all this I never used to touch his penis. He would concentrate wholly on me, making me cry with excitement, and he would talk to me, the language of lust: "Oh, you beauty, you lovely little cunt, those lovely soft hairs I'm going to bury my cock against them, right up your cunt. I'm going to fuck you, fuck, fuck, fuck you, and I'm going to wet all those hairs with my come, and after that you are going to suck it for me, all of it."

Then he would insert his fingers up my bottom and suck me to orgasm. While I was still crying with pleasure he would put his huge penis in me and with my legs around his waist would fuck me to at least two orgasms. He would still not have come yet, and would have an erection like an iron bar. He would push it against my lips until I opened my mouth and took it in and I would suck it. He was capable of withholding his ejaculation for as long as he wanted. Still not having come, he would take it out of my mouth and I would caress it with my hand, wrapping my fingers round it. Suddenly he would roughly grab my legs, put them onto his shoulders and force his cock into me

284

again and work hard and fast. Then he would come, and I would feel his warm semen spurting.

That then is my sexual fantasy. It never actually happened. I did have an affair with this married man, but most of the rest is just a daydream. [Letter]

ACTING OUT FANTASIES, PROS AND CONS

□ While only the woman herself knows whether acting out her fantasy would enrich her life, even knowing herself isn't a guarantee that what worked in fantasy is going to work as well in reality. It's a gamble; some women have told me that just talking about their secret desires—forget about living them—was not only disappointing, but ruined the effectiveness of the fantasy forever.

Some of the spine-chilling fantasies described back in the Pain and Humiliation Rooms at the House of Fantasy are enough to turn anyone off the idea of making their "dreams" come true. Luckily, the women who have these frightening sexual images usually say they have no real desire for the "Ouch!" treatment and would run a mile to avoid any real pain. Their gory fantasies would seem to be similar to the horrific, but beneficial, nightmares dreamed at night. (But if your nightmare fantasies aren't therapeutic—if they frighten you, not with the delicious thrills of a Dracula movie, but instead tempt you to find your own real-life monster—a little professional help might be in order.)

Women who see no conflict whatsoever in their fantasies, who want to get closer to them rather than further away, look around them and see everything changing and everything being tried; from films, magazines, and billboards, it seems life itself is full of fantasy, getting closer to each other every day; why not merge her life with her

285

fantasy? Here are some interviews and letters from women who've had various degrees of success at doing just that. ☐

Sylvia

I've been married for twenty years, have two children, and I've just celebrated my forty-second birthday. Both my husband, a newspaperman, and I have college degrees; we are middle-class people.

Years ago, discussing dreams and fantasies with my husband, we confessed to each other that we did, indeed, think of others during sex. Further, like many of my friends, I find it somewhat of a relief during the course of a hectic day to masturbate and fantasize about the red-haired producer and writer for television who is a neighbor of ours.

But I've had disappointing results in actually experiencing my fantasies. They both sort of just happened. The first had to do with a lesbian fantasy that's vague, in fact more just random thoughts about what it would be like ... after all, who knows women's vital sexual areas better than other women? Well, a few years ago a close friend paid me a surprise visit early one morning. Since I had not had the time to finish dressing, she caught me in my dressing gown. As we sat on the divan and had coffee, she gradually worked herself closer to me. That's when I began thinking about my fantasy, and wondering if this was it. But before I could decide if I even wanted it, like a bolt out of the blue she suddenly reached over and started fondling my breasts. I started to admonish her for such behavior, but she was not to be denied and gradually lowered her face onto my lap. I confess that while it was quite a shock at first, I wondered to myself whether she would be as good with her tongue as my husband (and a couple of other males I know) or as exciting as some of the lesbian scenes so prevalent in today's films. Did you see *The Conformist?*

Well, sadly she wasn't. She did bring me to a climax,

286

masturbating with her hand. I can still see her doing it. Fortunately, she has moved away. I really could never have brought myself around to seeing her again.

The other incident has to do with what I am sure must be a prevalent female fantasy: the male Negro and his reputed size and talent. This happened during the last presidential contest. My husband was called to Washington to cover some Senate hearings. During his absence, I attended a dinner party which brought together two presidential hopefuls and a group of pseudointellects (forgive me). One young Negro, well groomed and with a Ph.D. in political science, spent most of the evening with me discussing subjects from sales to sex. He offered to drive me home. By now, the fantasy had begun to play through my mind, and wondering what he was like sexually, I had already begun thinking about whether I wanted to find out. During the drive he pulled into a parking lot and proceeded to make advances. Of course you know what happened: he took out of his trousers his very hard and pulsing penis which he placed in my hand. I was actually holding it, this thing I'd imagined so often. He pleaded with me to let him "go down on you," and before I knew it, I was lowering my briefs and pantyhose. He ate as though it was his last meal. Fortunately, the children were away at school, and so I thought it best that we drive to my home and continue the action there. I'm not one who can relax in a sedan.

I don't know if Charlie was any representative of his race, but he was a *lousy* fuck. It was my first and last experience with the other race. But I shall never forget the experience. I thought it would also be the end of the male Negro as a fantasy for me, but I find it hasn't finished the fantasy, it's changed it. I may not do it again but I'll always remember it . . . in a way. One more thing: he begged me to suck him off—which I had done in fantasy —but which I naturally refused to do. I admit his instrument was mighty handsome to see and to hold, but beyond that, his sexual talents were zero. Incidentally, a close friend of mine also had intercourse with a black, and she, too, agreed that their sexual prowess is just so much baloney. It is a status symbol, I fear. Women would be smart to stick to their fantasies.

So, there's my story. I hope that it has been enlightening. Of course we mortals dream . . . for that is what life is all about. [Letter]

Babs

My fantasies are so personal, and the pleasure I get from them derives so much, I think, from the fact that they are private and locked away in my imagination, that I wouldn't dream of trying to make them come true. I've thought a lot about this, especially after writing this letter. I almost didn't write it for fear of diminishing this pleasure; I was afraid that putting them on paper would lessen their effectiveness. Luckily it hasn't, perhaps because I don't know you. I mean, if someone, even a close friend, asked me to speak them aloud so that the words actually made sound for someone to hear, I don't think I could do it. And if I could, it certainly would spoil them for me, especially the ones involving love. But act my fantasies out? Make them come true? No, absolutely not. My real life's not what they're about; I don't want those things to really happen to me, I simply want to imagine what it would be like. So that's where they'll stay. [Letter]

Elizabeth

I am twenty-five years of age and have spent most of my life in Kansas City. My husband and I have been married nearly five years and we have a son four years old. I am a college graduate, interested in painting and music, and after graduation I spent a short time working as an actress in summer stock. My present job is that of a telephone solicitor. Good luck in your research. Here goes.

Usually during sex I concentrate on what I'm doing and who I'm with. However, I sometimes fantasize that I am with an old boy friend or a complete stranger, that another man in addition to my husband is making love to me. There is a friend of my husband's with whom I once had a sexual encounter (at my husband's urging) and I often imagine him as the extra man. This fantasy happens when my husband and I are having anal intercourse. While I am stimulating my clitoris or my husband stimulates it for me, I pretend that the other man and I are enjoying vaginal intercourse while I'm having anal intercourse with my husband at the same time.

I sometimes think about the other women I know my husband has been with and wonder if he did the same things to them and how they reacted. I imagine that I am he, making love to one of these women. Also, when I am blowing my husband I try to imagine how it feels to have a penis with someone sucking it or tickling it with her tongue. I can almost feel the semen being sucked out when I would (when he does) obtain orgasm. I thoroughly enjoy my fantasies and find talking about them increases the excitement.

My husband encourages me to fantasize and urges me to describe my fantasies to him. He becomes very aroused, for instance, if I tell him that I masturbated that day and describe to him what I was thinking about while I masturbated. I have even at times told him of some of my fantasizing while we were making love. Any verbalization of this kind adds to his excitement. He has at times asked me to pretend he was an old lover and to describe my feelings and reactions. I have also asked my husband to pretend I am someone else while making love to me. I have once or twice pretended I was a boy and asked my husband to pretend the same while balling me anally. But although it excites him to hear me telling him my fantasies while we're making love, he later becomes depressed at the thought of what I've been thinking. He asks to hear my fantasies, but later I'm afraid they repel him; he becomes disgusted with himself for becoming excited by that kind of thing. All in all, I think I've decided

to keep my very pleasurable fantasies to myself in future.
[Letter]

Winnie

Okay, here goes . . . (I may have to go and masturbate
before I can finish this, as my mind goes blank.)

I have often thought it would be very yummy (and now
that I think of it, very messy, too) if somebody would pee
inside me (depends on who's washing the sheets). I never
had this actually occur, but often thought about it and
talked about it to men who seem to think it might be impossible. It is impossible—why? think I—because they
can't pee and have a hard-on at the same time? I suppose
this is destined to remain a fantasy, unless I can find some
physical wizard.

Also, I've been thinking about something and can't remember if I talked to you about it when we met: I recently was wondering if it isn't unpleasant to have all of your
fantasies played out and then you don't have any more.
See what I mean? Like . . . if a person does all those things
she thinks she would like to do, where will she get any
more fantasies? Just a thought. [Letter from a friend]

Loretta

The most significant thing I have discovered about my
fantasies is that they are far more exciting as fantasies
than as reality. I speak from experience. Carrying them
out was a disappointment. The fantasy was, in truth, more
exciting than doing it. I shall say no more than that my
fantasy was to be dominated, to be tied up. [Letter]

Sheila

I was left a divorcee with two daughters at the age of

twenty-five, and after a while I began having fantasies about young boys. I used to imagine them in bed with me, dressing and undressing me and all sorts of peculiar things, such as kissing me on the vaginal lips. It made me masturbate and also wear very sexy underclothes.

I used to picture the newsboy who delivered my papers having an affair with me. Then one day one of my daughters got lost and the newsboy eventually found her, and as a result a friendship started between us. Sometimes when he came to visit us he would sit in a chair opposite me. Staring at him "there"—as I was facing him—I used to imagine what his penis was like. Then one night after we had all gone to the pictures and the girls were in bed, he and I sat on the settee. Suddenly the urge came over me and I asked him if he was fond of me. I felt his hand moving under my dress, and before long one of my fantasies was realized and I actually found that his penis was in excess of what I had imagined. After two years we were married, even though I am twelve years older. We are very happy and have three children, one of which was the result of the night we came home from the pictures.

Fantasies tend to keep one going. I certainly enjoyed them, but the real thing is even more enjoyable. [Letter]

Claudine

My most exotic and rewarding masturbatory/copulative fantasy has remained a constant throughout my sex life, and this from the age of perhaps seventeen or eighteen when masturbation managed to find its way into my life more or less regularly every day for about two years. Where this fantasy comes from is still a mystery, but it has very often influenced my choice of lovers, and within the boundaries imposed by society on those relationships in which the fantasy has become a reality, I have truly been "living" my dream on several occasions.

It is possible that the Scorpio/Sado-Masochistic/Florence Nightingale superfuck that I imagine myself to be on

291

these noble occasions is a giant myth, but my ability to make it seem real is very unmythical, and it is in that way I manage to bring myself off to its sweet music each time it rears its lovely head.

The aberration explained away, I may now be capable of explaining the fantasy with the lucidity it demands.

I like gangsters. When I was a teen-ager, the masturbatory stories I told myself had to do with a sort of Mafiachief type of fatso who hired girls or even had them captured by his henchmen for his pleasure. Since all of the masturbation I ever do, or did, was clitoral and I then thought that was blatantly abnormal, the sequence of my fantasy is rather important.

These henchmen types would have me on a table and I never had the chance to do much talking. I was being masturbated in this artificial clitoral way to a peak of excitement which was designed to turn the gangster guy on when he actually poked his head through the door and suddenly got a whopping hard-on from seeing me ready to come. Needless to say, he always had a very big cock. He was dressed but would show me his hard-on because the boys told him I liked big cocks. He would then say that he wanted me to be brought off, because he didn't want to enter an "uncome" cunt. That gave me an excuse for having my orgasm, and that was usually the end of my story and I went to sleep.

Now . . . there are variations on this theme which have had to be dealt with throughout the years. This dangerous character of whom the whole world is obviously scared shitless sometimes comes through the door of the room where I am being masturbated to readiness by the "boys," and when he sees me and talks to me he decides he really thinks I am just the grooviest chick he has ever seen or met, and that I have the most delicious-looking pussy around, so he tells the guys to lay off and he fucks me good and proper and likes it and tells me that I will be his permanent old lady and get to have him every Thursday, for which I shall be handsomely rewarded. The boys are very surprised by this because the big boss never turns on to chicks, and they even stop to remind me that I am just about the luckiest girl in the world.

Aside from this variation, there are other things that occasionally swim into the scene. Sometimes he likes me enough to avoid entering me because his cock is so enormous as to have actually been rejected by many, many ladies, and he feels a little nervous about the possibility of hurting such a sweetie-pie as myself. I reassure him a lot and tell him it's perfectly dandy if he wants to enter me before I come because I can handle it. (I-am-a-champ sort of thing.) He's usually reluctant, but tells me that he will try it out first after I have come and am relaxed and wet enough to accommodate him, but that maybe next Thursday if we find it comfortable the first time . . . again this gives me the excuse I need to bring myself off with my hand and not introduce objects of unimportance into my vagina.

Anyway . . . this gangster guy is my friend and he would never hurt me but he hurts lots of other people 'cuz he's really a killer meanie. But . . . I am a nice chick and nobody would want to spoil such an adorable number as me. He used to be called "Joe," but sometimes now he is called by the name of whatever current lover is absent from my own scene and whose memory I am trying to call up.

I have had three gangster lovers in my real life, and all of them have been excellent lovers and fallen quite nicely into my preformed image of what a good gangster should be, i.e., they might be murderers on the outside but they would never hurt me. I never have bothered to tell any of them about this fantasy because they have all acted the part so well without a script.

I have gone off gangsters recently in both real and fantasy life, and have entered a period of recalling another fantasy which blows my mind sufficiently during times of extreme stress to enable me to have orgasms with myself: I imagine there are ten or twelve men in a sort of amphitheater who are being taught how to make a girl have orgasms. They all have to listen carefully to the nice man who is in charge of the lesson and who is showing them how to get girls to like them better. I get to be screwed by the one of these callow types (after I have come) who pleases me the most and whose cock is the hardest.

Boy, this really sounds stupider on paper than it ever does in my head, but I guess that's what fantasies are all about. Aside from the two fantasies I have mentioned, I have the eternal doctor-examiner, gynecological, freak-out number, and the very occasional recourse to horse or dog trips. In the main, though, doctors and horses I can do without. Generally speaking, it does not interest me much to carry out my fantasies in real life, as mostly when I have tried it has been a disappointment; morally and socially I can't go hanging around with gangsters all my life. [Letter]

Jocelyn

My fantasies have always concerned animals and nothing else. Ever since I was a teen-ager, the sight of dogs copulating or a horse in a field with his penis hanging down has excited me tremendously.

I am now divorced but have a lover, and most times when we make love I imagine it is the penis of a large dog or horse that is entering me, or a dog licking me and hordes of dogs all screwing madly. This really turns me on. I don't know why this should be or why it is only dogs and horses. My lover knows about this and likes to talk about it, but he does not understand either. While we are making love he says, "Don't you wish I were a large Alsatian or that this was a stallion's penis between your legs?"

When visiting a friend some time ago, his very large German Wolfhound was sitting beside me on the sofa when the pink tip of his penis began to appear, and this excited me so much I had to leave immediately. I dreamed about this dog for weeks afterwards.

I have never owned a dog, and much as I would like to I would be afraid of what might happen if I did get one. I am sure I would not be able to leave it alone, so I prefer to stick to my fantasies, which I really enjoy, and so I shall never buy a dog.

Another fantasy which I have, but which does not turn me on so much as the animal one, concerns a colored girl. My lover talks to me as he is stimulating me, asking me to imagine he is a young, slim, black girl and she is licking me, or that I am licking her and her creamy juices are pouring into my mouth. Although I have never had any homosexual experiences, I once saw a picture in a magazine of two girls, one white and one black, stimulating each other. Again, it was the little pink tip of the black girl's clitoris which got me excited, and it is this that I think about when I fantasize about a colored girl.
[Letter]

SHARING FANTASIES

☐ A sexual fantasy shared with an accepting, encouraging lover. What can I add? Like sex itself, it's more fun for two. ☐

Lynn

My fantasies during sex usually involve one or more men; whatever we are doing, there is invariably a group of people present, watching. In both fantasy and real life, I am an exhibitionist. I enjoy having men look at the crotch of my trousers, swim suit, or pantyhose. My husband knows of my fantasies, and encourages them. He also knows of my masturbation, which he considers heightens my sexuality. During masturbation, my fantasies are usually exhibitionistic. Before I was married I did have occasional lesbian fantasies, but no longer do.

If in real life I sit with my legs apart to show my crotch, in my fantasy it changes so that I'm wearing just a mini-

dress with nothing on underneath, and sitting wide-legged
so that I show my genitals. My husband is very understanding about my needs and encourages and helps me in
my fantasies. I give him a better time this way. For instance, he will kiss and suck my genitals for an extended
time so that I can fantasize about other men without any
vocal interruption from him. When I am ready, I will indicate to him and he will move up and put his penis in. He
will say, "Have you been fucked today?" and I will say,
"Yes, three men fucked me at the office," and he will ask
me if I showed my cunt on the way to the office, and I will
tell him I sat in the train with my legs apart so the men
could see. It's a game we play together and both get a big
kick out of this.

Here is my favorite fantasy:

It is evening. We are going to a party and I am in the
bedroom dressing. I put on a sling bra, then a short tunic
dress, and nothing else but shoes (I have a beautiful tan).
I stand in front of the mirror raising my arms so that my
dress lifts well above my cunt. We arrive at the party,
where there are about six couples, all handsome or beautiful, the men with tight trousers, the girls are all fully
dressed as far as their tits and crotches are concerned. I sit
down and enjoy knowing the men are looking up my skirt.
I stand up and bend over to pick up something from the
floor. I feel hands on my hips. I stay as I am and feel a
great penis go into me. I do not look around and he carries
on until he has finished. Then another man takes me and
lays me on the settee and fucks me. They all take turns in
different positions while the others watch. But none of the
other couples have sex. Eventually we leave. It is a warm
evening and we walk along with my husband's arm around
my waist. This pulls my skirt up enough so that men passing can see my cunt. We come to a grassy patch beside the
road and I pull my husband down to the ground so that he
is on his back. I take his penis in my mouth and then
mount him and we fuck in full view of the passersby. If I
had been fucking with my husband while having this fantasy we would now have reached the point where I would

be telling him of what was happening in my fantasy and that he was the man doing it so that we could work up to a wonderful finish. [Letter]

Jacqueline

It has taken me some time to write to you, even after consulting my husband, who had been in favor of my doing so since we first read your letter. The reason for my not making up my mind earlier was because of the results of my fantasies, and not so much because I practiced them. Whether you will find them surprising or shocking, only you, of course can say.

I am forty-two and have been married for twenty-five years, and have four children now grown up. Our sex life was, we think, reasonably satisfactory, except that I thought, for a long time, that something was missing, and that it was often rather humdrum.

About a year ago my husband apparently guessed this —probably from my attitude at times to sex, and also (and far more likely, I think) because he came to realize more and more that he could not give me enough to satisfy me. He had asked me often if he did have enough for me, and usually I said that he had—partly because I did not want to make him feel inadequate, and also, in retrospect, I am sure that I knew once I really started thinking of another man giving me more, that it would so obviously show in my reactions that my husband would notice, and might take serious exceptions to another man fucking me, even if it was only in my imagination. But one night, when he was trying to fuck me himself, he suddenly said that it was not of much use, and that I had become far too large for him to manage; that he could put what he had right into me without me feeling it and that what I now wanted was a man who was able to give me a thicker penis.

I amazed myself with my reaction to this, and he obviously felt it, because he then proceeded to talk to me about it, and we had the most wonderful fuck. I admitted to him that I had often imagined other men on top of me, and I even let him know which men I had imagined doing it. He became very worked up over my fantasies, and started going through our acquaintances, noting my variations in reactions as he mentioned their names. He knew I had a soft spot for at least two of them—his cousin and my sister's ex-husband—and we both reached a fantastic climax together, both imagining that I was being fucked by his cousin. He even made me call him by his cousin's name.

Having experienced this, we then of course practiced it more and more, and after about two weeks, during which time he had fucked me more than ever before, we were in bed one Sunday afternoon, which was about a week before we were going away on a holiday with his cousin and wife. This afternoon my husband was taking no precautions, as he normally did; he wanted to put it in bare, and he told me why once he had it in: this time he told me that when we were on our holiday he wanted it to be what he termed "a holiday of fucking," now that he had discovered how much nicer everything was, and that he wanted me to let his cousin fuck me if the opportunity arose. His idea being that if he put his cock into me bare, it would be reasonable, should I do as he suggested and let his cousin also fuck me, that if I became pregnant I could say that the baby was my husband's. He wanted me to agree to this and also to expose myself to his cousin, so I could find out what another man could do for me. Being miles away from home, he said, no one would know, and if I liked it, then there would be ample opportunity to enjoy it to the full, and as often as I wanted to.

By this time, of course, I was so worked up that I held him close to me with my legs around his back and for the first time in years I felt his come shoot right into me, as I promised to try what he had suggested. During that week before we went away, he rode me several times each night, and as I took his come every time, he could not say that if I was pregnant that it was not his.

He made certain that I was well-shaven before we went

on our holiday, and now I began to really feel like my husband did; I was far more ready to wear even shorter skirts and no panties, and found no difficulty in doing this once we got to Italy. We experimented to find out how I could expose myself without being too blatant, even though I knew in my heart that his cousin would not need much encouragement. We found it was easy for me to show what I had—bearing in mind that my cunny was absolutely bare, and that my slit would show clearly—and as soon as I found his cousin taking more interest and more liberties with me than ever, it was not long before we could slip away to our room and I was able to find out what another man was like.

The experience was something out of this world, and far better and easier than I had imagined. I also found that there are men with tools that can still open a woman, even after they have had several children, and I would have been content to have lain there for hours, watching myself being opened and really fucked. Although he was quite a lot bigger than my husband, it was not just this that gave me great satisfaction, it was the variation, and the different ways we did it—mostly with me lifted on pillows, but also often from the rear—a position I had not thought I liked, nor often indulged in. But with this man it took on a different meaning.

The history is that during that holiday I enjoyed both these men regularly and to such an extent that I was probably fucked more during those two weeks than in any year previously. My husband also enjoyed every moment, and what was surprising to me, even though he suggested it, was how much he liked to talk about it—to talk about me having had his cousin, and the fact that another tool had been in between my lips added spice, so that I had to promise him to continue our experiment. My sister's ex-husband was now brought into it, and I had to promise that I would take him if he showed interest after we got back home. Since he had parted from my sister he had lived alone in his house, and my husband now suggested that we ask him to come live with us.

We invited him after we got home from Italy, and he was put in a bedroom through which we had to go to reach ours; it was proposed by my husband that if things worked out, he would go on to bed earlier, and that I could then go to bed with my brother-in-law on the way to our own room. My husband could then enter me, immediately after I had taken my brother-in-law.

This also turned out as we had thought it might, but in this instance I really found out why my brother-in-law had parted from my sister. He was large enough to put off most women, particularly those who had not had children, as my sister had not, and I found my fullest satisfaction in having some difficulty in taking him, and in being stretched after years of being told I was too large. When I got into bed afterward with my husband, it was obvious to him what I had taken, and of course this gave him even more pleasure to insert his own tool only a minute or two after in the same place where I had just taken this larger tool.

I realize that this letter may not be exactly what you asked for, as in the main, it is an account of actions that followed *after* fantasies and not what occurred during them, but I would hope that you may be able to obtain some information from it. The point I would try to make is that it has benefited both my husband and myself. Him, because he is so much more a superior lover now than before, and quite frankly, I feel no regret or feeling of shame. [Letter]

Doris

My fiancé is writing this letter as I speak. This should give you some idea of how open we are with one another. I am nineteen years old and we are soon to be married.

My fantasies during intercourse and masturbation are always of him; he is always present in them. It is only during foreplay that I sometimes think of another man, in particular a man I work with. I imagine various situations that I have been in with him, but these thoughts end when I have intercourse, probably because I have never had intercourse with him.

Even when I think of another woman, my fiancé is present in my fantasies. He is usually watching as the woman goes down on me, or me on her. In reality, this would give us both a great deal of pleasure. In fact, anything I think sexually seems to turn him on. We don't talk too much during sex, but I do like him to tell me at the outset that he is going to "fuck me." Words like this can add a lot.

When I was about eleven years old, there was a rather good-looking young man, about twenty, who lived next door. Some weekends he used to have his girl friend come stay with him. In the evenings I could hear him in his bedroom with her—clearly the wall between our houses was not that thick. It did not take much imagination to know what they were doing, even for an eleven-year-old. My fantasy was very straightforward. I would simply imagine that he was doing, whatever it was, to me instead of her. I would lie there for hours listening through the wall and wishing I were in her place. I would never go to sleep till all was quiet next door. To this day I remember their lovemaking noises.

The only fantasy I've been able to put into practice has been one that indulges my exhibitionist tendencies. With my fiancé's encouragement, I will sometimes leave off my panties when I am wearing black stockings and a garter belt. With my mini-length skirts, it is not difficult to subtly reveal myself in public places. Later, I repeat all of this in great detail to my fiancé. I wouldn't think of leaving him out of my fantasies; having him involved or telling him about them heightens everything for me. Even when indulging in my favorite lesbian fantasies, I like to have him there watching, or in reality talking to me. [Letter]

Bonnie

I just recently became aware of my fantasies. I fantasize

301

far more about black men than white; they appeal to me more sexually. But this is not just fantasy; my husband is black. The only other man I balled more than once was white, and I rarely felt satisfied with him. Since I am very satisfied with my husband, I would imagine that this has much to do with my preference for black men in my fantasies. I should add that up until last night, the men in my fantasies were always anonymous.

In my fantasy last night—I've never had one like it before—the person I found myself fantasizing about was one of the three pastors at the church my husband and I attend. My husband is a student pastor at this church, and this man is his advisor. Physically, the man is not my ideal at all. My ideal is tall and slender (my best friend would call it "skinny"), whereas this pastor is no taller than myself, perhaps shorter, and stocky. He is middle-aged, which also hasn't before appealed to me. But last night was the first time the anonymous lover in my fantasy has ever been given an identity.

I do have another strange fantasy in which I walk into a store which deals exclusively in sexual aids and accessories —dildos, false breasts, sucking apparatus, etc. My desire is to buy a "mouth," though I never really picture what it would be like, just what it would feel like. [Letter]

Jessie

My husband and I do talk during sex, especially when he is feeling me. But the best sessions we have are when we both imagine that we are giving an exhibition on anything to do with sex. I usually strip while my husband lies on the bed describing every detail of me. I stand in front of our large mirror and have to do what he says. The language we use on these occasions really excites me. I end up caressing my titties and masturbating. When he strips, I part his legs and take the penis in my mouth. We have a session of oral sex, then we rub oil over each of us and go through a pattern of different positions. Rear entry in front of the mirror is best. Then we can see how we look to our imaginary audience and I can see it in me and also play with my clitoris, which by this time is really on end. [Letter]

Esther

I am fifty years old, and my husband is fifty-four. We have two children, both married. We are both college graduates, and my husband has an above-average income, which permits us to travel quite extensively. Since I was about twenty-eight, we have enjoyed a very active and varied sex life. My husband (I will use the name Bill) approves of all my sex activities, whether participating, assisting, or merely looking on. He would never be jealous or angry at anything I might tell him, if it enhanced my sex feeling. He insists that I mention the fact that my body is firm and trim, with about the same weight and measurements I had at thirty. We both believe that lots of sex is the best figure control a woman can practice.

I do not often fantasize during coitus with Bill, but it does happen on occasion. We vocalize a lot, giving directions, telling each other how it feels, etc.

I fantasize continuously while I masturbate. I conjure up many images at different times, depending how I am doing it. My most frequent image is of my boxer screwing me (this actually happens about every other day). Sometimes I fantasize sex with two men. I do it by alternating dildos between my vagina and my mouth, pretending that I am being screwed by one and Frenching the other. At times I have carried this further to include three men, by inserting a small dildo in my anus. Less elaborate fantasies have included my brother, my sister's husband, an uncle, and numerous attractive men we know.

When Bill or the boxer perform cunnilingus on me, I often just lie back with eyes closed and imagine all sorts of oral situations. They are often lesbian in nature, and mostly are concerned with a beautiful girl friend with whom I made love many times between the ages of fifteen and seventeen. Unfortunately, our family was transferred, breaking up our relationship. I had sex with other girls, but none were as lovely or skillful as my first friend. I have told Bill that if our paths should ever cross, I would go to bed with her, if she were willing, and I am sure she would be.

I began fantasizing at a very early age; at eight, I believe. At that time, my uncle, then about fourteen, showed me his erect penis, and showed me where it was supposed to go. He gave me a demonstration with his finger, which I enjoyed very much, and rubbed the head of his penis against my small hole. We engaged in similar sex play many times, and I began to masturbate regularly. Always, it was accompanied by thoughts of his finger screwing me, or his penis caressing my inner lips and clitoris. When I was thirteen, I began having sex with my brother, and this continued irregularly until about my sixteenth year.

I enjoy imagining that I am on exhibition. I have performed for Bill so often that I am accustomed to an audience, albeit of one. In our travels we have had several opportunities to view sex exhibitions, and strangely, perhaps, I always identify with the girls, and how, and to what extent, I felt that I could improve upon their performance. I am sure that I have a decided streak of exhibitionism in me. I love to pose for pictures; the sexier the better. In mild ways (with Bill's approval), I have indulged in exhibitionism. For instance, I have not worn panties in many years, except (honest injun) when I am expected to take them off; at the doctor's or the dressmaker's. I have given lots of strange men an unexpected peek at my pussy, while Bill and I observed their surprised and pleased reactions. Usually, this occurs on a motor trip, and I will have applied lipstick to my labia, to be sure they are unmistakably visible against the background of dark brown hair. Being rather moist and swollen, their visibility is enhanced. On trips, we always have a dildo handy and, of course, the boxer. I have let him screw me many times as we traveled, much, I am sure, to the surprise of passing truck drivers, who must have wondered what a large dog was doing with his paws on the back of the front seat.

Speaking our fantasies out naturally decreases the novelty of the particular situation to some extent. But we have discarded few, if any, of our fantasies. Actually, we have experienced many of our best fantasies, but even so, they remain effective sex stimulators. The most effective, the favorite, and the one which has withstood the test, is the one concerned with bestiality. It began about twenty years ago, and became a reality about three years ago. Our present dog is the third one, and he should be good for five or six years. The first two were German Shepherds, and we have trained all of them. Until the kids went away to college, dog-screwing was mostly reserved for special occasions, although I had cunnilingus often. I kept the dogs satisfied with masturbation and, when Bill was there to help guard against being surprised, I would fellatiate them. I know this may sound terrible, but it is really very pleasant, especially as I always thoroughly bathe that area with a nonirritating alcohol antiseptic which can be had in any drugstore. Precautions are unnecessary now, but I still enjoy giving him a suck sometimes.

I hope that none of what I have written has been offensive. Please use it in any way you wish, if it has any value. [Letter]

Posie

I am forty-seven years old and have only been married to my present husband for two and a half years. I was previously married for twenty-four years; he was a violent man and sex with him was something hateful. But my new husband is a very good and kind lover who has taught me that sex is a wonderful thing to be enjoyed. I find with him that talking about our fantasies makes them even more exciting when they happen again.

What I always like to imagine during sex with my husband is that I'm doing it with someone who doesn't belong to me. This "someone else" is no one in particular, and not always a man. Far from being jealous or angry, my lover tells me to talk to him and explain in detail things that go on in my mind, and it makes our lovemaking fantastic.

One of the favorite devices in my fantasy is to think that someone is watching me, and it becomes so real that it is this that heightens my climax. I do have lesbian fantasies, which really aren't great, as I'm a man's woman, but sometimes I do wonder how I would react to seeing another woman feeling her breasts and cunt, actually manipulating herself. I don't want to be doing it, I just want to watch her.

We often indulge in fantasies together, acting out little plays as though we had just met and he has never had a woman before. I seduce him, teach him what to do. Or we switch the roles around and he becomes the instructor. Either way it's enjoyable. [Letter]

Mara

I have actually acted out one of my fantasies, that of having sex with a colored man. When I describe this to my husband it really gets him going. If I add on top of this image the idea of being on exhibition, it gets me so keyed up I can even see the expressions on the faces of the people watching.

When my husband and I talk about these things it is easier to explain what we really think and feel, but of course most people, especially women, don't want to talk about taboo subjects. If you brought up the subject they would think you were sex-mad, when really it's the most interesting thing there is, and you are able by talking, and only by talking, to find out what makes people different. [Letter]

Joan

I think my fantasies began when I was quite young, but I have always remembered the first thing that really started me off. I still find it exciting to think about. I was about twelve and knew as much about sex as the next girl, I suppose. One day, two other girls and myself were in the park with several boys fifteen or sixteen years old. They bullied a younger boy to expose himself to us. This obviously fascinated all three of us girls, and as you might have guessed, the next thing that happened was an intensive petting session between us and the older boys. It may sound strange, but I can't really remember if one of those boys really got all the way inside me or not. But throughout it all, and still to this day, I can remember seeing that small red knob coming out through the foreskin, and I remember wondering whatever that little red thing was that was coming out toward me.

Seeing that first exposure got me started on fantasies as well as sex. I am fifty-five years old, and until quite recently kept secret my fantasies of exposing myself. In my fantasies it is I who expose my cleanly-shaven cunt to younger men, even youths, so that they can see what a real woman's cunt looks like. I have always wondered about the size of other men, because after our third child my husband felt like a finger inside me. It was then that I began to really look at men and to urge my husband to tell me what other men were like. I couldn't believe that some men were as large as he described, and in my fantasies I would imagine them, egged on by seeing my shaven cunt, mounting me. I would think of an abnormally large man, with a tool so big it would take me a long time to accommodate it. In my fantasy I would watch my bare slit being stretched further and further open, as his huge penis penetrated me to the hilt. (I have even pictured taking two men at once—as I know that this can happen.) And as my slit, totally free of hair, is visible in its entirety, the man in

307

my fantasy can watch me as well, the movement, the reaction of my cunt. I see him thrusting, stretching me, stabbing away and then withdrawing completely for our mutual inspection of the red shining knob, over which the skin is then forced back just as hard as the man can stand without too much pain, which broadens the knob, making it just as wide as it can possibly be made before reinserting it again.

Eventually, of course, when my husband began to see the reaction his stories of other larger men had on me, he began to suspect I fantasized. At first I was rather loath to admit them to him. I didn't want to talk back to him during intercourse; I wanted to stay with my fantasies. I also thought he might be hurt. But I soon realized how excited he got when I shared my fantasies with him, even told him that in them I was exposing myself to other men. He urged me to tell him more and our lovemaking suddenly took on a whole new excitement. He began to encourage me to think of other men. My husband is jealous of me, but he gets a definite kick from this "near attempt" at flaunting his wife before other men, even if only in fantasy.

Eventually, however, this developed to the point where he did, in fact, encourage me to have other men. We have also got so worked up at times that we have fantasized together about incest, which brings on a fantastic climax.

When my husband talks to me during sex—now that he knows that I have other men, and with his consent—he asks me all sorts of questions about the other cocks I have, and this gets him into such a state because, although he knows very well that he cannot fuck me like they can, he gets pleasure from at least trying. He now even encourages my real exposures to other men; in fact, he loves to shave me. These exposures later add a great deal to our sex as we fantasize together, talking back and forth, what it would be like if I had indeed taken on the man to whom he watched me expose myself—which, of course, is done simply by parting your legs a bit if you're sitting across the room from a man. Other times, of course, I do indeed take on the other men . . . and then tell my husband all about it. Now my husband even assures me that having other men regularly—and sharing the experience with him— makes me a better ride and far more relaxed and able to give of my best in bed. [Letter]

Adele's husband

I have read and reread your article, and having eventually decided your research work is a serious one, I have at last decided to write to you.

I am a heterosexual male, a widower, in fact, but I think you may find it quite interesting to read of the sexual fantasies of my dear late wife, who sadly died five long years ago.

We were married in the latter part of the last war, and when I was demobilized I was twenty-three years old and she was twenty-one. Right from the word go our married life was wonderful, both sexually and in every other way.

To come to the matter you're interested in. We had been to see a film with Alan Ladd in it at her instigation, because she always said how much she liked him. How much, I did not realize. The film had only been on ten minutes before she was kissing me very passionately and, of course, I slipped my hand in her blouse, undid her bra, and found her breasts hard and her nipples really erect. So naturally I went up her skirt with my other hand, having spread my raincoat over both our knees. She was wearing those silk panties without elastic—very handy—so I slipped my hand under and found her absolutely soaking wet. She had already come and as soon as I felt her clitoris, she came again. I finally had two fingers in her and she went wild. I hardly saw the film myself because she got my cock out and slowly tossed me off.

When we got home I asked her if seeing Alan Ladd always did that to her, and she replied that it was so and that she often fantasized about him when we were making love. But she said it wasn't the same as seeing him in a film because I wasn't tough enough with her. In fact, she

309

thought I was too kind with her, so there and then I
knocked her onto the settee, stripped off her clothes and
mine, switched out the lights and told her to call me Alan
and to do what she wanted with me or tell me what she
wanted Alan to do to her. It was fantastic! She told me she
had always wanted him to fuck her while he was on his
horse and she was sitting astride facing him. So we pretended this, with me sitting on the settee while she played
jockey on me. Unfortunately, that first time didn't last
long, as you can well imagine. Now I realize how totally
uninhibited we were then for such a young couple, because all the time she was crying out, "Fuck me harder,
Alan—what a lovely big cock you have," and so on and so
forth; no wonder I came quickly. As soon as I had come,
she knelt in front of me and said, "I've always wanted to
suck you off, Alan, and now I am." And my God, so she
did! We went to bed and she was insatiable. In fact, it was
so wonderful that next day I went to an army surplus store
and bought an army officer's trenchcoat and also a felt
slouch hat of the type he wore. I wore them home from
the office, and when I went in the house she burst out crying. Apparently she had been afraid of what I might have
thought about her behavior and would regret what had
happened the night before. May I say that I am one man
who never objected to my wife—I should say, my late
wife's—fantasizing with Alan Ladd. In fact, I must have
seen more of his films than any other man in the world.

This, however, was not the end. When Sean Connery
made his debut as James Bond in the films of the books by
Ian Fleming, she found that he "turned her on," as the
modern idiom says, and away we went again. Of course,
we had become more sophisticated as we grew older and
would have looked silly necking in the cinema. But as
soon as we'd left the cinema, and I was driving home, she
would have my slacks open and would suck me off, while I
was driving with one hand and bringing her off with the
other. This is not advocated in the Highway Code, by the
way, but as I always drive an automatic, there was no
hand brake or gear lever in the way.

310

I trust you do not mind my writing to you and I do think you may be surprised that there are some men who encourage their wives to fantasize while making love. It certainly enriched my life, and how lonely these last five years have been. [Letter]

CHAPTER SEVEN

QUICKIES

☐ This is as far as some women got in telling me their fantasies . . . just a fleeting thought or two off the top of their heads. ☐

. . . I imagine I am at the shore with the water running out from under my feet. The dizziness and the feeling of flight are overwhelming. I am being sucked out to sea. It is incredible . . .

. . . I am being raped by a Harlem gang, or seduced by my boyfriend's roommate, or I am seducing a virgin myself, or being filmed for a porno flick, or being discovered in bed by my parents or younger brother, or being in bed with other couples (that act works wonders!) . . .

. . . I think of my lover as a madman . . . or conversely as a virgin . . .

. . . I pretend that my lover is the boy I loved and wanted to marry when I was sixteen and we were separated . . .

. . . just knowing that this lover controls my life, since becoming pregnant again was something my doctor warned me not to consider . . .

. . . in my fantasies I always have my clothes on. I'm sure it has to do with rape, or why else would I be dressed?

Having my clothes on adds to the urgency; there is no time for preliminaries, or even time to think. But it's the most exciting sexual image I have . . . me dressed and being totally and fantastically raped by some unknown man, who will then disappear into the night, leaving me wonderfully satisfied and yes, dressed.

. . . I fantasize very typical stuff . . . our running through the fields, making love at the beach, whispered talks in bed, his asking to marry me . . .

. . . I discovered the existence of sex through a chance encounter with mating guinea pigs and was then filled in on the human details by a girl three embarrassing years younger than I. Once I knew the act existed, I did everything to try and visualize it: stuffing Kleenex up my vagina, then sitting down to watch hours of television, wondering if it felt like *that*. Picturing some crew-cut boy looking at me naked (he'd undoubtedly have been repelled by my almost non-existent breasts) and wondering what we'd do from there. Trying to imagine the actual penetration—painful? disgusting? joyous? I really couldn't picture it. When I tried, it seemed so intimate you could only do it with someone you really . . . cared for. But if you really cared for someone, how could you do such a terrible thing? It was a dilemma, and nearly stopped all my sexual fantasies . . . until I fell in love at sixteen . . .

. . . I imagine I am my husband's mistress while he is making love to me. I imagine I'm trying to seduce him away from his prudish wife. Or I think of myself as a call girl or prostitute. After my husband and I once went to an all-nude bar, I imagined for about a week that I was one of the girls we had seen. Strangely, when we are actually making love, I never fantasize that *he* is someone else. I'm always the one who is different . . .

. . . I used to have sex dreams, when I was reaching puberty; it all centered around the penetration. I was fascinated by how wonderful it seemed in my dreams, and thought I would simply die and go to heaven when I actually engaged in sex some day. The dream was so potent that I would engage in fabulous masturbation, which I loved, imagining that real sex between men and women would be even better. I ran into some trouble later on with priests who said it was "dirty" and a "mortal sin" to masturbate. So for a while I didn't, or if I did, I felt guilty. And finally I didn't do it anymore...

... I imagine what various men would be like in bed. I'm very happily married, so I would never go to bed with them, but if a friend of my husband's is attractive to me, I have fantasies about the two of us making love. As we are seated across from each other having cocktails, etc., I will picture him without his clothes. I get to the point where I am actually physically aroused by this...

... I had just broken up with a lover and in my masturbatory fantasies I would imagine I was making love with a woman, one of my best friends and a very attractive girl. In my fantasies the ex-lover would discover my friend and me and would be bitterly hurt...

... I wonder what it would be like to masturbate with a dildo and it always arouses me to see pictures in sex books of these devices in use. Explicit sex books (you know, the full-color pictures of men and women in all those positions) really turn me on. My husband and I have two of them and every once in a while we look at them. If we didn't make love after this, I would have to masturbate! However, I never fantasize about perverse sexual acts, like doing it with a horse. *That* turns me off...

... I began to have sexual daydreams about the age of four. There was a dark-haired, mysterious-looking man in the orchestra that played for Saturday night dances at my grandfather's country club. He played bass, and I would daydream from Sunday on through the week that he would come some night around dusk and whisk me off in the bass case. To this day I am attracted by dark-haired musicians, especially bass players, and have allowed myself time and time again to be carried off by them (not in their bass cases), only to discover that their lovemaking, no matter how wild, can never live up to my now quite grown-up fantasies of what I'd really like them to do to me . . .

. . . I am not with the obvious he-man muscular type. My sex orgies are with intellectual, almost shy men, who you think wouldn't know what to do in bed, but I picture them as experts under the surface. As if I'm the only one who knows their prowess . . .

. . . I am chained, being beaten, forced to make love against my will. This surprises me, because I'd never allow a man to lay a hand on me . . . yet I keep coming back to this situation . . .

. . . I just think how much I love him when we make love. But every once in a while, I play the pussycat and he the affectionate owner . . .

. . . I have had erotic dreams which have produced orgasm. I am making love with a black man, a mysterious stranger, teen-age boys, once, to tell all, even with a woman, and there was one with a stallion who looked like a man I know but was a horse all the same . . .

. . . I imagine, while I am masturbating, that I am being raped by a man who has just kidnapped me because he couldn't resist my fantastic beauty . . . or I imagine I am making love with an old high-school sweetheart who was maddeningly sexy but whom I never went to bed with because I was too virginal (my husband really is the only man I've ever been to bed with!) . . .

. . . I guess it's a submission fantasy, having my will overcome by sexual arousal. The man, my partner, has no identity, he is depersonalized. He never becomes another real person, like a movie star or my first love. He is not sadistic but he is not loving either—more like a cold unfeeling machine. Sometimes conditions are put on my achieving climax . . . I cannot make any noise or move or something like that. Sometimes there are two men . . . or more. I guess you would say my fantasies are somewhere between rape, victim and prostitute, sort of half and half. I never imagine being beaten or hurt in any way, and I never do anything myself; I am just acted upon. The man is an impersonal manipulator. There is no definite setting to these fantasies, no props or anything or fancy clothes. Sex fantasies are quite recent with me. I never had them when I was younger. I don't now have fantasies unless I know a man well and the sexual routine is familiar and comfortably old-shoe.

. . . I conjure up this ultramasculine, coarse, strong fellow, and in my most climactic moments he becomes very tender, very soft in his lovemaking to me, very, very much the right man for me. It turns me on to realize how fully this man can give of himself to me. Usually my men are totally indulgent . . .

. . . I am Queen Elizabeth (the First), ensconced in a castle with Hannibal, Rhett Butler, and Elke Sommer. The four of us do a variety of filthy things together. This is a serial fantasy, and I always take up where I left off. In my childhood fantasies I tortured various other women; but now that I am grown up, I don't have this particular type anymore . . .

. . . I'm spread-eagled on a huge roulette wheel that hangs on a wall. As my partner penetrates me, the wheel spins faster and faster and faster . . .

. . . I am attacked by a pack of German Shepherds (sexually, that is) . . .

316

... I have been smuggled into a male prison and am being passed from cell to cell. It is the "long-termer" section (they are ravenous!) ...

... I am completely passive having things done to me against my will. It is not actually rape, I don't struggle, I enjoy it but against my will. Sometimes I hear a voice, like on a PA system, describing what is being done to me and my reactions ...

... I am out on the street with no underwear. I approach two men walking together, lift my skirts, and offer to do anything ...

... I often borrow some of the more vivid scenes from *The Story of O,* like the one where she wears no underwear all day long and is constantly on call for her lover, who requests that she make love with other men while he looks on. And straight whipping scenes, like the bit from that same book where she is in the special beauty shop, sitting naked on the chair, having various interesting parts of her body prepared for sex. For orgies, I lean heavily on *My Secret Life* ...

... I am not very imaginative. I simply fantasize scenes that have actually taken place between me and my lover which I have found particularly interesting ...

... I am a stripper, performing on stage. Then I enter the audience and have sex with various men ...

... yes, I'm ashamed to say I've had fantasies about love and sex ever since I was at school. My headmaster never suspected it, but I was often *his* mistress in the most romantic surroundings. I sometimes fear that I am a nymphomaniac, but only in my "Walter Mitty" world. My favorite "trip," while plodding down our local Main Street, is into the harem of some virile potentate. When I awake, I am carrying ... a load of shopping.

. . . The men in my life have all been a bit wishy-washy. My fantasies are always about a he-man who knows how to put his foot down. In my dream, he puts me across his knee and wallops my bare bottom. Then we make love.

. . . I daydream about a certain bulky lump of male muscle I see pass up the road each day right in front of our house. He has a big black beard and marvelous twinkling eyes. Well, daydreaming's free, isn't it?

. . . my erotic fantasy is to walk stark naked through a spring meadow on a really hot day. A great "horny" hulk of a man (also stark naked) grabs me, and without a word spoken throughout, makes wild erotic love to me. (I think it might be as well if you only use my initials.)

. . . my fantasy love takes me for a trip up the Empire State Building. He knows of my love of music, my fear of heights. As we soar skyward, he calmly takes me in his arms, first very affectionately, then more possessively, until he becomes very demanding. Once at the top we make love, accompanied by Scheherazade type music. A wild, passionate affair, a conglomeration of sounds and sensations, all madly exhilarating. (How I've enjoyed writing this!)

. . . my secret fantasies concern sex in the air or on the sea. If I won the state lottery, I'd hire a plane and a boat, just to find out which rocking movement is better combined with sex.

. . . why is it when I'm a happily married mother of four lovely children and have a darling husband, why is it I always go off in a trance when I see our good-looking delivery man walk up the path on Monday and Wednesday mornings? My heart misses a beat as I open the door. While I wait for him to put down his packages, I stand there transfixed, my mind wondering what it would be like to make love to this six-foot hulk of a man. I'm sure I would die if he knew what I was thinking, as I'm only four feet ten inches tall.

. . . my fantasy finds me swimming in a pool, filled with champagne, along with two handsome men, one blond, one dark. I clamber out of the pool and lie on the table, while they massage me gently, but possessively, all over. The three of us dive back in, and I make love, right there in the champagne, to first one and then the other; tempestuously with the dark one, then languidly with the fair one.

. . . I go to my doctor and find a gorgeous Doctor Kildare type instead of my usual doctor. He asks me to go behind a screen and undress. I do so, and when I'm down to my bra and panties he comes behind the screen, looks me up and down, and compliments me on my body. I am embarrassed at first, but afterward feel flattered. He asks me to undress completely. I do so. When he examines me with the stethoscope, he repeats how much he admires me. When he says he would like to make love to me I willingly agree. Then he undresses and we make love on the examination couch. Afterward I dress and leave as though I had just paid a normal visit to the doctor. My husband, of course, knows nothing of my little daydreams and our marriage is a happy one.

. . . I'm lying on a low, large bed, wearing a long, bright red, see-through, antique Roman toga that would suit my long blond hair. Near me are two pet snakes and a cat. Lounging about are eight tall, slim, long-haired men, wearing short roman togas, pure white. They serve me and talk to me on erotic topics. Meanwhile, another eight sexy guys, wearing purple or red bell-bottom velvet trousers, black belts and flowered shirts, are singing and dancing to the sound of stereophonic, psychedelic music. I can choose any of them at any time to make love to me. (I'm not underaged.)

. . . whoopee for those delightful dirty daydreams. I often

319

dream about what sort of bed partners certain men would make, and my little mind went berserk recently when we had these lovely men installing a new central heating system. Our house may have been cold that week, but my thoughts kept me pretty hot.

. . . when sex got a bit mundane, I found myself imagining one night that I was "Jane" in a jungle hut being made love to. I screamed out "Tarzan!" and tore at my lover's hair. The fantasy ended miserably when some of hubby's last strands came away in my hands.

. . . I am being made love to in a huge, dimpled, whiskey bottle, hung from top to bottom in tiger skins. My lover is dressed as an executioner, with eyes glittering through his mask, and when he takes me, the tiger skins slither down to reveal my entire family gazing in shock, horror, and bewilderment. Please don't print my name or my family really will be shocked!

. . . I have only one romantic fantasy about men, and that is that I would love to walk out dressed to kill with my three children looking like TV model children. As I pass, every man looks at me and desires me, thinking how beautiful I keep myself for a woman with three children.

. . . my fantasy always takes place on a deserted beach. I am taking an evening stroll when I meet my heart-throb. I have had this fantasy ever since I was a teen-ager. Of course, the heart-throb changes from time to time.

. . . although I am over sixty, I am still a romantic at heart, and a very happily married woman. I must confess I often look at an attractive man at a social "do," or while waiting for the bus, and wonder what sort of partner he would make on a stolen week-end. I suspect not all the virile types make the best lovers! It is an exciting fantasy, and I'm thankful no one can read my thoughts, most of all my dear husband.

... I'm tall, elegant, and intelligent. I am always at a masked ball where I am made love to by every man I desire. I never take off the mask. Of course, in reality I'm short, thin, not very intelligent, and middle-aged. But I'm happily married.

... killing my daily traveling boredom, my mind always drifts to the jungle. Tarzan has me prisoner in his treetop home. He is wild, passionate, making love like the primitive man that he is. But how I enjoy every rough, clawing moment, so different from civilized delicacies. I've lost count of the times Tarzan has forced me to indulge in his animal sexual pleasures, but they keep getting better.

I'm the seventh wife of Henry Tudor,
Each night he comes to my boudoir.
By day I am Olde Englande's Queen,
But by night it's a different scene.
There's love, there's passion, and there's lust,
On Saturdays an orgy's a must.
I know I shan't go to the Tower,
For through my sex I have great power.
Of all his wives from one to seven
I only transport him to seventh heaven.

... I am a divorcee and live alone, but am not ever lonely, even though I do not go out and about much. My "fantasy" lover is always with me day and night, and I find *her* very exciting. She is a "masculine"-looking woman dressed in "drag" (men's dress). She is very sweet and she takes me out every Saturday and Sunday evening. She works in the Ambulance Services as a driver (senior). When we go to bed she is very gentle and understanding and a great lover—much better than a man. I would never exchange her for a man. Every time we have sex it is more exciting than the last time, and we manage to make love often (about twelve times per night—when I feel hot). Each action short, fast, but satisfying. Of course, this is just a fantasy or daydream, *but* the woman exists; howev-

321

er, not in *my* life (lucky devil who has her). I have only seen her in passing. I have been holding the "torch" for her for *nearly six years* now.

. . . there's this giant centipede or prawn, or a cross between the two, crawling into me head first, my legs being really wide apart to accommodate him. As he crawls into me, his thousands of fuzzy legs fall off onto the sheets around me. He tickles and excites me as he undulates and wiggles from side to side getting further and further in, and he becomes drenched with my nectar, which he licks up and is strengthened by. He goes on up and up. This all takes hours as he is ten thousand feet long, but I like every inch of it.

The next morning, happily exhausted, I begin the ritual of carefully gathering up the thousands of orange fuzzy legs that surround me, and take them in a wicker basket to the kitchen. There I dump them into my blue enamel jam-making pot, and add sugar, orange peel, lemon, nutmeg, banana peel scrapings, and a bit of hash when available (very optional). At the hard-ball, or so-called crack stage of cooling, I pour the orange mass into penis-shaped molds (can be bought in your nearest sex shop), and allow them to cool and harden. To be sucked later when desired, but I usually give mine away to my friends, as the penis-shaped mold itself is far more satisfying and I share him with no one. You'd be surprised how many of my friends drop by for their sucks.

As you can tell, these aren't things I really think about while fucking. They're not even masturbatory fantasies, just the kind of idle daydreams I have after a bath, while I'm lying down for an hour or so, half asleep, half awake, waiting until it's time to get dressed and go out for the evening.

. . . once every three or four months my husband trims off all my pubic hairs. He first uses scissors and then a small lady's electric razor. I always like him to be naked when he performs this task. Throughout the exercise I hold his

322

penis in my hand, and with gentle movement insure he maintains an erection. When I know he is nearly finished, I can feel in my mind a mounting impression of wanting to turn his penis like the throttle of a motorbike to make the noise of the shaver louder. This gets me so aroused that I almost climax, and so I turn the throttle even more to increase the noise of the motorbike in order that my husband will not be overwhelmed by my cries of passion.

. . . showering together, we occasionally have intercourse standing face to face. I like to lean back and watch as he puts just the tip of his penis into me. Then, as the water cascades down between our bodies, I imagine that I can feel an enormous quantity of his semen flowing out of the shower and into my stomach and pubic area. It heightens my sensations so much that I actually feel he is pumping gallons of semen into me and I always have a prolonged orgasm, even without there being any mutual motion between our bodies. I only experience this fantasy when he holds just the head of his penis inside me. I have to be able to look down and see some part of his penis between our bodies . . . if he is in too far and I can't see it, I can't have the fantasy.

. . . having sex with two men who are going down on me simultaneously. Or having sex with the television on inspires the fantasy that the TV performers are watching. Or masturbating in front of a crowd and turning them all on. Or fantasy of reaching down a man's pants on a crowded bus and masturbating him. Or being raped by a strong, handsome stranger, with constant profanity: "My cock is in your cunt and it's on fire," "I want to come all over you, in your eyes and your ass, etc.," plus assorted "Fuck me's."

"IN DEFENSE OF NANCY FRIDAY"

by Martin Shepard, M.D.,
psychiatrist,

author of *The Games Analysts Play*
and *A Psychiatrist's Head*

I

Frequently when we condemn, criticize, poke fun at or derogate traits in others, we are refusing to accept the same traits in ourselves. "I can't stand her being so dependent" often means "I'm ashamed of my own dependent feelings." "I think his rudeness is terrible" can be translated as "I won't accept my own rude moments." Similarly, "I think her fantasies are the products of a diseased mind" means "I would *never* allow such thoughts to enter my mind—for if I did I would be either sick or disgusting."

On the other hand, deepest contentment occurs at those moments when we are fully accepting of ourselves. At such times we respect our actions, feelings, bodies, thoughts. Failure to accept any of these aspects of ourselves is synonymous with self-alienation.

One of the highest states of consciousness attainable is that of the non-judgmental observer. In such a state, freed from the distortions of needs and value judgments ("If a pickpocket sees a Holy Man he will see only his pockets"),* he will begin to see WHAT IS, both in the world about him and within himself. Gurdjieff, the Russian philosopher-mystic, tried to teach people to develop "the Witness" within themselves. "The Witness" could detach itself and non-judgmentally witness and thereby accept both inner and outer events. Zen Masters and Yogis try to teach a similar acceptance to their students. All of these thinkers appreciate the fact that you don't think your thoughts, but rather that your thoughts think through you. They recognize that you are no more responsible for thinking than you are for digestion, breathing, for life itself. You may bear a certain degree of responsibility for what you do with your thoughts, but you certainly bear none for having them.

My Secret Garden is a compilation of uncensored data on women's most secret sexual thoughts. This is something that has not been done in our time. As a psychiatrist who has listened to such fantasies before, I consider it an honest accounting. It is also a useful book, for it can help other women witness and accept their fantasies and themselves. And yet I am certain that many people in our society will attack this work. They will do so by attempting to ignore it, condemn it, ban it, laugh at it, intellectually dismiss it, or psychoanalyze it. In doing so such critics will only reinforce their own and others' self-alienation.

The attacks on *My Secret Garden* will come from three directions. The most primitive charge will be that the women Ms. Friday interviewed are tortured or abnormal in some way and don't represent the average woman. The second and more sophisticated attack will be the intellectual/psychoanalytic approach, which will attempt to demonstrate why certain fantasies are not "healthy." Lastly there is the attack to be waged by the anti-Eros forces—those who regard such a frank sexual discussion as this work as either pornography or perversity. Both the nature of these lines of attack and the bankruptcy of such charges are themes I would like to explore more fully.

*Hari Dass Baba

1. The Women Interviewed Are Not Representative*

It might be argued that Ms. Friday's respondees were not representative of the average woman; that those who would talk about their fantasies are by nature exhibitionists or sexually preoccupied; that only the most "sensationalistic" fantasies found their way into print; that the sampling leaves out women who don't fantasize and therefore gives a misleading picture of female reveries.

There are two basic troubles with this argument. The first concerns the impossibility of obtaining a representative sampling in *any* study about *anything*. Indeed, there is an axiom in physics—the Heisenberg Uncertainty Principle—that recognizes that the very *act of measuring* distorts that which you are observing. And what is true of atomic particles is even more true of measurements in the field of human events.

Freud, for example, wrote books about the development of the psyche. Yet his samplings consisted not of "average people" but of patients he treated. Studies are presented of marital problems—and yet such studies, by their nature, omit marriages that don't have such problems. Still, the observations such works contain have a certain relevance for us all. Given the heterogeneous cultures of England and America—black/white, rich/poor, educated/uncultured, urban/rural, Christian/Jew, old/young—only a massive computer program could dare begin to claim a "representative sampling." And even then, the question arises of the biases of those persons who program the computer.

The second weakness of the argument that the "average woman" won't find herself in this book is that *there is no such person*. The "average woman" is an abstraction, a

*The 400-odd biographies and descriptions of the women do seem rather "average." No social or economic groups predominate. Ms. Friday has gotten a balanced sampling with the one exception that her subjects admit that they fantasize.

statistical fiction, not a reality. She has 2.3 children, had 11.6 years of formal education, married when she was twenty-one years three months and two days of age, is now thirty-two and a half years old, has intercourse 2.7 times per week, and will die at age 67.

Charges, then, that Nancy Friday's interviewees are unrepresentative are misstated. One should ask, instead, "Can a reasonable woman find fantasies within this book that she can relate to?" And here, I think, the answer must be "Yes." In my roles as therapist/husband/social being/lover, I have heard similar tales told by "ordinary" people. Dr. Seymour Fisher, author of *The Female Orgasm*, a book based on a more scientific study than Ms. Friday undertook, has found the same predominating themes in the fantasies his respondents reported. Not only that, but *he found no correlation between any given fantasy and the life style, education, orgasticity, sickness, health or any other life function of his respondents.*

2. It's Not Healthy

For all its liberating value, psychoanalytic thinking is also used (*misused*, in my opinion) in the service of containing and/or negating a healthy eroticism. I am sure some misapplied criticisms of this book will also come from this direction.

Yet how could it be any other way? For Freud, like all great teachers, taught best to others *that which he had to learn himself*. The essence of his message was that *our sexual urges are our prime motivaters* and that *this is how it should be*. He taught that sexual appetites and curiosities are okay. Indeed, his life work revolved about and satisfied his own exquisite sexual curiosity.

Still, as long as a message is being preached, you may be sure that the preacher has not yet mastered it himself. And such was the case with Freud. He showed a remarkable patience (inhibition?) in losing his own virginity (*after* he married at age thirty) and, as far as his biographers knew, ceased further sexual activity somewhat over ten years later.

Freud's ambivalent attitude about his own sexuality was naturally reflected both in his own life and theories and by his disciples. He paid homage to the immense motivating power of lust, yet seemingly blunted his own. He preached that the sexual appetite (Id) was natural, yet worked at fortifying the barrier (Ego) between lust and gratification. For he cautioned against abandoning oneself to one's pleasurable impulses ("acting out," as he called it) and preferred, instead, to analyze these forces. Why expect more? For a Viennese intellectual with a seductive mother, mind games might be more stimulating and less anxiety-producing than the mindless pleasures of the body.

Among his followers the story is not much different. Few analysts live what they teach. How many openly sexy psychiatrists have you seen lately? How many Freudian analysts would even dare to give a patient a warm embrace? How can one truly teach that Eros is okay if one is afraid to be erotic?

Still, analytic arguments (by sophisticated lay people as well as professionals) will be used to derogate and invalidate many of the fantasies expressed in this book. We will be told that it is unhealthy to fantasize. Or that fantasy is a substitute for reality; that if there is "real satisfaction," there is no "need" for fantasy.

Yet the term *psycho-analysis* means nothing more than an *analysis of psychological material*, as presented in word or deed. We can just as fairly psychoanaylze these analytically critical remarks.

The question ought to be raised: *Who are these arbiters of what constitutes "health" or "real satisfaction"?* Are the analyst's pleasures the only "healthy" ones? If he doesn't fantasize and you do, does that make him *healthy* and you *sick?* I would prefer simply to say that you are just *different.* "Real satisfaction" for one person is not necessarily "real satisfaction" for another. It takes a person of overwhelming conceit and arrogance to determine what "true pleasure" or "right pleasure" ought to be for others.

How can a critic state that fantasy is a *substitute* for reality? Isn't a fantasy as real as anything else? It is as *real* a thought as are the thoughts and words that the critic uses to dismiss it. And if the critic tells you that he, with his "real" or "healthy" satisfactions, has no "need" to fantasize, who is to determine whether it is the critic's inhibitions that prevent his adding pleasurable fantasy to his current pleasures or your "inferior" pleasures that cause you to fantasize?

This is a question for gods to answer, not men, and necessarily remains unanswerable. My point in raising it is to underscore the arbitrariness and the gamesmanship involved when dealing with the more intellectually oriented critics.

More traditional analytic remarks are bound to revolve around the theme of submission that runs through so many of the fantasies presented in this book. We will be told that these are examples of "masochism"—a label that conjures up images of mental illness or perversion. What of that charge? Is a woman who fantasizes being dominated, tied up, or forced to submit showing signs of mental disturbance? Does it "truly mean" (whatever *that* means) that she desires pain with her pleasure? Or that she needs pain in order to feel pleasure?

Writing in the journal *Medical Aspects of Human Sexuality*, a California psychologist, Dr. Andrew Barclay, reports a similar theme of so-called masochistic "I-am-being-exploited-during-intercourse" fantasies among women. But Barclay makes a less hackneyed interpretation of this phenomenon. He suggests that such fantasies serve the purpose of providing reassurance to the woman that she is being passive rather than aggressive sexually—thereby conforming to our cultural sexual stereotype.

I could suggest another interpretation of this submissive theme. Many women in their childhood have been strongly conditioned to say "No" to sex. They have been taught that the act is exploitative, naughty, indecent. To them, *willingly* to enter into such a lustful exchange with total commitment and abandon is not acceptable. But if someone else, by force, assumes total responsibility for the love-making by forcing them into it, they can finally lie back and enjoy it.

Neither Barclay's nor my "non-pathological" interpretation of this submissive element is more correct than the traditional pathologically oriented psychoanalytic one. But I do affirm that they are *equally plausible*. Besides which, it is important to bear in mind that psychoanalysts, by vocation, are trained to seek pathology everywhere. To paraphrase Hari Dass Baba: "If an analyst meets a Holy Man, he will see only his Oedipus problem."

The same reasoning applies to the other side of the submission coin—that of the dominator. Does a domineering fantasy mean that the dreamer has it in for men? That she wishes to humiliate, control, enslave, or torture them? Is it a sign of unresolved hostility?

Might it not *just as logically* be an attempt to mentally try on exaggerated cultural male stereoypes? Or a declaration of her own passionate sexual desire ("I am so horny I must capture and hold my frightened, reluctant stud"), or a way of affirming her responsibility for initiating the sex act ("I forced him into it")?

An analytically oriented critic could have a field day "proving" abnormality in the case of Stephanie (Chapter Four, *Seeing and Reading*), what with her preoccupation with tribal sexual punishments, Nazi tortures and sexual-organ mutilations. And perhaps such is the case. Yet, if the critic accepts the *reality* of Stephanie's fantasy, can he fairly omit or negate the *reality* of her statement that "although I might be a perverted sadist down deep, it doesn't seem to show in my daily life; in fact I am a gentle person, so I could afford to laugh, feeling secure in the fact that I have disciplined this part of myself"?

So again we have these unanswerable questions. Is a gentle woman who has sadistic fantasies disturbed? Might it not be nature's wisdom to enable her to handle and discharge negative feelings in dreams and fantasies instead of doing so in her interpersonal relationships? Would she be "healthier" if she were nastier in person and had less violent fantasies?

I contend that analytic criticisms of these fantasies do a great disservice to people. By declaring certain fantasies "No-No's" they reinforce self-rejection. (Your fantasy is as much *you* as any other part of you.) This is the direct opposite of the therapeutic goal. What is wrong with thoughts which improve one's sex life? The true masochist is one who avoids thinking "masochistic thoughts" once she has discovered, by accident or design, that such thoughts excite her.

There are additional factors to bear in mind in evaluating analytically oriented criticisms of these fantasies. One concerns the fact that psychoanalytic theory has been, by and large, formulated by males. Freud, Sullivan, Adler, Jung, Reich . . . became the arbiters and interpreters of what woman's "normal" sexual response should be. Yet, not being women, how could they possibly know on a cellular level what they were talking about? Is it really likely that these men were any more appreciative of what a "normal woman" might dare think than were the lover and former editor whom Nancy Friday mentioned in her opening chapter?

Another difficulty in interpreting these fantasies analytically is that the very act of analysis—of *labeling* ("Sadist, Masochist, Castrator, Oedipal, Self-destructive, Exhibitionistic")—creates a self-consciousness that is antithetical to the sexual mystique. One of the effects of sex is the self-transcendence that can be obtained by losing one's "self"—one's *ego*—in an act of embrace. To be conscious of self (*self-conscious*) and transcend self at the same time is an impossibility. Pity the bind that so many analysands are in who seek sexual freedom while being prodded by their analysts to be suspicious of and act analytically toward their erotic impulses.

The only "labeling" process that has impressed me in recent years came from a woman I met who only recently began enjoying her life. Painfully self-conscious during her first thirty-eight years, she woke up one day "and decided

331

to stop criticizing myself. I resolved, instead, to *label everything I do as 'good.'* Since then I've been doing exactly what I want to do and enjoying every minute of it." Self-conscious female fantasizers have more to learn from this woman's labeling process than from many of the followers of Sigmund Freud.

The greatest weakness in analytical evaluations of these fantasies, however, is that *such intellectual dissections represent a rational approach to what is essentially an irrational process.* For fantasies, like dreams, arise from the twilight zone of ancient experiences, future expectations, social conditioning, unfinished business, and complex biological and biochemical processes. The separation of these elements is possible if one recognizes that we make these evaluations as an intellectual challenge—much as one can find satisfaction in solving a crossword puzzle. But to suggest that such evaluations yield "truth" is either pretense or folly.

3. My Secret Garden Is Nothing More than Thinly Disguised Pornography

Paul Krassner, in his satirical newspaper *The Realist,* once wrote a story about a pornography case appearing before the Supreme Court. If the Justices got erections while reading the material, it was declared pornographic. This raised a very ticklish question. Might the Court next be asked to rule on whether or not Vaseline was pornographic?

Krassner's exaggeration was funny. Yet the reality of the situation is apparent. Society often considers that which turns you on to be wrong. Unless there is a "redeeming social function," such turn-ons are seen to be a threat to the morality or the fabric of our society.

As I write this I find myself in somewhat of a box. I do think that *My Secret Garden* performs a useful service in that this open sharing of various sexual fantasies might allow many readers to accept, without shame, guilt, or anxiety, various fantasies of their own. Yet, even if that were not the case—even if every purchaser of this book bought it *solely* to be sexually turned on—I would also say, "Well and good."

What is wrong with healthy erotic responses? Why should anyone have to justify a desire to "turn on"? If you believe in the right to turn on to your own fantasies, don't you also have the right to turn on to the fantasies of others? Is turning on some evil that requires a *"redeeming* social function" to justify it? I see more moral harm being done, *not* by the authors or publishers of "sexy" material, but by those censors and critics who attempt to foist and enforce *their* values upon others.

Bernardo Bertolucci, defending his film *Last Tango in Paris* against charges of pornography, put it well when he said, "Pornography is not in the hands of the child who discovers his sexuality by masturbating, but in the hands of the adult who slaps him."

The demand for a "redeeming" aspect of frankly sexual material puts those who would simply enjoy erotic pleasures on the defensive. For we then have to justify that which should be our birthright. We are told that an absence of erotic censorship would lead to social and cultural decay. But if that is so, why is it that so many members of our cultural aristocracy can and do respond to unadulterated erotic material?

The current craze over the movie *Deep Throat,* which consists of a thin story line to account for endless scenes of fellatio, underscores not only the absurdity of our anti-erotic critics but the absurd conditions that those who enjoy the film must also endure. *Throat* is an "in" film to see, and as such has been reviewed and commented upon by serious critics. Doctors, lawyers, members of Mayor Lindsay's administration, jet setters, and businessmen have been turning on to this movie for months. Yet they still remain productive members of society. And how do they justify their attendance at *Throat?* By pretending that the film is making a serious social point—that it is commenting on the morals of the day and/or poking fun at

333

our sexual foibles. Serious film critics have gone to court to make this very point. No one seems willing to be quoted outright as saying the simplest truth: "I went in order to turn on."

Throughout Nancy Friday's commentary, the gentle message is sent to *accept* these fantasies for what they are —poetic/erotic daydreams that provide enjoyment for the fantasizer. As a mental-health rule, such a message makes eminent sense.

Also, Nancy Friday attributes to fantasy the functions of foreplay, excitement, and the allaying of anxiety—thereby allowing excitement to grow. Fantasies can also be used, as she points out, as a rehearsal—a situation worked through in imagination before one actually lives it out. It is also true that fantasy can be used as compensation for a most dreary existence or as an escape—a way of procrastinating or avoiding taking more affirmative action in the outer world. Monica (Chapter Three, The Transformation Room) is a case in point. Described as a short, messy-looking over-weight nineteen-year-old who has toyed with the idea of suicide, Monica would rather fantasize herself as her beautiful sister than attend to prettying herself up.

Yet, even here, one can say "Why not?" After all, what alternatives are left? You can't make someone else's fantasies disappear anyway. And even if you could, would that cause Monica to make herself more attractive? Or would robbing her of a precious daydream make her even more despondent and more unkempt? Rather than discouraging her fantasy, I would prefer to see her live it out.

II

There are some types of fantasies that I've shared with others that have not found their way into print. This is no criticism of this book, for it does not claim to be a definitive encyclopedia of female sexual fantasies, but rather an attempt to show the range and variation of such material. One common fantasy left out is that in which the fantasizer thinks of herself as part of a machine, as an animal, as having the body of a man, as some creature from another world, as insect, or as God, or a part of the Buddha, or the petal on a lotus.

Many fantasies of this type occur under the influence of psychedelic agents (marijuana, hashish, mescaline, psylocybin) and are accompanied by exquisite sexual pleasure. So "real" are these fantasies that one truly *becomes* them —is not aware enough of "self" to realize that a fantasy is occurring until after the orgasm, which is often explosive and felt, seemingly, in every cell of the body.

III

While I feel quite strongly that the fantasizer ought to allow herself to accept, enjoy, and fully give herself over to her reverie, I also feel a word is in order lest *non-fantasizers* feel self-conscious over their lack of reverie. One should no more feel pressured to produce fantasies than be encouraged to avoid them.

It is, for example, quite possible and quite "normal" to be totally free of fantasy while making love. There are states in which a man or a woman may be so lost in bodily sensations that not only are daydreams absent but such people could not tell you where or who they are at that moment. This is not to say that such sexual experiences are better or worse—merely that they are different.

Finally, it is my belief that our interest in matters sexual —be it as critic or defender—is related to something far more basic and *inclusive* than deciding whether stimuli are "decently erotic," "pornographic," "perverse," "scientific," and so on. Whatever we are attracted by, we are always *looking, exploring, thinking.* These are the constants.

And these three constants have to do, I think, with the never-ending, unsolvable, and therefore always intriguing questions of creation and ego transcendence. How is it that motion and friction upon a small part of the body can make people for a moment oblivious of themselves, can cause—what the French refer to the orgasm as—*le petit mort* (the little death)?

If we are intrigued by the sexual appendages of the world, what could be more natural? We were all sired by an ejaculating penis, grew in the womb, passed through the vaginal vault, emerged between the labia, were nourished at a breast, and will most likely re-create again when we perform the rites of procreation ourselves. That the mysteries of life, death (ego transcendence), and intense pleasure are so closely linked with our sex organs is what, to my mind, makes these organs objects of perpetual curiosity.

My Secret Garden allows an important aspect of this natural curiosity to emerge from a locked closet. The bigger "secret," however, remains.

A LAST-MINUTE WORD FROM NANCY FRIDAY

I am presently at work on a new book of women's sexual fantasies. If you would like to contribute, you may write to me at the address below. Please be as detailed as possible about the content of the fantasy; include age, marital status, family history plus any other autobiographical sexual history. As always, I guarantee your anonymity. Write:

Nancy Friday
P.O. Box 1371
Key West, FL
33041